Jungian Thought in the Modern World

Jungian Thought in the Modern World

Edited by
Elphis Christopher
and
Hester McFarland Solomon

'an association in which the free development of each
is the condition of the free development of all'

FREE ASSOCIATION BOOKS / LONDON / NEW YORK

First published in Great Britain 2000 by
FREE ASSOCIATION BOOKS
57 Warren Street, London W1P 5PA

2 3 4 5   05 04 03 02 01 00

ISBN 1 85343 466 3 hbk; 1 85343 467 1 pbk

A CIP catalogue record for this book is available from the British Library.

Designed and produced for Free Association Books Ltd by
Chase Production Services, Chadlington OX7 3LN
Printed in the EU by TJ International, Padstow

Contents

Part IV Jungian Thought and the Religious, Ethical and Creative Spirit

Acknowledgements

In preparing the present volume, our aim has been to encourage the excellence that we knew resided in our authors. We thank them for their forbearance in responding to our insistent editing and the expectation that they would go the extra mile with us.

We would also like to express our appreciation for the advice and guidance, always generously and graciously given, of David Stonestreet, Psychology Editor for Free Association Books.

Elphis Christopher
Hester McFarland Solomon

Permissions

Chapter 11. Christopher MacKenna and the editors would like to thank Random House for permission to quote from *Memories, Dreams, Reflections* by Carl Jung for the territories of the USA and Canada. From *Memories, Dreams, Reflections* by Carl Jung, translated by Richard and Clara Winston. Translation copyright © 1961, 1962, 1963 by Random House Inc. Renewed 1989, 1990, 1991, by Random House Inc. Reprinted by permission of Pantheon Books, a division of Random House Inc. We would like to thank Harper Collins for permission to quote from *Memories, Dreams, Reflections* by Carl Jung for the territories excluding the USA and Canada.

Chapter 15. Figure 15.1 is reproduced by courtesy of the British Library. The other William Blake illustrations in this chapter are taken from *The Illuminated Blake* by David V. Erdman, Dover Publications, 1974.

Editors' Note

Throughout this volume, references to Jung's *Collected Works* appear in the abbreviated form *CW* followed by the relevant volume number. For full bibliographical details see 'Cited works of Jung' at the end of the book.

Notes on Contributors

Dr Elphis Christopher is medically qualified and has worked in the field of family planning and sexual medicine for thirty years. She is the author of a number of papers and a book, *Sexuality and Birth Control in Community Work* (1987). She has been a contributor to several books and has published papers on the unconscious factors influencing contraceptive and reproductive choice, psychosexual problems and psychotherapy. Her interests include history, comparative religion and studying different cultures. She is the consultant for Family Planning and Reproductive Care, Haringey Healthcare National Health Service Trust, a member of the Institute of Psychosexual Medicine, and Fellow of the British Association for Counselling. She is also a member of the British Association of Psychotherapists (BAP) Jungian Analytic Training Committee and a full member of the BAP, Jungian Analytic Section. She currently runs a small private practice.

John Clay read English and Modern Languages at Cambridge. He was a founder member and head of education at Peper Harow, the therapeutic community for disturbed adolescents in Surrey. He is the author of a number of books, including *Men at Midlife* (1989) and *R.D. Laing: A Divided Self* (1996). He is a fellow of the Royal Society of Literature and is on the Editorial board of the *Journal of the British Association of Psychotherapists*. He qualified with the Jungian Section of the BAP in 1992, and is in private practice and continues to publish. His most recent book is *Tales from the Bridge Table* (1998).

Warren Colman is a professional member of the Society of Analytical Psychology and a full member of the Society of Psychoanalytical Marital Psychotherapists. He has a background in counselling and social work and worked as a marital psychotherapist at the Tavistock Marital Studies Institute from 1982 to 1997, where he organised the clinical training of marital psychotherapists within the Institute and also in Sweden. He teaches and lectures widely, both in Britain and abroad. His publications include articles on couple therapy, sexuality, anima and animus and, more recently, on the self. He is now in full-time private practice in St Albans.

Geraldine Godsil read English at Cambridge and is an associate member of the BAP. She teaches on the Jungian analytic training and the MSc on the Psychodynamics of Human Development at the BAP and is involved in running seminars in infant observation in both these courses. She is also clinical manager of a large counselling service in London and her particular interest is in the application of Jungian and psychoanalytic ideas to literature.

Stephen Gross qualified as a social worker and has worked both as a general and as a psychiatric social worker in north London, before training with the Jungian Section of the BAP. He works in private practice and also as a supervisor and tutor at Westminster Pastoral Foundation, as well as being training coordinator with the Association of Independent Psychotherapists. He is the author of a number of articles on psychotherapeutic topics. His particular interest is in the place of psychotherapy within the wider social and intellectual context.

Ann Kutek graduated from Oxford University in philosophy, politics and economics, and went to Africa for Voluntary Service Overseas. She was caught up in a tribal war in Burundi in the early 1970s. After returning to England, she worked in local authority and commercial management and practised as a family therapist and cognitive analytic therapist before training with the BAP. She set up a nationwide network of therapists for a national charity to work in the corporate sector. She has lectured on child protection in the UK and abroad, and has published a number of papers. Her current interests include the process of conflict and the interaction of therapy and the world of work.

Dr W. Gordon Lawrence is visiting Professor of Organisational Behaviour, Cranfield University; managing partner of Symbiont Technologies, New York and London; Fellow of the Australian Institute of Social Analysis, and Fellow of the Bulgarian Institute of Human Relations. He was a senior consultant at the Tavistock Institute of Human Relations, London, for eleven years and is a past president of the International Foundation for Social Innovation, Paris. He is an organisational consultant and has practised in most continents of the world. Apart from articles, his most recent publications are *Roots in a Northern Landscape* (1996: Scottish Cultural Press), *Social Dreaming @ Work* (1998: Karnac Books) and *Exploring Individual and Organisational Boundaries* (1979, 1999: Karnac Books).

Canon Christopher MacKenna is a priest in the Church of England. He spent several years living as a Benedictine Monk before reading theology, with special subjects in psychology and psychology of religion, at Oxford. He has been Rector of Hascombe, Surrey, since 1980, and an Honorary Canon of Guildford Cathedral since 1998. A full member of the Jungian Section of the British Association of Psychotherapists, he works in private practice. His special interests include the psychology of religion and of religious organisations, and issues relating to the ethics of psychotherapeutic practice. He is currently a member of the Ethics Committe of the British Association of Psychotherapists.

Dr Dale Mathers trained as a psychiatrist at St George's Hospital, London, worked as a researcher, then directed the Student Counselling Service at the London School of Economics, before going into full-time private analytic practice. He is a Senior Trainer of the Psychosynthesis and Education Trust, London; trained with, and now teaches for, the Jungian Section of the BAP, and is also a member of the Association of Jungian Analysts. He is a member of the Scientific and Medical Network, a group actively exploring the interfaces of science and spirituality, a Buddhist, and a keen motorcyclist. He is currently working on *An Introduction to Meaning and Purpose in Analytical Psychology* for Routledge.

Helen Morgan studied physics and education at university before turning to mental health work. She worked in therapeutic communities with adolescents (the Cotswold Community) and adults (the Richmond Fellowship) for a number of years, finally becoming a trainer and then a regional director for the Richmond Fellowship. She is a full member of the Jungian Section of the BAP and now works in private practice, as well as supervising and consulting in the public sector. She is the author of a number of papers, and is particularly interested in the interface between the interior world of psychological enquiry and the exterior world of groups, organisations and society. Her most recent publication is 'Between fear and blindness – the white therapist and the black patient' (1998).

Jean Pearson has a first degree in psychology and sociology and a postgraduate diploma in applied social studies. She worked as a social worker in the field of psychiatry for a number of years. Concerned to make psychotherapy more widely available, she was instrumental in setting up the first free psychotherapy clinic outside the NHS, and worked for many years as its Director. She is a full member of the British Association of Psychotherapists, and now works in private practice in West London. She has a particular interest in applying Jung's ideas to issues of current social concern.

Dr Michael J.A. Simpson was a zoologist and ethologist, having carried out research on male grooming and dominance, and mother–infant relationships in free-living and captive primates, before training with the Jungian Section of the BAP. He is now in private practice. He has a long interest in how individuals of different species, including scientists, come to construe and construct their different worlds, and in how Jung's writing invites us to venture beyond the compass of any particular current scientific, religious or depth psychological world view.

Hester McFarland Solomon took her first degrees in literature and philosophy before turning to psychology and social psychology. She trained with the Jungian Section of the BAP where she is now a training therapist, teacher and supervisor, and a fellow of the Association. She is in private practice, and has published a number of papers linking Jungian analytic and psychoanalytic theory and practice. She lectures and pursues a variety of professional activities in Britain and abroad. Her current interests include the neurophysiological bases of early mental functioning and the ethical attitude as a developmental stage.

Foreword

It is a privilege to write this foreword because the thrust of the chapters in this volume is not only an analysis of the contemporary life of individuals in families, groups and other social configurations, but also an indication of how human life could become in the future. The experience of reading these contributions is transformational: the reader begins in one intellectual and emotional position but ends in another, enlarged one.

The chapters in this volume were originally delivered as an introductory course in Jungian analytic psychotherapy, some members of which went on to train as psychotherapists. The breadth and coherence of the contributions presented the audience with a way of thinking that is both rigorous and illuminating. An important, aspect of the chapters in this volume is that they lead the reader to develop his or her mental associations that further the engagement with society and its institutions. The leitmotiv running through this volume is 'only connect', an expression used by E.M. Forster as a protest about the nature of relationships. It is therefore a timely book which may cause us to pause and consider as we careen our way either towards massive destruction or towards forms of social creativity that, as yet, are accessible only through dreams.

Carl Gustav Jung was a contemporary of Freud, separated by a generation in time. It is well known that they started a substantial correspondence in 1906, met in 1907, and formed an intense personal and professional relationship, but parted painfully in 1912. Historians will always puzzle as to why this was so. Of course, we are aware of the manifest reasons, but what of the latent, unconscious ones? Two first-rate thinkers could not cooperate, except for a brief time. Was it because each had a vision of the workings of the psyche and the nature of the relationships in which it is embedded at the most profound of levels? I suspect that this is the case. Freud was a more conventional social scientist with a profound view of human nature based on a capacity to explore its roots in the personal unconscious. Jung was interested in the innate, spiritual and numinous qualities of the psyche and he made use of symbolism, the modern physics of quantum reality, alchemy and religion to substantiate this preoccupation. The erudition he brought to bear on the development of depth psychology is staggering and widens the mind in ways that leaves us aghast at his audacity, courage and creativity. Brought together, the combined completeness of Freud's and Jung's *oeuvre* is astonishing.

Jung's thinking and writing illustrate, at every point, his awe of and wonder at the qualities of the psyche and particularly of the unconscious, without losing sight of the need for evidence and scientific method. In many ways, Jung was anticipating the mysteries of the unknown of science at a time when the cultural climate of the day was grounded in a paradigm of scientific enquiry that was mechanical, constrained by what could be known only in finite, concrete terms.

By the eighteenth century Western science had adopted an ontological assumption of separateness. Science was separate from religion; mind from matter; man from nature; reason from emotion; self from object. This all rested on the assumption that there was a separation of the observer from the observed, that one did not affect the other. The observer was objective. This set of assumptions led to the idea that it was possible to reduce all phenomena to their fundamental particles. Thus, Western thinking could proceed on the basis that human beings occupied a gigantic Newtonian machine – not unlike a steam engine – that proceeded on classical physical methods. This resulted in an increasing amount of scientific and other knowledge. Such a scientific posture led to hubris on the part of humankind which came to believe that everything on earth existed for its benefit.

The sole basis for constructing this objective reality was the epistemological assumption that only our physical senses could generate data. Science was firmly grounded in the idea that the physical world was objective and could be studied at a distance. This was coupled with a positivist attitude that only data which could be measured physically was acceptable, and only when it was reduced to its elementary parts (reductionism) could it be understood. This has led to the fragmentation that is at the core of twentieth-century humanity's way of thinking, though it began a few centuries before.

However, Jung went against the grain of this well entrenched reductionist science. In the face of the intellectual climate of his times, he would never claim to have an absolute sureness and certainty of conceptualisation. He addressed this problem in his paper 'Synchronicity: an acausal connecting principle' (*CW* 8). Through his formulations on the nature of synchronicity and on dreaming he offered us access to the new science of relativity, uncertainty and intersubjectivity. These aspects of his thought I want to highlight briefly in this foreword, for they mark a distinction between the Freudian and Jungian perceptions of the world.

By discovering synchronicity Jung recognised that the order that exists in the human psyche is non-causal in that some human experience goes beyond simple cause and effect relationships in a temporal order. He saw that synchronicity was based on a universal order of meaning that was complementary to causality. Synchronicity, which Jung saw as being no more mysterious than the discontinuities of science, designates the equivalence or meaningful co-incidence of psychic or physical states, or events, that have no apparent causal relationship. It also applies to similar thoughts and dreams occurring at the same time in different locations. These two kinds of events, one inner and one outer, seem to have the same meaning and they occur almost simultaneously. The now classic example he cites is of working with a patient who dreams of a scarab and, at the same moment, a beetle flies into the window of the room. The meaning of synchronicity is available through knowledge of the symbolism embedded in the archetypes that are part of the inherited structures of the psyche.

Jung was very much attracted by the 'new physics' that had been introduced by Albert Einstein, Neils Bohr, John S. Bell and others, including Wolfgang Pauli who was Jung's collaborator in further developing the concept of synchronicity in 1952. Quantum physics gave us a new form of order that arises from the discernment of meaningful patterns in a context that went beyond the accepted temporal, cause and effect relationships, which was (and is) the accepted, taken-for-granted doctrine.

Jung postulated that there was an *unus mundus* that rests outside the human categories of space and time. This world lies beyond our accepted dichotomous categories of the physical and the mental and constitutes a wholeness, a oneness in which the psyche plays an integral part, and is not to be separated from what is conventionally called matter. This is a far cry from the atomistic, analytic approach, which is still pre-eminent in the twentieth century.

Here, Jung was pointing to the fact that scientists participate in the object of their observations in that they participate *in* what they observe by partaking *of* what they observe. All scientific investigators are subjectively involved in the phenomena they are observing and objectivity is essentially the clarification of the observer's subjectivity. He quotes C.A. Meir to make the point that both the object of research and the researcher, with his or her measuring instruments and procedures, are inextricably related. This complementary relationship between observer and observed is authentic and genuine, as is the relationship between physics and psychology.

There is a complementarity between space and time as there is a complementarity between causality and synchronicity. If these are drawn in the form of a matrix, the left-hand side of causality is memory when we link up events that are occurring now and those that are not occurring now. This we do intellectually. On the other hand, the right-hand side, which is grounded in synchronicity, is always experienced/felt, or sensed, is not thought about and is therefore known intuitively through synthesis, as opposed to the analysis and rationality that belongs to the left-hand side of the matrix.

The link between synchronicity and dreaming is found in the nature of dreams, which are experienced visually, often without words, and where events seem to be randomised, though they make sense at the time of dreaming. To follow Montague Ullman's formulation, dreams come from the unknowable depths of the psyche and are experienced as a blending of images

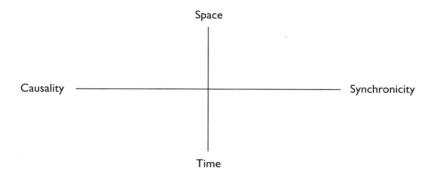

Source: Stein (1998), p. 217.

coming from personal and collective sources. Subsequently, we put the images into words. Using the concepts of physicist David Bohm, the explicate order of the dream as registered through images yields a discovery of the implicate order of meaning through articulation, association and amplification (Ullman 1975, p. 9). There can be a continual interaction between the implicate and explicate orders.

Dreaming, as Jung indicated, belongs to the domain of synchronicity. Dreaming belongs to the right-hand side of the matrix referred to above. Events are related in unprecedented ways in the dream, but from the context of the dream we can discern meaning. The only person who can find this meaning will be the dreamer, as Jung humbly insisted, though an analyst can offer help. There is a multiplicity of meanings, a multiverse as opposed to a universe of meaning, to a dream, as Jung makes very clear.

In a wonderful passage, which merits quotation, Jung writes:

> The dream is a little hidden door in the innermost and most secret recesses of the psyche, opening into that cosmic night which was psyche long before there was any ego consciousness, and which will remain psyche no matter how far our ego consciousness may extend ... All consciousness separates; but in dreams we put on the likeness of that more universal, truer, more eternal man dwelling in the darkness of primordial night. There he is still the whole, and the whole is in him, indistinguishable from nature and bare of all egohood. It is from these all-uniting depths that the dream arises, be it never so childish, grotesque, and immoral. (*CW* 10, para. 304)

In this passage, Jung was pointing to the unrecognised inseparability of mind and matter. I believe that in the process of evolution the simplest of organisms is engaged in dreaming, or proto-dreaming, as it reaches out to connect with its environment as part of the process of survival. In short, from matter arises mind. Mind, which is the seat of self-awareness and consciousness, is also where conception of I, differentiated from not-I, is formulated. Jung wrote:

> Individuation means becoming a single, homogeneous being, and, in so far as 'in-dividuality' embraces our innermost, last, and incomparable uniqueness, it also implies becoming one's self. We could therefore translate individuation as 'coming to selfhood' or 'self-realization'. (*CW* 7, para. 266)

In this process, dreaming will play a crucial part.

At a larger level, there is evidence that social systems dream (Lawrence 1998). This is shown in the forms of architecture they fashion as well as in the myths and legends to which they subscribe. Similarly, political systems dream in the form of statues, as used in the Third Reich and the former, communist, Russia and its then satellites: indeed, this is how any group creates its own identity over time.

A dream is a synthesis in that it is illustrating what we may not be aware of, but which is critical for our lives. Hall (1983) suggests three major steps in the Jungian approach to dreams. There has to be, first, an attempt to understand the dream by questioning and exposition to arrive at a state of detailed exactness. Second, there is the generating of associations and amplifications. This is done on the level of the personal, the cultural and the archetypal. Third, there is the situating of the dream in the context of the individuation process and the current life of the dreamer. Although dream interpretation is more complicated than this, it provides us with its essence and a place from where to begin the exploration.

What this emphasises is the richness and complexity of dreams. They have to be treated seriously. They are the major way by which we relate to the environment. They are also the means by which we think imaginatively through our connections, or non-connections, with the world. What comes across in Jung's writings is his respect for the dream, as well as the dreamer.

There is growing support for the idea that the brain operates on the basis of holographic memory processing. It does so by way of exciting, or agitating, the records of information that are stored in the brain – in the glial cells, to be precise. Essentially, it all works by association, which can be causal or based on synchronicity. Although some of these ideas were developed after Jung's death, I suggest that he was anticipating the quantum systemic qualities of the brain, seeing the possibility of connections that had never before been envisaged.

This is apparent when he wrote of the 'more universal, truer, more eternal man dwelling in the darkness of primordial night', for here he is indicating quantum connections in human beings. He is also saying, I think, that from the primordial matrix, or abyss, we have arisen, forming our consciousness over the millennia since the beginning of time. Our becoming is derived from the being of the dream. The Australian aborigine's conception of and belief in 'dream-time', from which all life is derived, reflects this notion. Out of the primordial night came life, which will continue to evolve in the same fashion. What appears to be a poetic truth turns out, on the basis of the research of the last few decades, to be literally so. There is a sense in which the current volume, a collection of chapters by a group of analytical psychotherapists sharing a common training and working together on a common project, creates a further example of the unconscious creativity described by the concept of social dreaming.

Freud and Jung were born in 1856 and 1875 respectively. They pioneered the systematic investigation and understanding of the unconscious mind. They were born at a time when Germany, Austria, Hungary, France and Switzerland were consolidating the triumphs of industrialisation. At the same time, they lived in a world that was comprehensible to, because it could be encompassed by, human beings that would have a high chance of being born and dying in the same location. Life was comparatively static and stable. By the time that Jung died in 1961 (Freud having pre-deceased him in 1939), Jung had experienced enormous changes in his life. Not only had there been the development of motor cars, aeroplanes, radio and television and all the other technological and medical benefits of the modern world, but also the world was moving inexorably to becoming what we now call a global society through the development of information technology.

Jung lived through two world wars and witnessed the monumental destruction associated with them. He also saw the rise of totalitarian states in different parts of the world. He had seen the imperial conquest of the world through colonisation. In other words, the boy born in Kesswil grew to be a man of Switzerland, internationally recognised, who had witnessed an almost total transformation of the way of life. Most people would simply have accepted this change as they lived out their lives. But Jung tried to understand it and what was happening to his fellow human beings. He situated it all in terms of human history, using ancient and medieval texts to link the old science of alchemy to his view of a new understanding in clinical work of the transference and counter-transference relationship. Although his writings on this subject are complex, they do provide a profound illumination of the phenomena that lie at the heart of the psychotherapeutic encounter.

Similarly, he explored human culture at first-hand by travelling to Algeria, Tunisia, New Mexico, Kenya, Uganda, Palestine and India to substantiate his thinking on the connection of myths, and other psychic phenomena, to modern mankind. For me, this level and quality of thinking was brought to bear in his book, *Modern Man in Search of a Soul* (1978), which details how modern humankind is in danger of losing itself as it races ahead on the crest of the wave of new technology. But to arrive at this kind of thinking Jung had experienced a period of torment – threatened by psychosis – at the beginning of the First World War. This was after he separated from Freud.

He writes movingly of this in *Memories, Dreams, Reflections* (1963), which was recorded by Aniela Jaffé. He recalls that he had a dream of Europe covered by ice, but, at the end of the dream, everything was in flower and he distributed a profusion of grapes to a large crowd of people. In another dream he was aware of the threat to civilisation from floods. What is most pertinent is the uncounted thousands of the dead in his dream.

Jung intuited the disasters that were to come in his lifetime, and was able to use them for understanding twentieth-century humankind and civilisation. Here we see a distinguished, scholarly, innately wise man become submerged in the unconscious and then resurface as a humane analyst of contemporary social life. He was able to speak to the rest of humanity in ways that were understandable. There is little doubt that this period of inner uncertainty was a major influence on his work in later life.

Jung is a writer and thinker who becomes more comprehensible as I become older. In particular, I find myself resonating with his ideas on the soul, on dreaming and on synchronicity, and have incorporated these in my own researches on social dreaming.

This volume continues in substantial measure the spirit of Jung's quality of thinking. It seems to me not to be didactic and full of certainty, but to be reaching out to grasp some meaningful understanding of contemporary life with its joys, its pains and its essential tragedy.

W. Gordon Lawrence MA Dr rer oec
Visiting Professor of Organizational Behaviour
Cranfield University, Bedford

References

Hall. James A. (1983) *Jungian Dream Interpretation*. Toronto: Inner City Books.

Jung, Carl G. (1963). *Memories, Dreams, Reflections*, recorded and edited by Aniela Jaffé. London: Collins/Routledge and Kegan Paul.

Jung, Carl G. (1978) *Modern Man in Search of a Soul*. London: Routledge and Kegan Paul.

Lawrence, W. Gordon (ed.) (1998) *Social Dreaming at Work*. London: Karnac.

Stein, Murray (1998) *Jung's Map of the Soul*. Chicago, IL: Open Court.

Ullman, Montague (1975) 'The transformation process in dreams', *The American Academy of Psychoanalysis*, 19(2): 8–10.

Introduction

Elphis Christopher and Hester McFarland Solomon

Carl Gustav Jung (1875–1961) was a man of the millennium. His personal history parallels the history of the twentieth century and is especially relevant to the current moment where themes not only from the twentieth century but also from other centuries of the second millennium in anticipation of the new era are being gathered.

Jung's life and work touch upon the twentieth century's two major themes: on the one hand, the discovery and mapping of the unconscious, an internal source of creativity and destruction for each individual; and, on the other hand, those outbreaks of dreadful violence and experiences of awesome creativity that can erupt from unconscious sources within groups and across humankind as a whole.

The stature of Jung relates to his capacity in the face of tremendous psychological distress and suffering to find authentic solutions within himself to heal and thereby to lay down the building blocks, which constitute his remarkable *opus*, for those who follow to use, develop and grow. The relevance of his contribution, contained in the volumes of his written texts and exemplified in his dramatic personal and professional life, offers an insight into new ways of addressing perennial human situations at the end of the millennium. These had previously been articulated within social, cultural, political and religious frameworks which are experienced by many as no longer viable, needing reinvention and renewal. Jung was prepared courageously to tackle the 'big subjects', the big problems of being human: the nature and workings of the psyche; the structure and dynamics of the conscious and unconscious; how the personality develops and expresses itself; the emergence of meaning; the significance of culture, religion, and spirituality; the problem of evil and the existence of God. Jung would say that the 'big problems' tackled him!

Jung provided us with a new, exciting and provocative map of the psyche. For Freud, there was the conscious mind and the personal unconscious in which repressed material unacceptable to consciousness was located. Jung expanded this view of the psyche to a third 'layer' shared by all humankind – the collective unconscious. The new geography of the mind necessitated a new language with which to orientate our explorations and explanations. Jung took many of his terms from the past but redefined and elaborated them in a new way such that many are now in common everyday usage – 'self', 'archetype', 'anima', 'shadow', 'introversion and extroversion', to name but a few. It is not possible to define all of Jung's terms here. For this, the reader is referred to a useful resource, *A Critical Dictionary of Jungian Analysis* (Samuels, Shorter and Plaut, 1986 (London: Routledge and Kegan Paul)). However, some of the terms used most frequently by the authors in this volume are offered here as an aid to the reader.

For Jung, the *psyche* was dynamic, flexible and capable of purposive change. He saw *libido* as related to the total life force or psychic energy of the individual, and not restricted to the energy of the psychosexual developmental stages as Freud posited. Jung understood that there is a natural tendency for the psyche to maintain a homeostasis, a balance, through the dynamic tension of the opposites. The resolution of this tension can take place psychologically through the emergence of a symbol, which is the vehicle for the creation of meaning and purpose for the psyche as a whole. This is the essential *teleological* nature of Jung's psychology.

The *self*, that peculiarly Jungian concept, thus represents an archetypal capacity to develop to one's fullest potential, a unifying principle within the psyche. 'The self is not only the centre but also the whole circumference which embraces both conscious and unconscious; it is the centre of this totality just as the ego is the centre of the conscious mind' (*CW* 12, para. 444). It is not value-laden, neither benign nor malign; rather, it should be regarded as the overall determining power of the individual.

The *collective unconscious* is a locus of psychological activity related directly to the phylogenetic instinctual bases of the human race. The contents of the collective unconscious reflect archetypal processes. The *archetype* is an inherited part of the psyche that structures recurrent patterns of psychological performance that are linked to the instincts. It is a hypothetical entity, unrepresentable in itself, and evident only through its manifestations; for example, in internal representations and outer behaviours that cluster around the basic and universal experiences of life. These are the major life events such as birth, marriage, parenthood, separation and death. Thus Jung speaks of the *archetypes of the collective unconscious*, and their accompanying images – images of the major life events and psychological developments – such as Madonna and child, the hero, the *puer/puella*, the anima and animus, the *coniunctio*, *hieros gamos*, and those images of the self that reflect potential wholeness, such as the mandala. Jung also referred to the collective unconscious as participating in the *objective psyche*, where spirit and matter find a common source, feeding humankind's knowledge, insight and imagination.

Jung conceived of the unconscious as a counterpole to consciousness and therein lay his theory of the *opposites*. The 'opposites are the ineradicable and indispensable preconditions of all psychic life' (*CW* 14, para. 206). The theory of the opposites represents a dialectic in which the dynamic within the psyche searches for a synthesis, a new creation. 'Nature does not halt at the opposites; she uses them to create out of opposition new birth' (*CW* 16, para. 534). It is the *transcendent function* that mediates the opposites, allowing for change to occur out of the dynamic tension inherent in opposition. By expressing itself psychologically through symbols, the transcendent function facilitates a transition from one psychological attitude or condition to another. Jung described the transcendent function as 'a natural process, a manifestation of the energy that springs from the tension of opposites and it consists in a series of fantasy occurrences which appear spontaneously in dreams and visions' (*CW* 7, para. 121). The *coniunctio* is an alchemical symbol denoting the union of unlike but not unrelated substances, a marrying of the opposites in an intercourse which has as its fruition the birth of a new element. This can be a real child, or it can be symbolised by a new creation that manifests potential for greater wholeness by transforming the attitudes of both opposing natures into an unpredicted synthesis. The *coniunctio* symbolises those psychic processes that lead to rebirth and transformation within the psyche. *Individuation* refers to the capacity of the individual to become increasingly separate, whole, and distinct from other people or the collective psychology. The person becomes conscious of the ways in which he or she is both a unique and at the same time an ordinary human being.

The above list of recurring terms to be found throughout this volume cannot be exhaustive and is offered as a 'rough guide' to those readers who may be relatively unfamiliar with Jungian thinking.

Let us turn now to this volume and how it came about. An introductory course entitled 'Jungian Thought in the Modern World' has been offered over a number of years by the Jungian Section of the British Association of Psychotherapists (BAP) to members of the public, most of whom are already practitioners in the mental health field with an interest in Jungian analytic theory and practice. The idea for the course originated from one of the authors, Stephen Gross, and Angela Bennett, another Jungian member of the BAP, was instrumental in establishing and organising it. An interested group of BAP members, all qualified Jungian analytical psychologists, practitioners of Jungian analysis and analytical theory, selected the topic(s) that they wanted to teach, and later to write about. All the contributors to the present volume, apart from Warren Colman, Geraldine Godsil, Christopher MacKenna and Michael Simpson, have taught on the course. All contributors are closely involved with the BAP as an organisation; each contributor is responsible for those ideas expressed in his or her own chapter.

The authors have been prepared to tackle Jung the man as well as Jung the thinker in all his complexity and paradox. In the process many have rediscovered Jung, or have read him in a new way. The book addresses through the sequence of its chapters some of the most pressing concerns facing individuals and societies today. Following this introductory chapter, the subsequent chapters track contemporary Jungian thinking, which spans a spectrum from the most individual to the most collective. As did Jung, so the authors push at the boundaries of human imagination, at the same time preserving the principles of discrimination and differentiation: this is where art and science meet. Rediscovering Jung's *opus* has enabled us to orient ourselves and develop our understanding at these various boundaries. The aim throughout this volume is to demonstrate the relevance of the extraordinary scope of Jung's contribution to the profound questions facing us today.

We are aware of having excluded certain key areas that Jung had already begun to explore in depth. In particular, there is no contribution in this volume regarding psychological types, and, although alluded to throughout the book, there is no specific chapter on the Jungian approach to the theory of dreams and dream interpretation.

Part I, 'Jungian Thought and the Individual', focuses on Jung's unique concepts concerning the structure and dynamics of individual psychology and the possibilities for change and transformation in the psyche.

It begins with Warren Colman's study, 'Models of the Self', as a way of introducing the reader to Jungian and post-Jungian thinking about the self. Jung's concept of the self is peculiarly his own and distinguishes him from other depth psychologists who may have been hindered by not having evolved a theory about the origins and development of the self. Colman explores three aspects of the Jungian self – the self as the totality of the psyche, the self as archetype, and the self as a personification of the unconscious. He then considers how some of the conflicts in the subsequent development of Jungian thinking can be understood in terms of the differing emphasis given to these three aspects. He proposes a fourth way of thinking about the self, as the process of the psyche. This raises important theoretical possibilities.

In the second chapter, 'Jung and his Family – A Contemporary Paradigm', Ann Kutek examines how Jung's own family history and experience shaped his thought. She considers how Jung's early emotional deprivation led to a search through the intellect to seek attachments in his professional life, most notably with Freud. The subsequent break with Freud, the 'father' of psychoanalysis, may have been inevitable, preceded as it was by Jung's conflict and disillusionment with his own father. Archetypal theory adds a further dimension to the nature/nurture debate, demonstrating that although the qualities and behaviour of parental figures and the child's environment are of pivotal importance to the child's development, the dynamic interaction between them and the child's archetypal experiences plays a decisive role in the child's capacity for socialisation and ultimately in how he or she fares.

The third chapter, 'Gender Issues – Anima and Animus' by Elphis Christopher, considers Jung's concepts of the contrasexual archetype, the anima (in the man), and the animus (in the woman), both directly from Jung's writings and also from post-Jungian contemporary analytical psychology and psychoanalysis. Psychological theories pertaining to sexual and gender identity development with particular emphasis on current feminist psychoanalytic critique are described. The concepts of animus and anima are briefly explored in relation to homosexuality. Clinical understanding together with Jung's view of marriage as a psychological relationship is illustrated by case material.

In Part II, 'Jungian Thought and the Collective', the focus turns towards a wider collective perspective.

In Chapter 4, 'Modern Western Society – The Making of Myth and Meaning', Helen Morgan looks at how and why societies develop myths to convey unconscious messages that have significance for the times in which they are evoked. She shows that, while Jung accepted the validity of the theories that Freud saw encapsulated in the myth of Oedipus, he also challenged its primacy and developed his theory of the collective unconscious and deep archetypal structures, which could be known indirectly through the pattern of myths that any culture tells itself.

Stephen Gross in Chapter 5, 'Racism in the Shadow of Jung – The Myth of White Supremecy', tackles the fraught issue of Jung's alleged racism and anti-Semitism. The relationship between Jung the man and his psychological theories are examined and the problems thereby posed are considered within a contemporary moral, political and intellectual context. Jung's thinking is appraised according to the notions of white supremacism examined by James Hillman and Frantz Fanon. The archetype of the shadow and the scapegoat are introduced, together with the concept of projection, as internal theoretical tools in our understanding of racism at an individual and sociopolitical level.

Ann Kutek in Chapter 6, 'Warring Opposites', takes Jung's concepts concerning the shadow and the collective unconscious further in the search to understand why some conflicts between nations, tribes and religions end in war, while others do not. Jung lived through two world wars and has been accused of Nazi sympathies. Ann Kutek explores how Jung developed his thinking in 1936 regarding the Wotan archetype as taking possession of the German people after the First World War. She also writes about the paradox that often, after a war, changes for the better can occur in some aspects of living. For example, psychiatric services and attitudes towards and treatment of the mentally distressed were improved as a direct consequence of the experiences of both world wars.

Part III, 'Jungian Thought and the New Sciences', takes up the challenge presented by current scientific thinking and its possible relationship to psychological theories, particularly those of Jung, concerning the structure and workings of the mind.

Thus, in Chapter 7, 'The New Physics through a Jungian Perspective', Helen Morgan explores Jungian thought in relation to the revolutionary paradigms of new physics, which challenge our previous divisions between mind and matter, the observer and the observed, and posits the interconnectedness of all matter. She considers some aspects of quantum mechanics, including David Bohm's ideas of the 'implicate order', where there may be echoes of Jung's concepts of the collective unconscious and synchronicity.

In Chapter 8, 'Recent Developments in the Neurosciences', Hester Solomon focuses on recent findings from psychoneurobiology in relation to the archetypal and developmental analytic traditions through an examination of the recent literature on early intersubjective processes and their neurobiological correlates. These have important implications for the nature/nurture debate regarding the origins of the self.

In Chapter 9, 'Creative Life in a Scientific World', Michael Simpson explores Jung's concept of the objective psyche and the individual's relation to it, and how new avenues of scientific investigation incorporate the scientist's creative relationship to his or her unconscious processes. He illustrates this through the double-bind situation that can occur in analytic work, a stuck situation where the way out of the impasse may emerge but cannot be predicted from what is consciously known.

Jean Pearson in Chapter 10, 'The Environment – Our Mother Earth', addresses present-day anxieties about the environment and humanity's destructive as well as creative relationship to it. She discusses the possibility that we may destroy our planet through our desacralisation of the material world, the result of our hubris. A possible way forward using Jungian concepts to heal the split between the 'masculine' world of ego consciousness and the 'feminine' world of unconscious relatedness is offered.

In Part IV, 'Jungian Thought and the Religious, Ethical and Creative Spirit', the final chapters are devoted to religious, ethical, artistic and creative concerns.

In Chapter 11, Reverend Chris MacKenna, a practising priest as well as a Jungian analytical psychologist, examines Jung's attitude towards Christianity in 'Jung and Christianity – Wrestling with God'. Jung wrote that his life's work was essentially an attempt to understand what others apparently believed. Chris MacKenna seeks to demonstrate how and why Jung took ambivalent, confused and at times defensive stances towards Christianity.

In Chapter 12, 'The Ethical Self', Hester Solomon places philosophical and ethical questions concerning good and evil – in particular, the need to restore to consciousness the unconscious shadow – firmly within psychological enquiry. She demonstrates how the central Jungian concepts of transformation and individuation include the idea of integration of both good and bad aspects within the self and the recognition of these in others. She goes on to explore the ethical attitude as a developmental position, and how this may be reinforced or thwarted by the child's primary caregivers. Links are made to the ethical position that should obtain in the consulting room.

In Chapter 13, 'Spirits and Spirituality', Dale Mathers studies Jung's life as the background to his religious and psychological preoccupations. Jung came to see religion as an archetype of meaning that developed throughout life, particularly at *rites de passage*. Analytical psychology offers ways of under-standing religious experiences and religious systems, noting whether they are open or closed, opening or closing. It can comment on their reality testing ability, using qualities of self – agency, coherence, continuity and emotional arousal – to measure a religion's adaptive capacity.

John Clay in Chapter 14, 'Jung's Influence in Literature and the Arts', describes the historical background to Jung's association with the arts, both in his personal life and via his influence on his contemporaries and later practi-tioners. He cites Jung's view that 'art' applies widely to all fields of creative endeavour, and not just the well known and well trodden artistic paths. John Clay sets out to show what lies behind the notion of creativity and to demon-strate the unconscious forces underlying artistic production. Examples from literature and painting are used to illustrate these processes.

Finally, in Chapter 15, 'Winter's Ragged Hand – Creativity in the Face of Death', Geraldine Godsil uses Jungian theory as a frame to show, through Jung's life experience and through a detailed study of Blake's *The Gates of Paradise,* that the recognition of death can stimulate creativity. This creativity of old age may be a critical factor in maintaining relationships of interest, love and warmth right to the end. The paradox of diminishing bodily powers still being accompanied by fecundity in symbolic life is not that uncommon, although the ageism of modern Western culture can make us blind to it, both as a reality and a possibility. Blake's illuminated text shows us the complex interrelationships sustained in the dialogue and argument he establishes between three core myths. Erasure, as an act of obliteration, is countered by the perpetual work of remembering and recreating loved figures from the past and lost aspects of the self as they reappear in shadowy configurations.

Thus the progression of the chapters represents a circumnavigation of the *unus mundus,* Jung's idea that psyche and matter, the individual and collective, the inner and the outer, are deeply interconnected in meaningful ways. So the progression of the chapters charts a sequence from the individual to the collective and back again to the individual – from the intimate to the ultimate, from life to death through to rebirth. Thus, also, Jung's personal and often perilous quest to understand the workings of the unconscious, both as a source of conflict but also as the source of humanity's creativity and highest endeavours, speaks out to us as we seek to come to terms with the multitude of internal and external pressures of life lived in the modern world prior to the beginning of the third millennium.

Part I
Jungian Thought and the Individual

1
Models of the Self

Warren Colman

Introduction

The self is the centre and the circumference of Jung's psychology. Its realisation through the process of individuation was, for Jung, the ultimate goal towards which we strive as human beings; indications of its presence can be found in all aspects of human endeavour, but especially in religion and mythology. Unlike Freud, Jung did not regard religion and spirituality as illusions or sublimations of some other basic instinctual force. He recognised religion as expressing in itself a fundamental and irreducible need of human beings for purpose and meaning and the recognition of something greater than themselves. It was this 'something' that Jung termed the self, taking the term not from its customary usage in Western psychology but from the Hindu notion of the Self or 'Atman', that aspect of divine power which resides in every individual as the source of being.

This usage sets 'the Jungian self' apart from almost all other Western conceptions of the self. These tend to equate the self with 'the sense of self' or the capacity to possess a sense of self.[1] This, after all, is the ordinary everyday usage of the word: it is what I mean when I refer to 'myself' and what I mean when I stop to think about who this little word 'I' refers to. In this sense, having a self is equivalent to the development of a capacity to understand the meaning of 'I' and is concerned with the experience of subjectivity as a coherent and continuous sense of being a particular person. Jung regards this as *the personal self*, which he refers to as the ego. It is the self of which we are conscious and, as such, forms a *content* of consciousness as well as being its centre. By contrast, the Jungian self is always that which *transcends* consciousness, that which is *greater* than what I take to be 'my self'.

3

Jung's thinking on the self is full of complexities, paradoxes and uncertainties, many of which are inherent in any attempt to discuss something which, by definition, transcends human comprehension. It is perhaps inevitable that he used 'the self' to refer to several different but overlapping conceptions, just as 'the God-image', which Jung regarded as indistinguishable from the self, has a potentially infinite range of meanings. There are various ways of categorising these different usages (see, for example, Gordon 1985, Redfearn 1985). In this chapter, I shall outline three aspects of the Jungian self: the self as the totality of the psyche, the self as an archetype and the self as a personification of the unconscious. I then consider how some of the conflicts in the subsequent development of Jungian thinking can be understood in terms of the differing emphases given to these different aspects of the self. Finally, I propose a fourth way of thinking about the self, as the *process* of the psyche.

Contrasts and Comparisons: The Self is Not Myself

Jung was ahead of his time in recognising the shifting and multiple nature of ego consciousness. He saw the 'ego-complex' (that which I take to be me, my personal identity) as only one amongst many complexes or 'sub-personalities', any of which could invade or disrupt the conscious mind or even act independently of it.[2] Jung's psychology is therefore well in accord with recent trends towards 'decentring' or 'deconstructing' the self. The difference is that Jung goes further, reaching towards some overarching view of a self which encompasses and can potentially unite the multiplicity within it.

Jung would also have recognised the arguments of social constructionism and discourse theory that the self is a socially constructed fiction maintained via a complex web of interweaving social narratives: he would have said that this was what he meant by the *persona*. The persona (from the mask worn by actors in Greek drama) is the face that we put on for the world. It is how we appear to others and, sometimes, to ourselves. But it is not who we truly are (*CW* 6, para. 370). Thus Jungian psychology takes issue with social constructionism when the latter maintains that there is no self *beyond* social appearances.

The closest parallel to Jung is the concept of 'self-actualisation' in humanistic psychology, particularly associated with Abraham Maslow. This is certainly close to Jung's concept of individuation and Maslow's description of 'peak experiences' undoubtedly refers to experiences of psychic wholeness such as Jung describes, as well as those described in the literature of spirituality and mysticism. These experiences, though, are best thought of as intimations of a wholeness which ultimately transcends them. The Jungian self thus refers not only to what is actualised but includes all that which is not actualised and never can be actualised.

The Self as the Totality of the Psyche

As a totality, the self can only be partially represented in consciousness, either through experiences of wholeness or through symbolic images which represent a wholeness greater than oneself. This does not necessarily mean that experiences and feelings of wholeness actually *are* 'the whole person'. Since the self includes the unconscious as well as the conscious mind, and the unconscious is by definition unknown to consciousness, the greater part of the self must remain forever unknowable. Even though we may become conscious of hidden aspects of ourselves, even though we might realise considerable aspects of our potential, the unconscious (in Jung's conception of it) is like an inexhaustible reservoir, a living stratum that continually regenerates itself and is therefore infinite. Furthermore, the unconscious also includes the archetypes, fundamental structuring factors of the psyche that underlie conscious experience but can never themselves become conscious. We do not know the archetypes – we only know the multiple representations of them in consciousness. To remain true to the hypothesis of archetypes, we must remain true to their ultimately irrepresentable nature: that is, we must always keep in mind that what we see are *images*. Perhaps it is like looking at a movie screen: if we try to see where the images come from, we are blinded by the light of the projector and see nothing.

Jung regards the symbolic representations of totality which appear in consciousness as indistinguishable from the God-image. This is not to say that all such representations appear in the form of 'God', nor that 'God' and 'the self' are the same thing – something that psychology is not in a position to establish in any event (*CW* 9ii, para. 308). What Jung does claim is that religious imagery is concerned with the symbolism of psychic wholeness and that religious aspirations are identical with the goal of individuation. He particularly cites the image of Christ who represents 'the whole man' that each of us might become. 'In the same way that Christ represents a personality greater than the average man, Christ, as a symbol, represents something greater than the average ego – the self' (Samuels 1985, p. 98; *CW* 11, para. 414). However, since the defining feature of the self as a totality is that it is infinitely greater than the ego, *any* symbol which is greater than the individual may be a symbol of the total self (*CW* 11, para. 232).

For example, a woman whose life had previously been severely restricted in various ways told me of a dream in which she released a genie which grew to enormous size, filling the entire horizon. I saw this as an image of her unrealised self: the genie has enormous power, far beyond that of its master, the ego, and yet it is in the service of the ego and can only do what the ego commands. This is a clear example of how a symbol of the self may nevertheless represent a *part* self. A symbol of totality would actually have to encompass not only the genie but also its master, and perhaps the lamp as well. We might even take the entire story of Aladdin as a symbol of the self: the cave, ·the evil old man, the princess and her father could all be seen as archetypal aspects of an individual personality so that we might have to consider the story as a whole to get a sense of the total self.

Ultimately, symbols are always indications of a reality beyond themselves. So, for example, when Jung spoke of his experiences with mandalas, saying: 'in them I saw the ultimate' (Jung 1963, p. 222), he did not mean that the mandala itself expresses the ultimate but that his contemplation of mandalas enabled him to see 'the ultimate' through them. Someone else might see only a mandala. Symbols depend on a relationship between the object and its perceiver. As in physics, the observer influences the observed and the observed influences the observer.

The same problem of how to represent the irrepresentable has been a consistent theme in Western philosophy and theology since before the time of Christ.[3] The Jewish philosopher Philo first distinguished between God's *ousia*, his unknowable essence which lies beyond our reach, and his *energia*, his activities in the world. Philo's project was to reconcile the abstract, eternal and immobile divinity of Aristotle – the Unmoved Mover – with the God of the Jews who was very much an actor in human affairs. Later in their formulation of the doctrine of the Trinity, the Cappodacian Christians also took up Philo's distinction, arguing that God has one *ousia* but three *hypostases* – the exterior expression of God's internal (and unknowable) nature. Thus the Trinity is actually not God himself but merely the only way that God can manifest himself to our human comprehension. Similarly, the Gnostics regarded the God of Creation as a lower God or demiurge, behind whom stood a series of higher levels of being before the true God himself could be reached. In the Kabbalah, this higher God is called *En Sof*, 'that which is infinite'. This inner aspect of God is so hidden, so impersonal and inconceivable that he is not even mentioned in the Bible (Scholem 1941, p. 12).

Many religious thinkers and mystics such as Dionysius the Aeropagite, Maimonides and Meister Eckehart have argued that since God is unknowable he can only be defined negatively by that which he is not. Meister Eckehart distinguished between the God of the Trinity and the unknowable Godhead whom he called 'Nothing'. This echoes Jung's suggestion that the self does not exist as such. All these distinctions refer to the impossibility of achieving any representation of 'the thing in itself' which is, in any event, not a 'thing' (therefore it is 'no-thing'). If we regard God's *ousia*, *En Sof* and the Godhead as referring to an infinite totality, then all representations of it are necessarily partial. Negative theology attempts to school the mind out of its habitual tendency to form images and concepts which it then takes for reality by making it attempt to think the unthinkable. In this way, it may be possible to go beyond the limits of thought to an experience in which 'this' and 'that' dissolve in 'that which is and is not'. Zen koans utilise a similar method.

In mystical experience, the distinctions between partial and total, conscious and unconscious, subject and object cease to have any meaning. There is no longer a state in which I, the subject, am conscious of something (the object); rather there may be a state of boundless infinitude which the subject/object dualism of language that structures our normal consciousness is unable to capture. This would be an experience of the self's capacity to unite the opposites which constitute its structure or, to put it the other way, that the opposites which structure the psyche are united in the self.

Although such experiences are rare, even for those who dedicate their lives to the spiritual discipline of achieving them, partial experiences of wholeness and moments in which the unity of all things is glimpsed are not unusual. These moments offer an *intimation* of wholeness, an incontrovertible inkling of a psychic totality that remains forever out of reach and unknowable.

The Self as an Archetype

It is confusing that Jung refers to the self as both the totality and an archetype within the totality, albeit the central one. Fordham, in a careful examination of the way Jung talks about the self, points out the contradiction between these two usages (Fordham 1987, pp. 1–33): if the self is the totality of the psyche including all the archetypes, how can it also be one of them? Furthermore, as an archetype, the self cannot be the totality since it excludes the ego which perceives it and is structured by it. Nevertheless, the symbolic images which represent the self in consciousness are clearly archetypal and therefore presumably structured by the archetype which they represent – that is, the archetype of the self. This is where the notion of archetypes as discrete entities 'in' the psyche begins to break down. Archetypes are better thought of as modes of experiencing, tendencies to experience the world and ourselves in particular ways. This enables us to recognise the dual nature of archetypes: they generate particular symbolic images but these images also refer to particular psychic functions. The image of the hero, for example, refers to the struggle to achieve psychic separateness, particularly in relation to the mother. When a particular archetype is 'constellated', that is, when a particular psychic function needs to be undertaken or developed, the psyche 'throws up' the relevant symbols that galvanise the conscious mind towards action. These images may occur spontaneously – in dreams, for example – but there may also be 'ready made' images in the culture which assume a particular fascination and importance for the individual at specific points in his or her development.

From this, we can see that archetypal symbols of wholeness (indicators of 'the archetype of the self') may occur more strongly in *fragmented* individuals than in more integrated ones. They are generated by the compensatory function of the unconscious which acts to balance the conscious situation. While it is paradoxical to think of 'the archetype of the self' as somehow separate from or contained within the self, it is possible to think of archetypal processes directed towards wholeness and of a 'central archetype' whose centring functions involve the organisation and integration of the psyche as a whole. Symbols of psychic wholeness therefore function to draw the individual towards wholeness and, especially, towards becoming more centred; for the closer one is to the centre, the more panoramic one's view of the periphery and the less one is thrown around by the oscillating turmoil of psychic life. Eventually, perhaps, one arrives at 'the still point of the turning world', an image of the self *par excellence*.

In his later work, Jung also came to think of the self as the archetype of the ego. He seems to have recognised that the sharp distinction between ego and self could not always be maintained since the more individuated one becomes, the closer the conscious ego approximates to psychic wholeness (although this is an ever-receding goal). The self is also akin to consciousness in that both can be described as a circle whose centre is everywhere and whose cir-cumference is nowhere – a description originally applied to God. While the ego is the totality of consciousness ('I' am in everything I experience), the self is the totality of conscious *and* unconscious and, in the same way, is omnipresent. This suggests that the archetype of the self can be thought of as the archetype of subjectivity – that is, as a basic principle which underlies the experience of a subjective self out of which the ego gradually develops. This line of thinking has recently been developed by Polly Young-Eisendrath, whose work I discuss later in this chapter.

The Self as a Personification of the Unconscious

Jung recognised that the archetypal figures that appear in dreams, mythology, fairy tales and other symbolic systems such as alchemy or the tarot were per-sonifications of psychic functions. It is therefore not unreasonable to assume that some archetypal figures, especially those concerned with leadership in some way, might be personifications of the *totality* of psychic functions – that is, the self. Just as the king represents the whole nation, so the king or lord or God might represent the whole psyche. But here we see the paradox of part and whole creeping in again: the king not only represents the people, he is himself one of them, albeit a particularly powerful one. Jung often sees the relationship between king or God figures and one of their subjects as symbolic of the relationship between the self and the ego. But then it becomes hard to sustain the notion that the king is a personification of the *whole* self since what we see are two parts in relation to one another that *together* make up the whole. There is a blurring here so that ego/conscious is seen in opposition to self/unconscious and in this way the self takes on the guise, not of totality, but of a personification of the unconscious.

The clearest example of this is in 'Answer to Job' (*CW* 11, paras 560–758) where Jung takes Job's conflict with Yahweh as a metaphor for the relationship between the ego and the self. However, Yahweh is more like a personification of the elemental powerhouse of the unconscious while Job represents the puny but essential forces of consciousness. Yahweh is presented like an omnipotent infant who cannot contemplate any check to his own importance and becomes consumed with world-shattering rages when his own wishes are thwarted. The self is thus seen as identical with the primitive, undifferentiated unconscious, full of raw potential which needs to be refined by the ego, here represented by Job's challenge to his almighty God. Jung sees Job as forcing God to recognise – and justify – his own injustice, thereby bringing about an increase in consciousness, represented by the birth of Christ.

This has led to a model, developed further by later Jungians such as Erich Neumann and Edward Edinger, in which ego development is seen as a progressive emergence and differentiation from the self (equated with the unconscious). This makes it especially difficult to hold on to the way that the ego is at the same time part of the self and, furthermore, in the course of development becomes *more* like the self through greater assimilation and realisation of unconscious contents. This leads Edinger to assert an 'ego–self paradox' by which the 'dialectic between ego and self [leads] paradoxically to both greater separation and greater intimacy' (Edinger 1960, p. 18). This apparent paradox can be unpicked if we distinguish between self as totality and self as unconscious. Through the individuation process, greater consciousness naturally produces greater intimacy with assimilated psychic contents precisely because there is also a greater separation from unconsciousness. The more separation from unconsciousness there is, the greater the awareness of self.

In addition to their paradoxical part/whole nature, there is a further difficulty with symbolic personifications of the self: they produce a misleading attribution of subjectivity. This can result in a failure to distinguish between personified symbols of the self and the unknowable reality to which they refer. Edinger gives a clear example of this when he argues that since the self includes everything that we are, the self also *accepts* everything that we are (Edinger 1960, p. 10). This is rather like saying that the periodic table accepts all the elements because it includes them. It begs the question as to whether the self can have this kind of personal, emotional subjectivity or whether this view is a sort of anthropomorphic 'category mistake' on the part of the ego. This issue is also strongly echoed in theological controversies about the nature of God. Is God remote, impersonal and ineffable like Brahman and the Unmoved Mover, or is he a personal God, like the Judaeo-Christian God who has a personal, emotional relationship with his creation (cf. the ego)? If God is too remote, we become unable to relate to him at all. Yet if he is too personal, there is a danger that we (the ego) attribute to God (the self) our own human attributes and thereby reduce the awesome infinitude of the All. Even for Jews and Muslims, the Christian idea of a God-man was a step too far: the attribution of human form to the divine infinitude was regarded as blasphemy.

The three aspects of the self I have considered are held together in Jung's thinking by the overall sense of the self as 'the greater personality'. For example, he describes it as 'a more compendious personality' that takes the ego into its service (*CW* 11, para. 390). Jung regards the development of this kind of relativity and humility as crucial to the process of individuation: the ego must renounce its arrogant omnipotence and recognise its dependence on forces greater than itself. This view is certainly in accord with the self as a greater totality of which the ego is only a small part. It also recognises that the greater part of that totality resides in the unconscious, and it is the task of the ego to acknowledge unconscious archetypal forces and to bring into consciousness the potential inherent within them. Perhaps most important of all in this view of the self are those occasions in which the self seems to speak to us, when we hear 'the inner voice' or feel 'the will of God', a greater power possessed of far greater knowledge and intelligence to which our own small conscious purposes must bow. It is easy to see how such experiences promote a view of the self as possessing personal subjectivity. However, they may more accurately be construed as *messages* in personified form, messages that indicate the existence of a larger overall organisation and purpose that encompasses the ego: the archetype of the self.

In the subsequent development of Jung's thought, the accentuation of these different aspects has produced several conflicting models. Much of the controversy has been played out in a series of furious debates about the role and nature of the self in infancy. Jung himself had little interest in infancy and childhood, perhaps because he regarded that phase of life as belonging to the Freudian territory from which he had become an exile. As later Jungian analysts have turned their attention to the first half of life, they have taken differing views on whether, and in what way, the self is present from the beginning of life and/or only emerges in the course of development. The three developments I shall now consider roughly correspond to the three models I have outlined:

1. the mythological approach (represented by Neumann and Edinger) which emphasises self as unconscious;

2. the biological approach developed by Michael Fordham, whose concept of 'the primary self' is a model of the self as a pre-existing totality;
3. the constructivist approach, represented by Polly Young-Eisendrath and Louis Zinkin, who, in slightly different ways, concentrate on the archetype of the self as the organising principle underlying personal subjectivity.

Jung and Neumann: Primary Union

Neumann, who most closely follows Jung, believed that the infant exists in a state of primary undifferentiated union with the mother who 'carries' the infant's self in projection. In this model there is a symbolic equation between unconscious, self and mother. The mother represents the self to the infant who is like a dependent ego carried in the maternal matrix of the unconscious self. As ego consciousness grows, so the child gradually separates from the mother (and later, the father) through a series of archetypal conflicts. Neumann sees the world's great myths, particularly hero myths and creation myths, as symbolic depictions of the development of consciousness on both a collective and an individual level (ontogeny recapitulates phylogeny) (Neumann 1954).

This theory represents the self as being similar to what Kleinian analysts refer to as 'the good internal object'. The mother initially acts as a container, which later becomes internalised. This aspect of the mother is particularly well suited to represent the self since container symbols are amongst its most characteristic symbols, such as the castle, the city and especially the alchemical vessel or *vas*, in which symbolic transformations take place. The mother's womb contains the infant as the self contains the ego, surrounding it on all sides, while the mother's breast, like the self (and the unconscious) is the source of all its nourishment and is itself a circle symbol *par excellence*. Symbolic linkages between mother, self and unconscious are therefore particularly strong and it is hardly surprising that the mother features as a particularly powerful symbol of the greater totality and our dependence upon it. This is a good illustration of the way that archetypal representations are often fused so that one image can represent many archetypes, just as one archetype can be represented by many images (Freud called this 'over-determination'). Only in the course of later development do the archetypes of self, mother and child differentiate out from each other in the way they are perceived by the conscious mind.

Fordham: The Primary Self

Michael Fordham approached the study of the self in infancy from a completely different point of view and, as a result, was sharply critical of Neumann's approach. His background and interest was in the Cambridge empirical school of biology – worlds apart from the German mythological Idealism of Neumann. Fordham was interested in the analysis of actual children and took an empirical approach to what could actually be *observed* in their behaviour as well as their fantasies. He particularly objected to the implication that the infant has no autonomy and is merely a function of the psychology of the parents. In his view, the child is an active and separate individual from the start. In recent years, child development studies have amply confirmed Fordham's view that the mental capacities of infants had been grossly underestimated. It is therefore idealistic, romantic and sentimental to believe that infants exist in a state of primary union and have no self of their own.

Fordham's approach takes the infant as primarily a biological organism, a psychosomatic entity, rather than a symbolic or social being. These elements are not denied but are understood within an overall conception of psychic development that parallels the unfolding processes of biological development from the simple fertilised egg to the complexity of a fully developed human creature.

Fordham uses 'self' in terms of an organism's capacity to initiate psychic and somatic activity. Fordham's interest is therefore primarily with the *total self* and, in particular, with its earliest form, which he termed the *primary self*. He proposes the existence of a primary psychosomatic integrate which contains everything that the self will become in potential. The primary self is 'a blueprint for psychic maturation from which the behaviour of infants may be derived' (Fordham 1976, p. 11). The primary self 'deintegrates' when it meets environmental triggers that produce a 'readiness for experience'. Such readiness is typified by the new-born infant's rooting for the breast. When a deintegrate is 'met' by the environment, an experience takes place and the self 'reintegrates' with the new experience included in it. This rhythmic alternation between deintegration (going to meet the world) and reintegration (returning to the self) continues throughout life.

Fordham's model allows for the unending development of a self of increasing complexity and sophistication out of the most rudimentary elements. It also enables us to understand how increasing differentiation of psychic elements and discrimination of environmental experiences develops in parallel with increasing levels of integration. The integrated adult self is therefore (ideally) like a symphony orchestra: many different parts operating in a coordinated way to produce a richly layered, complex texture of meaningful sound. The model also allows us to understand (a) *dis*-integration, where the parts do not cohere and some instruments are either silenced or busy 'blowing their own trumpet' in disregard of the whole; and (b) failures of development where the self does not deintegrate sufficiently and the personality remains stunted, unable to form the internal experiences out of which a meaningful relation to the world can develop. Fordham suggested that infantile autism could be understood as the most extreme example of such a failure to deintegrate (Fordham 1976).

Zinkin and Young-Eisendrath: The Constructivist Critique

Where Fordham starts from the innate activity of the infant, constructivists start from the intersubjective interaction *between* mother and infant. Thus, Louis Zinkin, Fordham's colleague in the London Society of Analytical Psychology, objected to the notion of a primary self that was *pre-given*. He pointed out that there never is a point *prior* to interaction with the environment when some undifferentiated entity could be said to exist: 'one would have to go back to the earliest beginnings of the universe to find ... the intellectual necessity ... of an original undifferentiated state' (Zinkin 1987b, p. 177). Therefore, he argued, 'there never is an objective entity which corresponds to [the primary self]' (Fordham and Zinkin 1987, p. 142). In fact, Fordham agreed that the primary self 'has no date' and confirmed that he was talking about 'cosmic experiences extending to the limits of space and time' (Fordham and Zinkin 1987, p. 143). An apparently hard-nosed scientific concept has suddenly become, at the same time, a highly mystical one. The dialogue between Fordham and Zinkin echoes the Zen Buddhist question 'What is the face of the Buddha before you were born?' The primary self is the original Buddha face. Once again we find that we are brought up against the limits of what is thinkable.

For these reasons, Zinkin believed that 'the self only comes into existence through interaction with others' (Zinkin 1991, p. 6) and that it was meaningless to speak of a self that exists prior to the infant having any conception of 'myself'. In other words, the self is constructed, not by the individual in isolation but through an interactive field out of which 'the individual' emerges. At the risk of oversimplification we might say that Neumann puts the self 'in' the mother, Fordham puts it 'in' the infant and Zinkin puts it *in between* mother and infant.[4]

Polly Young-Eisendrath, an American Jungian with a strong interest in realigning Jungian thought with postmodern trends in philosophy and psychology, is also a firm adherent of a constructivist position. She is particularly opposed to the tendency to attribute subjectivity to the self as if it is a person, and to reify the self as if it were a substantive entity. She identifies these tendencies as stemming from the epistemological errors of 'realism' and 'essentialism', as a result of which 'we may sound as though we can know the unknowable in saying the Self has intentions, views and desires' (Young-Eisendrath 1997a, p. 162). Instead, she emphasises the aspect of archetypes as *predispositions* to particular forms and images of psychic functioning. Following the philosopher Rom Harré (also an influence on Zinkin), she has identified what she calls 'the invariants of subjectivity': coherence, continuity, a sense of agency and affective relational patterns. Since these are universal features of subjectivity, within a wide range of different ways of thinking about and experiencing a personal self, she concludes that they must be archetypal. Therefore, she suggests that, especially in his later work,

> it was Jung's own intention to present his concept of Self as *a universal pre-disposition to form a unified image of individual subjectivity*. This predisposition arises out of a transcendent coherence, that unity of life that is not personal and may be called God, Tao, Buddha Nature, a central organising principle (of the universe) or other names. (Young-Eisendrath 1997b, p. 54; original emphasis).

Since the form that individual subjectivity takes is that which Jung calls the ego, Young-Eisendrath is arguing that the self is the archetype of the ego. As such, it is not the totality, far less a personification of the unconscious, but an abstract principle of organisation and coherence which structures human subjectivity as it is constructed 'in a context that includes culture, language, and other persons'(Young-Eisendrath and Hall 1991, p. xii). Young-Eisendrath and Zinkin emphasise different aspects of the same overall project: both stress that the archetypal self cannot be divorced from the personal self and that the personal self is acquired through mutual interaction, not a given that arises in and of itself. However, where Zinkin is interested in the detailed dialogue that takes place between mother and infant, Young-Eisendrath takes a more abstract, philosophical approach and has been able to realign constructivist thinking with Jung's view of the self as an archetype. The self-as-totality is not a relevant consideration for either of them.

Self as Process

Here I want to begin to sketch out a view of the self which is both totality and archetype, both organising principle and that which is organised. In this view, the self is best understood as the overall *process* of the psyche. That is, it is not simply an organising principle *within* the psyche but is better thought of as the organising principle *of* the psyche.[5] There is no principle or archetypal structure which is in any way separate from that which it is organising. The structure is inherent in itself – the self is both a tendency towards organisation (the process of individuation) *and* the structure of that organisation (the self as archetype). In other words, the psyche is self-structuring and the name for that process is the self. What misleads us is our tendency to isolate elements of thought into 'contents': then the self-as-archetype becomes a 'content' 'within' the psyche-as-the-total-self, creating an artificial paradox. If we think of the self as the process of the psyche, this paradox disappears. This also avoids the tendency that has dogged religious thought and has cropped up again in Jungian psychology: the tendency to hypostasise the self as a 'thing' to be known. In her postmodern 'campaign' against reification, realism and essentialism in Jungian psychology, Young-Eisendrath is a direct descendent of Philo, the Cappodacians and all negative theologians. In fact, she does indeed draw on another kind of negative theology: the Buddhist doctrine of 'no-self' which was originally a corrective against the Hindu tendency to concretise Atman as a substantive self.[6]

However, Brahman (and Atman as its individual aspect) is also, properly conceived, not a discrete entity but something that pervades everything. In a Hindu parable, Brahman is compared to salt dissolved in water. It cannot be seen nor can it be distinguished from the water in which it is. It is thus everywhere and nowhere. This may seem to be an essentialist view, as if there is a definable essence of being which is Brahman. But here the essence is inseparable from the element in which it is found – lived existence. It is as if the self is not an experience and certainly not a *content* of experience, but rather the *taste* of experience, its *quality*.[7] Brahman is that which 'cannot be spoken in words, but that by which words are spoken ... What cannot be thought with the mind, but that whereby the mind can think' (from the Upanishads: quoted in Armstrong 1997, p. 40). If we apply this to the self, we might say that the self is not subjectivity but the condition by which subjectivity is possible. It is not myself, nor the experience of myself but the very possibility of my having self-experience. This, I think, is what Jung means by the larger personality that is the self. It is a recognition that our self-organisation is not bounded by our self-awareness but is the overall purpose and organisation of our existence as human organisms. If there is anything which qualifies as archetypal, surely this is it.

This way of thinking is also surprisingly close to developments in Darwinian biology and the burgeoning field of consciousness studies. This linkage is particularly interesting since two of the key proponents in this field, Richard Dawkins and Daniel Dennett, are vigorously atheistic and reductionist, apparently the very antithesis of the Jungian *Zeitgeist*.

In his book *Consciousness Explained,* Dennett (1991) proposes an explanation of consciousness based on what he calls 'the Multiple Drafts Model'. This model is strikingly postmodern in that it eschews the existence of any single point at which consciousness takes place in favour of a multiplistic, decentred view of both consciousness and the self. He argues that we must rid ourselves of the homuncular fantasy in which neurophysiological processes are somehow all directed towards and served up to a 'Central Meaner' who receives 'inputs' from sensory data and the body in 'the Cartesian Theatre' of consciousness. Rather, he suggests the brain is like a serial processor in which multiple versions of events, meanings, emotional and sensory states and language coexist in such a way that it is not possible to distinguish any boundary between those that become conscious ('mental') and those which do not. Consciousness is therefore a field which is in continual flux, rather like Jung's view of the psyche as a multiplicity of complexes.

Rather than the self as an 'inner person' (homunculus), Dennett suggests, like Young-Eisendrath, that the self is an abstraction. Furthermore, it is one which, in rudimentary form, is attributable to *all* life forms: even the lowliest amoeba must make a distinction between 'me' and 'the rest of the world' (not-me):

> This minimal proclivity to distinguish self from other in order to protect oneself is the biological self, and even such a simple self is not a concrete thing but just an abstraction, a principle of organization. (Dennett 1991, p. 414)

This seems to me to recognise that *all* organisms are driven by an overall sense of purposive intelligence that is beyond the conscious mind. It is simply that in human beings, the self is inevitably of a far more complex kind and, appropriately, its contemplation inspires awe. So, while the self may not possess subjectivity, it becomes unremarkable to attribute to it an overall purposive intelligence with coherent intentions and 'needs' that transcend consciousness. How else could we function at all? We have only to consider the complex functioning of our internal organs (and our brains most of all) to see this. Why should we expect the psychic aspect of ourselves to be constructed any differently? This is the basis for Jung's teleological view of the psyche as a holistic system of purposive self-regulating functions. Conscious realisation of the processes at work in ourselves may well make us feel humble and small and offer a rebuke to the hubris of the ego, but must also provide that deep-rooted, inalienable reassurance of what Winnicott (1971) calls 'going on being'. We do not need to know *how* we do it, we just discover that we *are* doing it.[8]

Dennett applies the same kind of thinking to the construction of a personal self. As he puts it, we find ourselves 'spinning a self' just as the spider finds itself spinning a web. We do not know what we are doing or why we are doing it; it is as if it is doing us. Dennett proposes the construction of the self as an example of what the biologist Richard Dawkins has called the 'extended phenotype' – extended effects of genetic activity through which a creature's environment is altered. Examples include spiders' webs, beavers' lakes and the stone shells created by caddis flies (Dawkins 1982). There is a very close parallel here to Fordham's argument for the primary activity of the self. Fordham, too, argues that the infant is able to 'create' aspects of his or her environment by his or her own activity. Extended into the intersubjective view, we might say that all of us act on each other to promote the development of our individualised personal lives which are therefore part of the extended phenotype of the human organism. I suggest that 'the self', like God, is an image of this process. The God-image appears to be the *source* of our existence but it is also the *result* of the processes it represents. The God-image is the image, not of the self that is spun (myself), but of the process by which it is spun – that through we live and breathe and have our being. As individual subjects, we are subject to the self.

If the self is the process of being human, it follows that the self is in everything we are. This view also offers a reconciliation of the part/whole paradox. The thrust of Dennett's philosophical critique is against the conception of a conscious agent who somehow exists in the Cartesian Theatre of consciousness, observing and making decisions separately from the processes of awareness through which it exists.[9] Similarly, we need to get away from the idea of a self 'in' the unconscious – or anywhere else, for that matter. So, for example, when Fordham says the self deintegrates and reintegrates, we might see the self *as* deintegration and reintegration. Indeed, Fordham states that 'a deintegrate is endowed with and continuous with the self'. This means that parts of the self are endowed with the qualities of the self since, as I indicated earlier, the self *is* the quality of experience.

Louis Zinkin uses the analogy of the hologram to refer to the way that parts of the self are not distinct from the whole self, but rather are merely different forms that the self takes. In the hologram, the whole image is present in every part of it since the image is a function of wave patterns that form the holo-movement. Zinkin concludes that

> [m]ovement is primary and the appearance of forms as they emerge from the movement is secondary ... It would be better understood if the movement of the psyche in individuation is taken as primary, not the structures such as the archetypes, the ego and the self or the unconscious, which are only comparatively stable and autonomous forms. (Zinkin 1987a, p. 124)

I want to take this just a little bit further and suggest that the self *is* the holo-movement. Therefore, the whole self is present in every part of it. It is omnipresent from the very start. Furthermore, since it is never a discrete entity, there is no need to postulate starting from a self-contained system, as Fordham does in the hypothesis of the primary self (Fordham and Zinkin 1987, p. 138). The nascent individual may be a system but it is perpetually in interaction with other systems, and is itself made up of myriad part-systems down to the level of the genes and further down to their atomic constituents, until the search for origins disappears once more into the nothingness of the unthink-able and becomes infinite. The self emerges out of this primary wholeness and develops towards a discriminating consciousness capable of asking from whence it came. Our individuation involves our becoming distinct and discrete individuals to the point at which we can confront the universe from which we have sprung as discriminated but intrinsically connected parts of it. Then, if we can grasp it, we might once again know the experience of wholeness at a different level: at the level of *consciousness,* the highest level of differentiation known to us. At this level, we might become differentiated enough to *perceive* our interconnection and oneness with the universe.

Notes

1. This is true of the concept of the self in psychoanalysis, for example, where the concept has been mainly used in America, by followers of Heinz Hartmann's ego-psychology. Some Jungians feel that Kohut's view of the self as 'the centre of the psychological universe' is similar to Jung's, although he does not refer to its potential connection with the image of the divine. For a detailed elaboration of this view see Jacoby (1985).
2. The term 'sub-personality' has been used by Joseph Redfearn in his book *My Self, My Many Selves* (Redfearn 1985). Redfearn's work is a comprehensive elaboration of the multiplicity of the self in terms of the shifting identifications of 'the I' and its relation to 'the Not-I'.
3. I am indebted to Karen Armstrong's *A History of God* (1997) for most of the information in this and the following paragraph.
4. These views may also be combined. For example, Hester Solomon (1997, 1998), while adhering closely to Fordham's view of the primary self, has sought to demonstrate that Jung's notion of the self in transformation is both primary *and* relational.
5. Similarly, Rosemary Gordon refers to the self as a structure within the psyche, whereas I think it would be more accurate to describe it as the structure *of* the psyche (Gordon 1985, p. 269).
6. Following a hint from one of Jung's letters, she refers to the self as an 'empty centre' around which the personality is organised (Young-Eisendrath and Hall 1991, p. 61). I have developed this view elsewhere in relation to the 'heart of the mystery' in *Hamlet* (Colman 1998).
7. Robert Pirsig has made 'Quality' the centre of a philosophical system, supraordinate to the subjective reality of mind and the objective reality of matter. He equates Quality with Tao which, in turn, Jung equates with the self (Pirsig 1974).
8. While I was working on this paragraph, I received a letter from an ex-patient telling me how she had been hijacked at gunpoint and fully expected to be raped and killed. The fact that neither had happened she attributed mainly to an inexplicable feeling of wholeness, calm, and inner confidence that she experienced as she faced death head-on. As a child, she had been devastated when she realised that no one, not even her mother, could prevent her from dying and she had suffered from fears of dying ever since. The strange thing, was, she told me, that as she was driven for several hours at gunpoint into the middle of nowhere, she felt, for the first time, *a certainty that she would go on breathing and that her body was capable of sustaining her.* It must have taken the presence of death as an external reality to shock her into an experience of the self.
9. It seems to me to beg the question to refer to such a Cartesian agent as either 'he' or 'she'. How does it know that it is gendered in the first place?

References

Armstrong, K. (1997) *A History of God*. London: Mandarin.

Colman, W. (1998) '"That within which passes show": *Hamlet* and the unknowable self', *Harvest*, 44(1): 7–23.

Dennett, D. (1991) *Consciousness Explained*. London: Penguin.

Dawkins, R. (1982) *The Extended Phenotype*. Oxford: W.H. Freeman.

Edinger, E. (1960) 'The ego–self paradox', *Journal of Analytical Psychology*, 5(1): 3–18.

Fordham, M. (1976) *The Self and Autism*. London: Heinemann.

Fordham, M. (1987) *Explorations into the Self*. London: Academic Press.

Fordham, M. and Zinkin, L. (1987) 'Correspondence between Louis Zinkin and Michael Fordham', in H. Zinkin, R. Gordon and J. Haynes (eds), *The Place of Dialogue in the Analytic Setting: The Selected Papers of Louis Zinkin*. London and Philadelphia: Jessica Kingsley, 1998, pp. 133–48.

Gordon, R. (1985) 'Big self and little self', *Journal of Analytical Psychology*, 30(3): 261–71.

Jacoby, M. (1985) *Individuation and Narcissism. The Psychology of the Self in Jung and Kohut*. London: Routledge.

Jung, C.G. (1963) *Memories, Dreams, Reflections*. Reprinted Glasgow: Fountain Books, 1977.

Neumann, E. (1954) *The Origins and History of Consciousness*. Reprinted London: Karnac, 1989.

Pirsig, R. (1974) *Zen and the Art of Motorcycle Maintenance*. London: The Bodley Head.

Redfearn, J. (1985) *My Self, My Many Selves*. London: Academic Press.

Samuels, A. (1985) *Jung and the Post-Jungians*. London: Routledge.

Scholem, G.G. (1941) *Major Trends in Jewish Mysticism*. New York: Schocken Books.

Solomon, H. (1997) 'The not-so-silent couple in the individual', *Journal of Analytical Psychology*, 42(3): 383–402.

Solomon, H. (1998) 'The self in transformation: the passage from a two to a three-dimensional world', *Journal of Analytical Psychology*, 43(2): 225–38.

Winnicott, D.W. (1971) *Playing and Reality*. London: Penguin Books.

Young-Eisendrath, P. and Hall, J. (1991) *Jung's Self-Psychology. A Constructivist Perspective*. London and New York: Guilford Press.

Young-Eisendrath, P. (1997a) 'The self in analysis', *Journal of Analytical Psychology*, 42(1): 157–66.

Young-Eisendrath, P. (1997b) *Gender and Desire: Uncursing Pandora*. College Station, TX: A & M University Press.

Zinkin, L. (1987a) 'The hologram as a model for analytical psychology', in H. Zinkin, R. Gordon and J. Haynes (eds), *The Place of Dialogue in the Analytic Setting: The Selected Papers of Louis Zinkin*. London and Philadelphia: Jessica Kingsley, 1998, pp. 116–34.

Zinkin, L. (1987b) 'Correspondence (Response to a previous comment by James Astor)', *Journal of Analytical Psychology*, 32(2): 177.

Zinkin, L. (1991) 'Your self: did you find it or did you make it?' Unpublished paper for discussion at the Analytic Group of the Society of Analytical Psychology, 4 November.

2
Jung and His Family –
A Contemporary Paradigm

Ann Kutek

The purpose of this chapter is to examine how Jung's own early family history and experiences may have contributed to shaping his thought in adulthood, and thereby to increase our understanding of families and the process of individuation. It will relate his early emotional deprivation to his search through the intellect to seek attachments in his professional life, most notably with Freud. The subsequent break with the 'father of psychoanalysis' may have been inevitable. Its roots lie, after all, in the conflict with his own father. A parallel deficit in the relationship with his mother possibly accounts for the ensuing quest for a female muse and the attachments he formed to important women outside his marriage. These were women of high intellect: in particular, Sabina Spielrein, Toni Wolff, Aniela Jaffé and a circle of other patients, professionals and students who included Edith Rockefeller McCormick. They served as replacements for his own extended family, who had often turned out to be a disappointment to him.

Jung has been called a precursor of modern family therapy (Samuels 1985a). Research in that field, as well as in attachment theory and in child psychotherapy has helped to broaden our understanding of human development and family life, especially through the contributions of Klein, Winnicott, Anna Freud and Bowlby. None the less, the relevance of Jung's thinking in this area may be underestimated since, despite his own inauspicious beginnings, he demonstrated both in his personal life and through his depth psychological 'method' how it is possible to rise above them. Jung instigated the hypothesis of the archetype, which helps to deepen the study of contemporary family life in its many and diverse forms (Kutek 1983).

In his book *On Jung*, Anthony Stevens (1991) traces back the idea of the archetype to Plato, a debt acknowledged by Jung (*CW* 8). He describes archetypes as 'active living dispositions, ideas in the platonic sense, that perform and continually influence our thoughts, feelings and actions'. They are seen as common to all mankind, 'yet each person experiences them and manifests them in his or her own way ... Unlike Plato's idea, the Jungian archetype is no mere abstraction, but a biological entity' (Stevens 1991). Jung refers to them as, 'a biological organism, endowed with generative force' (*CW* 6), 'existing as a centre in the central nervous system which seeks its own activation in the psyche and in the world' (Stevens 1991). It is possibly something like a *prion*, or what modern neuropsychologists have called 'mental modules', (see Schwartz's obituary notice of Marie-Louise von Franz (Schwartz 1998)). Marie-Louise von Franz, analyst and long-time associate of Jung, predicted that, as with Galileo's discovery,

> future generations of researchers would discover these self-same structures without reference or acknowledgement to Jung. This she felt would be only right and proper, for the fact that they made this discovery independently would prove that Jung's work was not at all hypothetical but was based on the objective facts of psychic life. (Schwartz 1998)

Adaptations to life are achieved through the development of those parts of the personality accessible to daily social intercourse, which Jung called the *persona* (after the name given to the mask worn by actors in ancient Greek drama). Those developments that are 'hidden' in the unconscious and often projected outside the self were grouped by him under the term 'shadow complex'. He proposed that the two aspects of the personality complement and counterbalance each other. Jung felt that the shadow stood for the dissociated sub-personality, but he regarded it as only part of the unconscious psyche and, as Stevens notes (1991, p. 43), not the rough equivalent of the whole Freudian unconscious.

If Jung's influence on child and family work may seem less obvious than that of later psychologists, it is nevertheless significant and has filtered through to us in at least three distinct ways. First, as Samuels (1985a) has indicated, Jung proposed an outline concept of individual neurosis caused by family dynamics through a description of how the child's development results from an interaction with the parents' psychology and psychopathology. The child may be thrust into the parents' 'unlived life'. In this connection, Skynner, an early pioneer of family therapy, observed:

> from the beginning, [Jung] regarded children's psychological problems as usually expressive of difficulties in the total family system, whereby relief of symptoms in one individual might lead to the development of symptoms in another. (Skynner 1976, p. 373)

Moreover, Jung points out that the birth, development and personality of the child have their counter-influence on the parents (*CW* 4, paras 91–2). As will be discussed later, the 'absence of the child' has an archetypal influence on childlessness which is reflected in the current preoccupation with inter-country adoption, technological advances, *in vitro* fertilisation, gender selection, frozen embryology, surrogacy and the potential for cloning.

Second, by formulating the notion of homeostasis, Jung opened up a parallel with material science, particularly with biology. This idea also lies at the heart of General Systems Theory (GST), upon which so much of modern family therapy is based. Just as nature hates a vacuum, so it is hypothesised, a missing psychological component is filled by what is available.

Third, Jung's impact on the study of child development was facilitated by his British collaborator and editor, Michael Fordham, and colleagues at the Society of Analytical Psychology, who established a clinic for Jungian training and child psychotherapy in London (Sidoli and Davies 1988).

Jung's approach adds a further dimension to the nature/nurture contro-versy by bringing the two sides into cooperation through the archetype (see Solomon 1994). Thus, although the actual qualities and behaviour of parental figures and the child's environment are of pivotal importance, their interplay with his or her archetypal experiences as activated by them, have a decisive role in socialisation and ultimate success in life. The child's archetypal experience is not only part of the child's individual nature but is also integral to a family's character. At the same time we have little useful means beyond depth psychology and aspects of sociological theory, to explain how some children raised outside a 'standard' family manage to adapt to societal norms, while others remain dysfunctional or outcast.

In Western culture, we lay much store on individuality. When we refer to 'me', we generally have in mind that there is only one 'me', one 'I', one 'myself'. This is less obviously inferred from other cultures where perceptions of individuals are more conditional on group determinants, role and gender. Jung conceptualised the self in three ways: his inner explorations, his travels to other continents and his wide reading of anthropological and non-European texts. Following earlier attempts to explore his own unconscious, in 1913, prompted by a dream, he began a systematic enquiry during a period of severe inner disturbance, probably some form of breakdown. During that time, he monitored his dreams and consequent influx of imagery. He hypothesised that he had chanced upon 'sub-personalities'. This opened up the notion that the psyche can 'personate', that is, produce complexes which relate to one another as if they were separate people participating in a drama. In this idea the subject is not only an onlooker but an active interlocutor who may seek various opinions from the different voices or have arguments with them. This is a common phenomenon in pre-adolescence when children relate to one or several 'imaginary' characters of their private acquaintance (Hobson 1985).

In his self-analysis, Jung came to know various sub-personalities who were eventually labelled, amongst others, 'the shadow', the 'anima', the 'trickster' and the 'Old Wise Man'. They were not only inhabitants of Jung's psyche, but were visitors from a 'place' he was to term the 'collective unconscious'. Not until 1919 did Jung emerge from a long night in which he had encountered and brought to consciousness the most intimate and buried elements of his personality. He sensed that an integration of his so called No. 1 and No. 2 personalities, his inner and outer worlds, had occurred through a process he was to call 'individuation'. He was forty-four.

The process suggests that he was involved in a titanic struggle not to be engulfed in but rather to bring light into dark areas of his personality which could have stymied his creativity and left him beyond the reach of understanding and resolution. How had he become so threatened by these inner contents and processes? One answer might be found in an understanding of the dynamics of his dysfunctional family. How was it that he could make sense of such an invasion? Another possible answer to this resides in the richness of his family heritage and the familiarity of those close to him. His own family, intimate friends and colleagues were all engaged, wittingly or not, in his process. The resulting legacy to us is his immense *opus*, the *Collected Works*, which amounts to a contemporary *Odyssey*. He left no formal autobiography, except for fragments and the first three chapters of *Memories, Dreams, Reflections* (1963), curiously redolent of his near contemporary, James Joyce's *Portrait of the Artist as a Young Man*. Several biographies have appeared in recent years, ranging from the sympathetic (Wehr 1987), through the speculative (McLynn 1996), to those frankly courting controversy (Noll 1997). There still remains a mass of material 'embargoed' in Jung's family archives. We have not exhausted the sources of further information about Jung's life.

The reluctance of some to take Jung's narrative seriously, or in any way to see it as relevant to modern thought except as an historical curiosity, is doubtless due to an idealisation of scientism and to the grip of a pervasive materialism. If it cannot be directly observed or computed, it is no more than a chimera or a system fit only for a coterie of believers. Perversely, the construct of quantum physics, in many respects as hypothetical as Jung's description of the personality, labours less under the weight of scepticism. Yet, if our enquiry into his life and method can yield observations of a normative order, we can apply them to some of the most intractable areas of contemporary psychological and social observation. As a way into such enquiry, it is possible to imagine the young Carl Gustav as if he were a current case of concern to the local education authority or a social services department.

The Case of Carl Gustav

This boy might have been referred to the educational psychologist. Evidently bright, he was not achieving his potential. Though well grown, he was physically inept and shy, often absent from school due to sickness or family problems and frequently coming off worst in scrapes with other boys. His numeracy was well below his verbal and comprehension levels. Teachers observed that he veered between clowning and orchestrating pranks, and absences in prolonged day-dreams. An enquiry into his background revealed a number of significant factors to account for his at once sad and perplexing demeanour.

He was the elder of two surviving children of a country parson and his wife. The first child, a son, lived only a few days and died two years before Carl was born. A sister was born when Carl was nine. Carl's extended family was large by contemporary standards. Both his parents were the thirteenth children in their reconstituted families, as both grandfathers had been widowed at least once. Both parents came from professional and therefore comfortable backgrounds. Carl's paternal grandfather was a man of some eminence, being a professor of medicine. The other grandfather was a university chaplain who had previously followed an academic career.

Carl's father, Paul, himself had a promising academic career as a student of oriental languages, but, being prone to depression, he decided to study for the ministry and accepted a living in a rural backwater. The marriage to Emilie, herself the daughter of a parsonage, was not a happy one. Apparently, there were difficulties of a psychosexual nature. When Carl was three, his parents separated. His mother became an in-patient in a mental hospital. Carl was sent to live with an aunt and was found to have developed eczema. He was often left in the care of maids and, at the age of four, was subject to nightmares and morbid preoccupations.

He was described as a day-dreamer and accident-prone. He fell so badly around the house, that, on a couple of occasions, he scarred himself permanently. A child psychiatrist who reviewed his notes suggested that he was suffering from childhood schizophrenia triggered by parental separation (Winnicott 1964). Even after his mother returned from hospital and his parents were united, Carl was frightened of her mood swings – at times she was quiet and remote, and at times powerful and dominating. His early memories of her were only vague. He remembered her dark clothing more than her face. The women who figured more prominently were the maids and his father's erstwhile companion, Bertha.

As the household was strictly Protestant, Carl developed a deep suspicion of Catholicism and especially of Jesuits who wore dark 'frocks' reminiscent of those worn by his mother. As a result of his father's moves to different parishes, Carl found it difficult to maintain connections with other children. He was quite solitary and would amuse himself with toy soldiers. He lived in a phantasy world of his own. When he started school at six, he was soon bullied and did not make friends easily, possibly because the majority of the other children came from more modest homes. One way he found to disarm his tormentors was to act the clown and play tricks. As he was big for his age, it was surprising that he did not take advantage of his size and strength. When he was seven, he suffered from croup and choking fits. His night fears continued. His parents again led 'separate lives'.

The birth of his sister Gertie when he was nine years old was a great shock, for it was unannounced and posed a great disruption to an only child and to the life of an already uneasy family. However, just two years later, through his innate ability and possibly his family's social connections, he joined the academic stream of the local grammar school. He did well in classics and the humanities but consistently struggled with maths and was excused from PE following several fainting fits.

After a further bullying incident in which he was knocked unconscious, Carl was off school for six months and went to stay with relatives. The suggestion of returning to school brought on school phobia and a recurrence of fainting fits which led to the possible diagnosis of epilepsy. If confirmed, the outlook was bleak, but Carl seemed to take matters in hand and the fainting fits 'disappeared' completely. He was able to resume his studies.

However, his continuing outbursts of bad behaviour suggested a personality split. Much of the time, he displayed extreme arrogance and an exaggerated view of his own importance; for instance, during an outing, when told off by the father of a friend. In between his own father's fits of rage or depressive withdrawal into his book-lined library, Carl managed to achieve a level of closeness with him, especially on an intellectual plane, but there was deep underlying conflict and, doubtless, disappointment on both sides. They avoided sensitive subjects, especially that of his father's occupation and all it stood for. It was apparent that Carl would not be following his father and many other uncles into the Church.

In adolescence, Carl was typically morose and inspired deep hostility in his peers – especially his literature master, who branded him glib and a liar (McLynn 1996). He was plagued with self-doubt and was hypersensitive to criticism, especially when he thought it undeserved. His occasional flashes of brilliance were mocked, which isolated him further and increased his reservoir of rage. Fortunately, one of his maternal uncles, a parson, intervened by encouraging his intellectual pursuits and introduced him at the age of sixteen to the great writers and philosophers, such as Plato, Aristotle, Kant and Schopenhauer. This resulted in his being labelled a braggart and invited the sobriquet of 'young fogey' from fellow pupils. However, even the breakthrough with the special uncle proved illusory, for he cultivated only those philosophies which supported the party line, that is, theological rectitude. Carl felt rebuffed once more.

Carl's sexual awakening also proved unhappy. A brave attempt at self-revelation to a pretty girl in his father's social sphere ended when he perceived no reciprocity or even recognition between them and he concluded that it was, after all, meaningless. At the age of eighteen, Carl was a strapping six-footer, well built with a resonant voice. His first sexual experience occurred when a friend of his father, a man whom he had earlier idolised, seduced him and left him with a horror of (homo)sexuality. In spite of continued tribulation at home, failing parental health and dwindling finances, Carl passed his school leaving certificate and managed to gain not only a place in medical school , but also a maintenance grant from the authorities, thus scotching his conviction that those in power were against him.

Carl's father was immensely proud of his son's achievement and shared in it briefly before dying at the start of the second term at university. His mother opined that it was a timely death, inferring that had he survived, he would have become a hindrance to Carl's career prospects. In fact, his father left a sum of money equivalent to about £200 in today's terms, and plunged the family into poverty, inferior accommodation and the real prospect of a premature end to Carl's academic career. However, three relatives eventually rallied in Carl's support and, through a combination of allowances, loans and the selling of family antiques, lifted the family out of penury. Carl completed his studies in five years and took a first 'house job' in psychiatry. He thus left his mother's house. (See Figure 2.1.)

The case of Carl approximates to what Eva Seligman, Jungian analyst and long-time marital therapist at the precursor to the Tavistock Marital Studies Institute, has described as a 'half alive' patient (Seligman 1985). She has studied the inner world of patients who have used this as a self-description and who presented themselves as inhabiting a 'permanent state of twilight, of non-differentiation and inexorably trapped'. She recalls a woman,

> recently divorced, suffering from an acute phobic condition, obsessed with a fear that the sun will never rise again, and that she would spend the rest of her life in everlasting darkness. In the course of her analysis it transpired that, on the one hand, she felt herself to be almost irresistibly pulled back into the powerful, but suffocating, dark embrace of her mother, represented also by her husband, and on the other, she longed to come alive as herself, discovering and developing her own atrophied identity. It was an interminable tug of war. (Seligman 1985, p. 70)

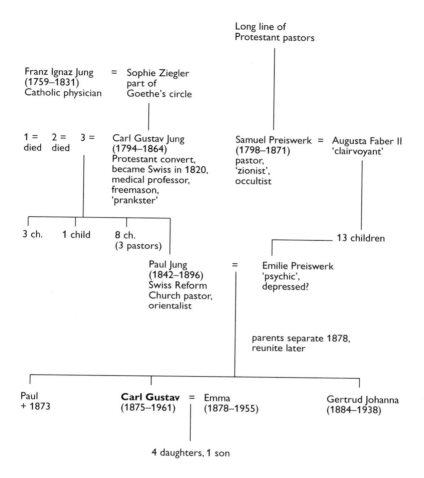

Figure 2.1 Jung's family tree

The tug of war is characteristic of the young Carl's life, too, with the difference that he was not observed early in life and his internal world can only be inferred. One reason for the radical splitting in the personality is the absence of one parent, often the father, but sometimes either parent and sometimes even both. This has vast implications for the personality development of the child and his or her future chances and those of the child's own progeny. The effects on children of broken families or those where, in effect, only one parent has ever been available is sociologically well documented (Robinson 1993).

The Missing Parent

This century might be characterised as a matriarchal epoch by default – men have been slaughtered massively in wars, relationships realign at an accelerated rate, and families reconstitute, expelling their young both symbolically and literally in the process. In addition, many young men have no obviously assigned role in society other than to be marginal, and significantly more single women than men rear their children alone. Moreover, through the centuries, fathers have tended to leave child rearing to women and some have never formed anything more than a nominal relationship with their children. Effectively, 'single-parent' rearing is more the norm than the shared upbringing of children.

A symbolically 'missing' father may be accompanied by the 'all-too-present mother'. Seligman's thesis, reflecting Jung's, is based on the idea of homeostasis. In her work with patients, she describes the frequency of ego-damaging mothers, who can be withdrawn, self-absorbed, or efficient but affectionless. Sometimes they can be inferred as anxiously over-solicitous and over-protective, rigidly controlling, domineering and intrusive. Other presentations are of seductive and castrating mothers who are puritanical and guilt-inducing, or who tyrannise their children by their own illness, more feigned than real. Seligman can only conclude that the more unconsciously destructive a mother is, the less the child can bear to be separated from her. Even when the father is present physically, he may be excluded by the mother–child pair and exclude himself. Seligman continues, 'I have evidence that there is an unconscious collusion between mother and child to maintain and prolong their mutually interdependent omnipotence thus avoiding the conflicts of the oedipal triad' (Seligman 1985).

It is possible that the missing parent can be reinstated by various routes which include multi-parenting, substitute parenting, transference analysis, systemic family or group therapy, and friendship, and through sustained relationships where complementary archetypes can operate. On the whole, these circumstances cannot be made to order. But once the gap is recognised, so the opportunities which can be utilised, are also seen and spontaneous examples of reinstatement and recovery abound. Some startling examples of children with missing parents include Alexander the Great, Isaac Newton, Marcel Proust and Jean-Paul Sartre. The level of success achieved is, of course, dependent upon timing, how early the deficit is spotted, the time of life, the ability to relate and the extent to which the repair experience is adulterated or sustainable – in short, upon its quality. In a few cases the adjustments are so ill-matched that the outcome can have perverse or even catastrophic effects. This is a likely explanation for the notorious British child molesters and murderers like the Wests, Brady and Hindley, and many less infamous prison inmates.

Robin Skynner (1976) states there are two fundamental principles common to all psychotherapeutic work:

1. nature balances automatically what we do not balance consciously, a condition clearly expressed by Jung in respect of complementarity and homeostasis of the conscious and unconscious;
2. aspects of the psyche excluded from conscious awareness operate autonomously, continuing to find expression but doing so in a manner disconnected from and often harmful to the personality as a whole.

Thus, denied or dissociated parts of the personality, like sexuality and aggression, do not cease to exist when they are put 'beyond the pale'. They simply disappear from view but find continued expression in disguised form or appear in other behaviour or in someone else instead. In the individual or in the family, such emotions may be expressed as apparently meaningless symptoms in one or more members, or the emotions denied expression may burst through in one member who acts as a safety valve for the whole group, although he or she may have to be expelled, or expel him- or herself from the family system in order to facilitate this.

The streets of most British towns, cities and rural areas attest to the isolated and homeless individuals whose history frequently contains 'expulsion' from an uncontaining environment or institution such as a mental hospital, a children's home or the armed forces. All of them will have fallen out of a broken relationship or family. Skynner likens the dissociated psychic contents of social isolates to soldiers who, cut off from their army and from central control,

> become marauding bandits seeking only their own satisfaction and neglecting the welfare of their comrades. A constructive solution requires re-establishing connections between the parts and the whole as such errant soldiers may again serve a useful function if accepted back and reintegrated into military discipline. (Skynner 1976, p. 12)

The Missing Baby

Just as we have identified 'half alive' people who inevitably suffer from a 'missing parent', so we are now confronted more graphically with the child-lessness of individuals and couples. Adoption, technology and the age-old phenomenon of surrogacy, are pursued in order to fulfil the aching desire to have a baby. There is no doubt that this desire is generally met with compassion. When the baby is procured, however, it is less clear what might be its psychic legacy. It is possible that the 'barren' adult seeks identification of his or her early self with the denied and longed for child. What this spells for the child can be gleaned from adopted people who have come into psychotherapy, or from 'replacement children'. 'Carl', the story of the young Carl Gustav Jung, shows he was such a child. We know that the individuation task of many adoptees is made harder when they are deprived of sources that lead them back to their roots, complicated as it already is by two sets, or more, of parents. The question then is, can two sets of parental imagos merge into one set of parental archetypes? Here is a contemporary instance that shows a different outcome to Jung's own.

The Case of 'Diane'

An overweight woman in her thirties was referred by her surgeon to the psychological department of a general hospital. Having given birth to children early in her marriage, she underwent a complete hysterectomy. She returned to the hospital complaining of abdominal pain for which no cause could be detected. Eventually, the surgeon decided that a rare intervention might solve the chronic condition. The patient continued to complain that the pain was acute and reported blood in her urine. She was on a repeat prescription of pain-killing drugs.

Over time, the surgical wound became so infected that further surgery was undertaken. While in hospital on one of her many visits for check-ups, Diane was surprised by one of the medical staff as she was nicking her finger and introducing blood from her finger into her urine. When challenged, Diane explained that this was necessary to persuade the surgeon to really pay attention to her continuing pain. She was referred for psychotherapy as a result of the incident. As a result of her persistent seeking of medical treatment, mostly unnecessary, she was diagnosed as suffering from Munchausen's syndrome, a condition characterised by the feigning of disease or injury in order to undergo medical treatment.

Diane had been raised by a childless couple who adopted her when she was six weeks old. She was their only child. Although Diane recalled her childhood as 'happy', both parents succumbed to ill-health and died one after the other, having been nursed through their long illnesses by Diane. At around that time, legislation was passed in Britain to enable adopted people to trace their biological parents. Diane set out on her search, helped by friends. She discovered that she was in fact born to a couple who wanted a son after having had daughters. As another daughter was not welcome, she was placed for adoption. She eventually discovered that the longed-for son had been born, but she was unsuccessful, despite her efforts, in re-establishing contact with her surviving natural parent.

During the early phase of psychotherapy, Diane was cut off from her feelings and only related to her continuing pain that could not be stemmed. When the possibility arose that she could, after all, have some contact with her siblings, she became much more engaged and was able to express her hostility not only to the hospital staff who had looked after her, but also to the therapist. As she gained contact with her siblings and their families, she found she was welcomed and was able to recognise many family similarities between herself and them. She remained in therapy for a further period when she developed interests outside her illness and eventually suggested that she did not need to attend therapy sessions as her lengthy hospital journeys were too onerous.

Although Diane could not have access to her biological parents, her experience with her adoptive parents probably sufficiently activated the archetypal energy of her internal parents to enable the cooperation of the symbolic hospital parents to heal some of her catastrophic pain. Coupled with the rediscovery of her siblings, co-lateral products of the same parents, she regained a possibility of recovery and re-entry into the original family system. Sometimes the child's genetic and psychological ancestry is wilfully obscured. In the case of artificial insemination by donor (AID), or when there is non-biological surrogacy – that is, when a woman acts as host to the embryo of another couple – the effects on the baby's psyche are not yet known. It is likely that some will turn out to be 'half alive' in the sense described by Seligman (1985).

The dreaming Carl Gustav

Resolution of inner conflicts and losses can be achieved in ways other than through clinical therapy, and may be helpful through focused attention to dreaming. This is illustrated in an incident from Jung's own life. In 1938, at the invitation of the British government in India, Jung went to participate in the celebration of the twenty-fifth anniversary of the Indian Science Congress. On this trip he was distinguished by three honorary doctorates. It was also the occasion for the following dream:

> I found myself, with a large number of my Zurich friends and acquaintances, on an unknown island, presumably situated not far off the coast of southern England. It was small and almost uninhabited. The island was narrow, a strip of land about twenty miles long, running in a north–south direction. On the rocky coast at the southern end of the island was a mediaeval castle. We stood in its courtyard, a group of sightseeing tourists. Before us rose an imposing Belfroi, through whose gate a wide stone staircase was visible. We

could just manage to see that it terminated above in a columned hall. This hall was dimly illuminated by candlelight. I understood that this was the castle of the Grail, and that this evening there would be a 'celebration of the Grail' here. This information seemed to be of a secret character, for a German professor among us, who strikingly resembled old Mommsen, knew nothing about it. I talked most animatedly with him, and was impressed by his learning and sparkling intelligence. Only one thing disturbed me: he spoke constantly about a dead past and lectured very learnedly on the rela- tionship of the British to the French sources of the Grail story. Apparently he was not conscious of the meaning of the legend, nor of its living presence, whereas I was intensely aware of both. Also, he did not seem to perceive our immediate actual surroundings, for he behaved as though he were in a classroom, lecturing to his students. In vain I tried to call his attention to the peculiarity of the situation. He did not see the stairs or the festive glow in the hall.

I looked around somewhat helplessly, and discovered that I was standing by the wall of a tall castle; the lower portion of the wall was covered by a kind of trellis, not made of the usual wood, but of black iron artfully formed into a grapevine complete with leaves, twining tendrils, and grapes. At intervals of six feet on the horizontal branches were tiny houses, likewise of iron, like birdhouses. Suddenly I saw a movement in the foliage; at first it seemed to be that of a mouse, but then I saw distinctly a tiny, iron, hooded gnome, a cucullatus, scurrying from one little house to the next. 'Well,' I exclaimed in astonishment to the professor, 'now, look at that, will you ...'

At that moment a hiatus occurred, and the dream changed. We – the same company as before, but without the professor – were outside the castle, in a treeless, rocky landscape. I knew that something had to happen, for the Grail was not yet in the castle and still had to be celebrated the same evening. It was said to be in the northern part of the island, hidden in a small uninhabited house, the only house there. I knew that it was our task to bring the Grail to the castle. There were about six of us who set out and tramped northwards.

After several hours of strenuous hiking, we reached the narrowest part of the island, and I discovered that the island was actually divided into halves by an arm of the sea. At the smallest part of the strait the width of the water was about a hundred yards. The sun had set, and night descended. Wearily, we camped on the ground. The region was unpopulated and desolate; far and wide, there was not a tree or shrub, nothing but grass and rocks. There was no bridge, no boat. It was very cold; my companions fell asleep, one after the other. I considered what could be done, and came to the conclusion that I alone must swim across the channel and fetch the Grail. I took off my clothes. At that point I awoke. (Jung 1963, pp. 310–12)

Jung was impressed by the fact that the idea of the Holy Grail was still alive amongst the British, and von Franz (1975) comments that the Grail story is not only about the vessel itself, but also about the theme of healing the 'old sick king', Amfortas, who suffers from a wound that cannot be healed. Jung felt that the spiritual and psychological suffering of his own father, who was assailed by doubts about his faith, was a depiction of the fate of Amfortas.

> My memory of my father is of a father stricken with an Amfortas wound, a 'fisher king' whose wound would not heal – that Christian suffering for which the alchemists sought the panacea. I, as a 'dumb' Parsifal, was the victim of this sickness during the years of my boyhood, and, like Parsifal, speech failed me. I had only inklings. (Jung 1963, p. 242)

Perhaps in contemplating his childhood self from the perspective of the adult, already in his sixties, Jung had achieved an understanding of his 'missing father' and a resolution to his lifelong search for him.

In Jung's view of the psyche's dynamics, dreams have the function of promoting a better adaptation to life by compensating the one-sided limitations of the conscious. For Jung, the psyche is a

> self-regulating system that maintains its equilibrium just as the body does. Every process that goes too far, immediately calls forth compensations, and without these there would be neither a normal metabolism nor a normal psyche. In this sense, we can take the theory of compensation as a basic law of psychic behaviour ... Similarly, the relation between conscious and unconscious is compensatory. (*CW* 7, para. 330)

Jung rejected Freud's notion that the dream is a façade that hides its true meaning. For him, a dream is an illustration of the dreamer's situation and mobilises the psyche's potential to meet it. Jung's dream of the Grail castle illustrates that, at a particular moment in his life, when he had attained those personal and professional achievements which had been denied not only to his missing brother but also to his father in his own lifetime, Jung's archetypal dream afforded him an internal connective experience.

Conclusion

Jungian thinking has provided us with a science of the psyche which is directly adaptable not only to understanding personality development and family life, but also to the spheres of therapy and social policy. The damaging role of the 'missing parent' has been identified, whether through physical absence or psychological withdrawal. Contemporary Jungian thought has highlighted the critical role of the father in each child's development. Difficulties are potentially compounded if a 'missing baby' is replaced by a child, as Jung was, or one with a technologically assisted or out-of-family genetic inheritance. The study of this phenomenon is made urgent by new developments in human fertilisation and embryology.

The fruit of Jung's thinking, which has been deployed by followers and others both in and beyond the therapy consulting room, makes the outlook for people of any inheritance optimistic, provided that the archetypal opportunities of their unconscious can be recognised in time and galvanised for the process of individuation.

References

Hobson, R. (1985) *Forms of Feeling*. London: Tavistock.

Jung, C.G. (1963) *Memories, Dreams, Reflections*. London: Collins/Fontana and Routledge, 1967.

Kutek, A. (1983) 'Families – A partnership of strength', in J. Lishman (ed.), *Working with Children*. Aberdeen: University of Aberdeen.

McLynn, F. (1996) *Carl Gustav Jung*. London: Bantam Press.

Noll, R. (1997) *The Aryan Christ*. London: Macmillan.

Robinson, M. (1993) *Family Transformation through Divorce and Remarriage*. London: Routledge.

Samuels, A. (1985a) *Jung and the Post-Jungians*. London: Routledge and Kegan Paul.

Samuels, A. (ed.), (1985b) *The Father – Contemporary Jungian Perspectives*. London: Free Association Books.

Schwartz, C. (1998) Obituary Notice on Marie-Louise von Franz, *Independent*, 23 February.

Seligman, E. (1985) 'The half alive ones', in A. Samuels (ed.), *The Father – Contemporary Jungian Perspectives*. London: Free Association Books.

Sidoli, M. and Davies, M. (1988) *Jungian Child Psychotherapy: Individuation in Childhood*. London: Karnac.

Skynner, R. (1976) *One Flesh, Separate Persons*. London: Constable.

Solomon, H. McFarland (1994) 'The transcendent function and Hegel's dialectical vision', *Journal of Analsytical Psychology*, 39(1): 77–100.

Stevens, A. (1991) *On Jung*. London: Penguin.

von Franz, M.L. (1975) *CG Jung: His Myth in Our Time*. London: Hodder and Stoughton.

Wehr, G. (1987) *Jung – A Biography*. Boston, MA: Shambala.

Winnicott, D. (1964) Review of *Memories, Dreams, Reflections, Journal of Psychoanalysis*, 45.

Suggested Reading

Samuels, A. (1989) *The Plural Psyche*. London: Routledge (especially Chapters 3–8).

Stevens, A. (1991) *On Jung*. London: Penguin (Chapters 4 and Part II).

3

Gender Issues – Anima and Animus

Elphis Christopher

Introduction

Exploring anything to do with gender issues can be controversial, and even potentially damaging, for both men and women, in different ways.

Women have been and are both idealised and denigrated for their 'femininity', seen as weak and irrational. Men and masculinity have been overvalued and prized. Thus, for example, in some patriarchal societies there is an illicit trade in foetal scanning, such that if the foetus is shown to be female it may well be aborted to save the family expensive dowries. While the differences between the sexes can be a source of delight and celebration, they can also be the target of conscious and unconscious attacks. Both men and women can project opposite sex characteristics on to the partner of the other sex. These can be 'shadow' projections (of the parts of ourselves we do not like and hence project on to others) such as weakness, vulnerability, sexuality, brutality and violence. More recently in the West men seem to be carrying shadow aspects for women as in the feminist view that 'all men are bastards', potential rapists and sex abusers. Boys are currently doing less well in school than girls. Women may be seen as sexually seductive and alluring but also as ensnaring and engulfing. There has been a resurgence of the archetypal *femme fatale*, the deadly woman; for example, in films such as *Fatal Attraction* and *Disclosure*.

Exploring gender issues then can raise more questions than offer answers. Perhaps this is inevitable in the current climate of rapid societal changes, especially with regard to the role of the sexes. Under the impact of feminism, some women have chosen or been forced to identify with men, attacking their own femininity and despising relatedness. Some men in self-defence have exaggerated their masculinity (the so-called 'laddish cult'), or have tried to disown their aggression and be more 'sharing and caring', running the risk of being despised as 'wimps'. Is there a separate feminine and masculine psychology? Do the sexes undergo a different psychological developmental pathway? If so, how far are these determined by innate factors or psychosocial, culture-bound conditioning – the blue/pink phenomenon? Core gender identity, the sense of being male or female, is established by the age of two and a half years and is difficult to change (Stoller 1968). Would it be more helpful to speak of masculinities and femininities? Are there primitive and more mature forms of these? For example, it could be argued that over-population is not only a consequence of lowered death rates but also the operation of an unthinking primitive feminine and masculine psychology. This is not to deny that the decision-making concerned with the control of fertility is most complex, involving conscious and unconscious factors (Christopher 1987). Even raising it as an issue can be seen as contentious both socially, due to fears of eugenic control, and psychologically by being asked to acknowledge and bring to consciousness what is kept at an unconscious level by virtue of the fact that it is primitive. However, over-population is one of the factors that threatens our continuing existence on the planet and has to be addressed.

Are there risks that, when femininity and masculinity are discussed, what is being examined are stereotypes rather than true differences? Certainly Jung has been accused of this. However, what cannot be overlooked is Jung's important contribution to a deeper understanding of male and female psychology in discovering the unconscious contrasexual aspects (the anima in the man, animus in the woman) of each sex. When these are made more conscious they can provide a way of enriching the personality and redressing the balance between the sexes. This will be explored later.

Jung, of course, 'spoke out' of his own psychology and 'life experience'. In his early childhood he was abandoned by his depressed mother who had to be hospitalised. He was cared for by an aunt and a maid servant, 'a dark haired olive skinned woman', who left a deep impression in Jung. After this time he felt mistrustful whenever the word 'love' was spoken. The feeling he associated with women was for a long time that of innate unreliability, whereas 'father' meant reliability and powerlessness (Jung 1963, p. 23). Despite this, Jung empathised strongly with the aspirations of women who were, or felt, misunderstood. Women were his first disciples. Emma, Jung's wife, wrote in a 'secret' letter to Freud that 'naturally all the women were in love with him' (*Freud–Jung Letters* (1974), p. 467). Jung had his own 'anima problem' or complex, feeling the need for inspirational live anima figures. The two most well known were Sabina Spielrein (see Carotenuto 1984) and Toni Wolff, with whom he had a sexual relationship.

Bearing the foregoing in mind, I propose to let Jung speak for himself through his writings on the contrasexual aspects of each sex, and to indicate how he arrived at these discoveries. The views of some later Jungian analysts will be explored, together with those of psychoanalytic writers. The concepts of animus and anima are briefly explored in relation to homosexuality. Clinical understanding, together with Jung's view of marriage as a psychological relationship, is illustrated by case material.

Jung's Concepts of Anima and Animus

In *Memories, Dreams, Reflections*, Jung (1963) described his mother as having two sides to her personality – a warm, motherly, feminine side, and a hidden unconscious masculine side with traits and modes of behaviour generally ascribed to men, such as ruthlessness, rationality and power. From his clinical work, his experiences with his own family, and his own self-explorations, Jung observed that beneath his conscious masculine personality there seemed to lie an unconscious feminine side with its own particular way of acting. His self-explorations began in earnest after his break with Freud in 1913, when he began to 'confront his unconscious' through dreams, images and fantasies. A young female figure, Salome, who was blind, appeared in these, along with Elijah, an old man. Later he found himself struggling with an inner female voice telling him that what he was writing was 'art'. He disagreed with this and described it as the struggle with the anima in her negative aspect. Later he became aware of her positive aspect when she communicated the images of the unconscious to his conscious mind (Jung, 1963, pp. 211–12). Because these sub-personalities existed at the unconscious level and, in Jung's experience, seemed universally present, he considered them to be archetypes of the collective unconscious. He called the man's feminine counterpart, *anima* (the Latin word for soul), and the woman's masculine counterpart, the *animus* or spirit. The anima and animus are symbolic modes of perception and behaviour within the psyche, which are represented internally by figures of the opposite sex. Since they were unconscious, the femininity or masculinity represented by the anima or animus was generally ill-developed. Despite this Jung thought that their role was to mediate between the ego and the inner life. Evidence for this mediatory function came from dreams wherein the anima/animus figures served as helpers to the dreamer, echoing folk tales and myths (Hopcke 1989a). Some individuals identify with this inner figure, others project it on to women or men they know.

In the General Index to Jung's work there are six columns of references to anima and two to animus. This is perhaps explicable because Jung was a man and knew his own sex better. Jung has been criticised because the anima appears in a more positive light than the animus. Although references to the anima/animus concepts are scattered throughout the *Collected Works*, Jung's four most complete formal statements are to be found in *CW* 6, *CW* 7, *CW* 9i,

9ii. Perhaps Jung's clearest exposition of the anima/animus concept can be found in *CW* 17, para. 338:

> Every man carries within him the eternal image of woman, not the image of this or that woman but a definite feminine image. This image is fundamentally unconscious, an hereditary factor of primordial origin engraved in the living organic system of the man, an imprint or archetype of all the ancestral experiences of the female, a deposit as it were of all the impressions ever made by women, in short an inherited system of psychic adaptation. The same is true of the woman: she too has her inborn image of man. Actually from experience it is more accurate to describe it as an image of men whereas in the case of the man it is rather the image of woman. Since this image is unconscious it is always unconsciously projected upon the person of the beloved.

Jung was at pains to emphasise that the anima is an *empirical* concept, not a theoretical invention, nor 'sheer mythology'. Its sole purpose is to give a name to a group of related or analogous psychic phenomenon (*CW* 9i, para. 114).

Jung saw the anima falling basically into two parts. First, in his personal unconscious a man has qualities generally considered feminine, such as relatedness, softness or receptivity, which he needs to integrate into his ego consciousness in order to be whole. The second aspect is archetypal and more complex. The anima in her archetypal aspect is both a symbol of the entire collective unconscious and also the personifying factor that bestows anthropomorphic form and affect on all archetypes and manifestations, including herself. She is concerned with life and meaning. Jung also equated her with Eros, naming it a feminine principle despite, of course, being a male god of the ancient Greeks. Anima is first mentioned as a psychological idea in the sixteenth century, although its earliest ancestor was the concept of *anima mundi*, the World Soul as elaborated by Plato in *The Timaeus*. To the men of antiquity the anima appeared as a goddess or witch, while, for the medieval world, the goddess was replaced by the Queen of Heaven and Mother Church. This illustrates that there is a change not in the archetype but in the projected image.

Jung thought that the animus corresponded to the paternal logos. As anima and animus are archetypes, they have positive as well as negative aspects. The positive aspect of the animus expresses 'spirit', philosophical or religious ideas in particular, or rather the attitude resulting from them. The 'anima gives relationship and relatedness to a man's consciousness, the animus gives to a woman's consciousness a capacity for reflection, deliberation and self knowledge' (*CW* 9 ii, para. 33). Although the above may appear stereotypical, it was how Jung organised his thinking about the masculine/feminine aspects of men and women.

In its negative aspect it is possible to be 'possessed' by the archetype that is determined by an internal image. Possession by the anima or animus leads to a transformation of personality and gives prominence to those traits which are characteristic of the opposite sex. In the state of possession both figures lose their charm and their values; they retain them only when they are turned away from the world in the introverted state when they serve as bridges to the unconscious. Turned towards the world, the anima is fickle, capricious, moody, uncontrolled and ruthless. The animus is 'obstinate, harping on principles, laying down the law, dogmatic, world-reforming, argumentative and domineering' (*CW* 9i, para. 223).

Jung laid a great deal of stress on the process of individuation – that is, the process by which the person becomes more of him- or herself, a whole individual and distinct from others, from not-self. He saw analysis as aiding this process. This self-realisation needed the person to distinguish what he or she is and how he or she appears to self and to others. To do this requires work on the personal shadow. Jung described this work as the apprentice-piece of analysis (*CW* 9i, para. 61). However, understanding was also needed of the anima (for a man) or the animus (for a woman) in order to distinguish him- or herself from them, because while they remained unconscious they could operate as autonomous complexes, as a law unto themselves, with mainly negative effects. If they are made more conscious, through self-reflection or analysis, their effect can be creative, adding purpose and meaning to life. This Jung described as the masterpiece of analysis (*CW* 9i, para. 61). The loss of the anima, or rather, the loss of the relationship to her, especially in the second half of life, resulted in a diminution of vitality, flexibility, human kindness and consequent premature rigidity, crustiness, obstinacy and pedantry (*CW* 9i, para. 147). Thus it is important to consider the *function* of anima and animus.

Jung explored the particular relationship between anima and animus, which he called the syzygy, the divine pair, a term used for any pair of opposites whether in conjunction or opposition. He wrote of the linkage between anima and animus as being psychologically determined by three elements: 'The femininity pertaining to the man and the masculinity pertaining to the woman, the experience man has had of women and vice versa (here early childhood events are of prime importance); and the masculine and feminine archetypal image' (*CW*9 ii, para. 41). Jung concluded that images of the pairing of male–female syzygy were as universal as the existence of man and woman, citing the recurring motif of male–female pairs in mythology and pointing to the pair of concepts designated as yang and yin in Chinese philosophy.

In early alchemical illustrations the male and female are conjoined sym- bolically to form an hermaphroditic figure, suggesting that as part of the alchemical process they must be differentiated and then reunited as an androgynous pair. Bisexuality is not implied, rather, the male and female principles are held in conscious balance, conjoined but without a fusion of their characteristics (Samuels et al. 1986). This conjoined but differentiated figure is designated the *androgyne*. Jung saw this metaphorical being as symbolising the end product of the alchemical process. The image of the androgyne is, therefore, relevant to analysis in that it seeks to reintegrate after a process of differentiation the component parts of the personality as a whole.

Jung considered that the anima and animus not only influence relationships, and marriage in particular, but also the choice of partner which may result from anima and animus projections. Because these personifications are influenced by childhood relationships with the parent of the opposite sex, choices of marriage partners often reflect the psychological condition of the parent (and their anima/animus) with whom the child is unconsciously bonded. Jung (CW 17, paras 332–4) put forward the idea of a 'container' and a 'contained' in marriage. Thus the simpler personality is contained emotionally by the more complex personality. This can refer to either sex. The relationship can be threatened when the 'container' becomes bored and resents the 'contained' partner. When relationships break down or couples quarrel, this may be caused by a battle between the animus and anima of each partner, hurling 'vulgar abuse, misapplied truisms, shop-soiled platitudes' at one another (CW 9ii, para. 29).

Thus the two partners find themselves in a banal collective situation, in the grip of archetypal forces. The concept of container/contained has had useful application in couple therapy, in the relationship between therapist and patient and, most importantly, mother and baby. Although Jung's description of anima/animus, feminine/masculine may appear culture-bound and stereotypical at times, nevertheless he was well aware that the position of women in the modern world was changing. As early as 1927, Jung wrote of women, in 'Woman in Europe', that their

> newly won masculinity makes it impossible to believe in marriage in its traditional form ... masculinity means knowing what one wants and doing what is necessary to achieve it. Once this lesson has been learned it is so obvious that it can never again be forgotten without tremendous psychic loss. The independence and critical judgement she acquires through this knowledge are positive values and felt as such by the woman. She can never part with them again. The same is true of the man who with great efforts wins that needful feminine insight into his own psyche often at the cost of much suffering. (CW 10, paras 259–60)

Jung was also well aware of his debt to women patients. 'I have had mainly women patients who often entered into the work with extraordinary conscientiousness, understanding and intelligence. It was essentially because of them that I was able to strike out on new paths in therapy' (Jung, 1963, p. 167). A similar debt that Freud owed to his women patients was emphasised by Appighanesi and Forrester (1992).

For Jung, of central importance to the ongoing health and creativity of the psyche as a whole was the capacity for relationship, which he denoted in archetypal terms as the *coniunctio*. Jung stressed the importance of the coniunctio or 'internal marriage' as the internal union of opposites. Since it was his conviction that the 'entire range of psychological possibilities is available to everyone ... [it] follows that personality can be described in terms of a *balance* between masculine and feminine factors' (Samuels et al. 1986).

There are therapeutic implications in Jung's concepts of anima and animus. Jung (*CW* 16, para. 423) writes of the complex relationship between analyst and patient. Where the analyst is male and the patient female, there is the conscious relationship, then the relationship of the man to his anima and of the woman to her animus, the relationship between the anima and the animus, and finally the relationship of the woman's animus to the man and the man's anima to the woman where each person is identified with their contrasexual archetype.

Views of Later Jungian Analysts

Since the bedrock of Jungian psychology is the concept of a collective unconscious with its deep archetypal structural images and processes, most Jungian analysts have something to say or write about the anima/animus concepts, whether they are interested in the development of the self, in its infantile origins, in the details of personal history, in working with the transference/counter-transference; or whether they are more interested in archetypal psychology, focusing on religious, mythological and alchemical themes. The issues explored are the concepts themselves as contrasexual aspects of the psyche, whether they are linked to gender, whether and how far they are culturally or stereotypically determined, whether each sex has both an anima and animus, how useful the concepts are to clinical work, their manifestations in each sex and in their relationships.

There are crude polarities – the orthodox view that what Jung said was true (even though he was aware that he was involved in pioneering work on the anima and animus), and the 'politically correct' view which dismisses his theories on the basis that he was a 'male chauvinist', stereotyping male and female attitudes and behaviours conditioned by his upbringing and culture. For the former, difference is all; for the latter sameness is stressed. Zinkin

(1992) summarised the orthodox and revisionist schools of thought, each calling on clinical, biological and mythological evidence.

The Revisionist Group

Whitmont (1969) noted that the moody woman who is anima possessed as well as the opinionated man who is animus possessed are often seen in clinical practice. This and other clinical observations led him to question, not Jung's descriptions of anima and animus, but rather whether they could be differentiated between man and woman, when the man is without animus and the woman without anima.

For Hillman (1985), an archetypal psychologist, anima and animus are archetypes with the status of a Greek goddess and god. He rejects the notion of contrasexuality. Anima, he states, appears in the psychology of women. Both women and men have an anima and animus in some kind of relationship within their psyche, although one side may be more dominant than the other depending on the individual, the culture and the society.

Samuels (1989) argues that there is no such thing as a feminine principle. He takes into consideration anatomical and physiological differences, but questions whether they need to form the basis of feminine or masculine psychology. His position, difficult to prove or refute, is that there are no innate differences in the psychology of any group of individuals and that whatever differences might be found are attributable to culture, with the important consequence that they can be modified.

All these authors reject the idea of the contrasexuality of the anima and animus but retain Jung's idea that they are archetypes.

Orthodox Views

More orthodox views are presented by Grinnel (1973), a Zurich analyst who writes about the alchemical phenomenology of male and female figures and about a feminine psychology referring to the nature of his female patients. Shuttle and Redgrove (1986) base the idea of feminine psychology firmly on biological differences. Since women menstruate (have 'periods') they understand periodicity in a way that men cannot. Through the experience of their own bodies, including the rotting smell of their menses, they are closer to the cyclical nature of birth and death than men can be. Drawing on the myths of Semele, Eros and Psyche, and Beauty and the Beast, Dunne (1989) reaches similar conclusions. The contents of myths and dreams are not just patterns of archetypal imagery arising from the collective unconscious but are expressions of the real differences between male and female psychology which result from their real bodily differences.

Zinkin himself (1992) takes the view that there are specifically different male and female psychologies, even though Jung's ideas of what these differences are need to be reconsidered. He considers that Jung's descriptions now seem dated and stereotyped to the point of caricature.

Rosemary Gordon (1993) disputes the idea that the anima figure inhabits the man only. She believes that the anima figure is possessed by, or in the absence of sufficient consciousness, possesses, both men and women. What distinguishes men and women is their *relationship* to this internal figure. A man will tend to relate to the anima through *projection* on to a woman, while a woman will tend to relate to the anima through *identification* with her. However, there can be no real and genuine personal relationship unless enough conscious personality has developed so that the influence of the archetypal anima figure is modified and restrained. Gordon also tackles the issue of the confusion of Jung's description of the anima with his conception of woman. Anima is *not* the woman. The anima figure as carried in the psyche of man and woman is really a hybrid derived from both archetypal as well as collective and cultural influences. Gordon sees Jung's essay 'Woman in Europe' referred to earlier (*CW* 10) as an enlightened and *prophetic* view of the development of modern woman and man.

Gordon also contrasts 'mother' with anima. Mother is the elementary character and function of woman, whereas the anima has a transformative character and function. She is the archetypal beloved one. In that role she fascinates, instigates, drives and encourages the man to act, to seek adventure, to change, to create. In myths and fairy tales she demands to be wooed and won through trials and tests. She lives far away from the parental home. The anima is at the opposite end to the mother whose love cradles, comforts and consoles, but who, if left unchallenged and undisputed, may crush and consume her offspring. While the ideal relationship to the *mother* is sought in the form of *fusion*, the ideal relationship to the anima is in terms of *coniunctio*, the coming together of the two discrete entities.

Verena Kast, a Zurich-trained analyst (1984), explores various patterns of human heterosexual relationships such as 'mother'/son, 'father'/daughter, goddess of love and her youthful lover; wise old man and young girl, and couples in conflict. She, too, thinks that each sex has an anima and animus, that images of both appear in the dreams of both sexes; for example, good fairies, witches, whores, saints, nymphs and little girls, compelling patriarchs, mysterious strangers, divine youths, fascinating thinkers, emerging prophets. For her, one person does not assume the anima role and the other the animus role; instead, an entire couple constellation can be experienced in the psyche of each person. Kast says that seeing anima and animus as a *couple* constellation could have a therapeutic advantage. We would not have to speak reproachfully of a woman analysand 'caught in the animus'. Such reproaches are not therapeutically effective. Instead, she suggests, we could ask what internal female figure would have to join such a male figure so that the patient could feel more balanced, more satisfied. The vital feeling that is linked with this anima figure could then be imagined and experienced.

What about Anatomy?

Freud, famously or infamously, depending on one's point of view, used the phrase 'anatomy is destiny'.

The foetus starts its first six weeks of life as neutral, without a defined gender. At around seven weeks the presence of the Y chromosome (inherited from the father) causes the gonad to develop into a testis. The testes produce testosterone which brings about the distinctively male bodily characteristics. The testosterone also influences brain structure leading to differences between the male and female brain. Durden-Smith and de Simone (1983) have explored the physical and psychological differences between the sexes and the evolutionary reasons for these. There is much greater thickness of the corpus callosum, that is, the fibres connecting the two hemispheres in the female, although in cross-section the posterior end of the corpus callosum is thicker in the male. Language centres are more widely dispersed in women than in men, in whom there seems to be greater specialisation of functions between the two hemispheres. Anatomical remnants of the opposite sex genitalia are reminders of the neutrality of the early foetus. Psychological and physical differences between the sexes emphasise that men are better at activities requiring muscular strength and visual motor skills, such as locating objects in space, although women are better at the visual motor skills. This should make them better surgeons! Men tend to be better at abstractions and mathematical ability, whereas women tend to be more sensitive in intimate relationships, more responsive to changes in the expression of the human face and to use more non-verbal expressive gestures in conversation. They are better at nurturing. Much of the differences can be attributed to the long evolutionary period in which men were hunters and women were gatherers.

The serious study of sexual or gender difference is now academically respectable in university psychology departments under the impetus of feminist critique and has generated a considerable amount of literature (for example, Sayers 1982, Frosh 1994). Frosh, a practising clinical psychologist as well as an academic psychologist, writes that

> sexual difference is something one has somehow to be involved in; it cannot be dismissed or avoided. 'Masculinity' has been marked by closure throughout its history, holding things in place, symbolised by the unitary sexuality of the penis. 'Femininity' has always challenged this but in the various voices of contemporary, psychoanalytic feminism it has managed to articulate this challenge in an unavoidable form combining seductiveness

with content. This has left masculinity in a void and men at something of a loss ... While we may choose to deal with the anxiety this produces by withdrawing into the fixed positions of the past, we have at least been exposed to the possibility of constant everlasting change. (Frosh 1994, p. 144

Several authors, such as Johnson (1989), Rowan (1987) and Tatham (1992), have specifically explored new definitions of masculinity and what it means to be a man. For example, Tatham takes the 'craftsman' Daedalus as a model for masculinity rather than the 'hero'.

Psychological Development of Sexual/Gender Identity

Freud drew attention to infantile sexuality that culminated in the oedipal phase when the child chooses the parent of the opposite sex as the object of his or her erotic aims and wishes to replace the hitherto strong identification with the parent of the same sex. This arouses both guilt and anxiety. The boy's conflicts are resolved by re-identification with the father. Freud saw this as an easier developmental task for the boy than for the girl, since later he has only to transfer his love from mother to another woman. The girl would like to possess and give a baby to mother. As this is impossible because she lacks a penis, her sexual longings are focused on her father, with mother as a sexual rival. Her secret wishes have to be suppressed, as she also fears the loss of her mother.

Stoller (1968), an American psychoanalyst, considered masculine identity as more fragile.

In contrast to Freud's decision that masculinity is the natural state and femininity at best a successful modification of it, I feel that the boy's relationship to his mother makes the development of feminine qualities more likely ... The boy must manage to break through from the peak of his mother's femaleness, a task so frequently incomplete, to judge by the amount of effeminacy, passivity or forced hyper-masculinity one sees. (Stoller 1968, p. 263)

Jessica Benjamin (1990), another American psychoanalyst, looked afresh at Freud's theories of infantile sexuality. In particular, she approached the oedipal complex from a feminist perspective. Like Freud, she saw the development of masculinity as less problematical than femininity, but considered this as much more culture-dependent. Masculinity and femininity become associated with postures of master and slave. These postures arise in boys' and girls' different relationship to mother and father. Girls are identified as objects and boys as subjects in the Oedipus situation. Father is the exciting other in the child's life who allows for separation from the mother. For the boy, the identificatory love for the father allows for recognition and a special erotic relationship with him. Through this, the boy sees himself as the subject of desire. The identificatory love is the psychological foundation of the idealisation of male power and autonomous individuality. Separation from the mother is not so easy for the girl. Benjamin links the little girl's desire for the penis as evidence that she is seeking identification with the father, the representative of the outside world. However, father's own misidentification with his mother and his continuing need to assert difference from women make it difficult for him to recognise his daughter as he does his son. He is more likely to see her as a 'sweet adorable thing', a nascent sex object. His withdrawal pushes her back to mother, turning inward her aspirations for independence. A further consequence of this is that many girls are left with a 'lifelong admiration for individuals who get away with their sense of omnipotence intact. They grow to idealise the man who has what they can never possess – power and desire' (Benjamin 1990, p. 109).

Benjamin believes that with substantial alteration in gender expectations and parenting, both parents can be figures of separation and attachment for their children, and that boys and girls can make use of identifications with each parent without being confused about their gender identity. Intriguingly, though without reference to Jungian concepts, Benjamin believes that individuals ideally should integrate and express both male and female aspects of selfhood (as culturally defined). The core sense of belonging to one sex or the other will not be compromised by cross-sex identifications and behaviours. The wish to be and do what the other sex does is not pathological nor necessarily a denial of one's own identity. The choice of love object, homosexual or heterosexual, is not the determining aspect of gender identity, an idea Benjamin states, that psychoanalytic theory does not always admit.

It is difficult for any theory of gender identity development to do justice to the complex nature of the subtle interactions taking place within the individual, between the parental couple, and between the child and the parent. There are internal as well as external realities. Jung's concepts of the archetypes that are unchanging but whose images are constantly changing both in projection on external figures and modification by them, especially the parents, envisage the potential for almost endless possibilities, permutations and variations in the personality. However, it does seem to be generally accepted that each person carries aspects of the opposite sex in their psyche and that these need to be made conscious and integrated within the personality. The degree to which this happens can determine the extent to which masculinity and femininity appear in their more primitive and defensive forms. The child not only has to relate to the 'conscious' parent but also to those unconscious contrasexual aspects within the parent. Gee (1995), a contemporary Jungian analyst, considers that the anima and animus in a man differ constitutionally from those in a woman. Thus it is easier for the boy to identify with a man's animus (and the girl with the woman's anima) because of the similarity. In Gee's view the boy projects his animus on to a male figure, usually an older boy, as part of his 'apprentice love' and then goes on to identify with that figure as part of integrating his animus in a modified form. The boy will go on to develop his anima in relation to his mother and then with another woman. The girl will develop her animus in relation to her father and then other men. The intensity of the anima and animus functions varies between individuals.

When a person is stuck developmentally through early damage to the psyche due to poor or inadequate parenting, he or she may only be able to behave in limited, often stereotypical ways. Indeed, these may appear to be the only options open to the person, a necessary part of his or her defensive system. For example, the individual may be fixed in an heroic mode, always battling and striving, unable to relate, or else he or she may behave as an 'innocent' victim, always put upon (the fault always lies elsewhere), denying his or her own aggression and destructiveness. These negative feelings are projected on to others. Insecurity about gender identity may lead the individual into exaggerated overcompensatory identification with a primitive masculine or feminine stereotype; for example, the stiff-upper-lip man who may not allow himself to show his feelings, or the frivolous, empty-headed woman who may not be able to think. Such extremes may lead to collusive couplings that break down when one or other partner does begin to change and develop.

In the unconscious factors that draw a couple together there is often the hope and wish that what is problematical for one partner can somehow be compensated for or managed better by the other. When this goes well then each partner can develop and grow. When the hope is not realised, there is disappointment which can lead to rejection and the end of the relationship.

Clinical Applications of the Anima/Animus Concepts

Colman (1995), another contemporary Jungian analyst who has worked for many years as a marital therapist, looks at *cross-gender identifications* where there is shared gender insecurity used defensively in heterosexual couples, which may cause the relationship to break down. Both partners are 'possessed' by the contrasexual archetype (anima and animus) and have been unable to integrate their contrasexual potential. He proposes three aetiological factors which may predispose an individual to cross-gender identification. These are: (i) an over-close relationship during childhood with the parent of the opposite sex; (ii) a negative identification with the parent of the same sex; and (iii) inappropriate use by their mothers as substitute caretakers (narcissistic objects).

In both sexes masculinity is idealised while femininity is denigrated. Colman stresses that cross-gender identity is not necessarily indicative of homosexuality. Sexual orientation and gender identity are relatively independent.

With animus possession the girl expresses her rage and disappointment with the mother, who has failed to meet her basic need for affirmation and unconditional love, by turning to the father. There is inevitable disappointment for the girl at the time of passage through the Oedipus phase. There then appear three routes to the development of a masculine identity for the girl. First, she may identify with father as a protection against the loss of both parents. Second, with a negative Oedipus complex she may hope to regain the lost mother by identifying with father (the route followed by some lesbians). Third, by behaving in a coquettish way as an attempt to seduce the father, she may offer to meet his anima fantasies in return for her own need for recognition. This is the origin of the *femme fatale* who wishes not to love but to be loved (for example, Carmen). She may seek revenge on men by trying to humiliate them as she was humiliated in her original oedipal love affair (Hedda Gabler, for example).

While the animus-possessed woman typically idealises her father, the anima-possessed experience of the man is often one of being idealised or idolised by mother. Initially this relationship with the mother appears to offer limitless gratification. Stoller (1968) believes that in the most extreme cases the infantile gratifications are so great that no masculine core gender identity develops at all – this is the genesis of the male transsexual. In less extreme cases the boy exists as a boy, but only on condition that he remains mother's creature. This situation is symbolised in the mother–son myths of antiquity (Neumann 1949; *CW* 5, p. 424, para. 659). These sons are destined to be the *puer aeternus* – the eternal boy (*CW* 9i, paras 193, 268, 269). They can never leave mother as her seductive power is too great. They fear their masculinity as something dangerous and destructive. The female equivalent is the *puella* – the eternal girl who is unable to leave her parents. She is strongly attached to father. No other man can take his place. She is both dependent on and hostile to mother and cannot identify with her as a woman. Thus she may never see herself as a potential mother, only a virgin daughter.

Homosexuality: Anima and Animus

Hopcke (1989b), a Jungian analyst who is also gay, has thoughtfully and deeply explored the ideas and concepts relating to male homosexuality of Jung, Jungians directly influenced by Jung and latterday Jungians. He notes that there are few references in the *Collected Works* to homosexuality, and certainly Jung did not propound a theory of homosexuality. However, Jung did put forward some mixed views on homosexuality. On the one hand, he considered that homosexuality should not be a matter for the law and that an individual's homosexuality should be distinguished from other aspects of his personality (*CW* 10, p. 112, para. 251). He also considered that homosexuality could be the result of psychological immaturity, that is, an unconscious identification with his anima or inner feminine figure. This could lead to a projection of his persona, that is, his outer masculinity, on to another man (*CW* 6, paras 471–2). Nevertheless, Jung counterbalanced this by stating that an individual's homosexuality has a *meaning* peculiar to that individual. Psychological growth consists in becoming aware of that meaning. Hopcke thinks that the three variables of sexual identity – anatomical gender, sociocultural sex roles, and sexual orientation – have become confused in analytical psychology. He stresses the importance of both personal experiences and archetypal elements, and proposes that the sexual orientation of an individual is determined through a complex interaction of the archetypal masculine, the archetypal feminine and the archetypal androgyne. Some gay men may identify and be identified by society with the inner feminine seen in its shadow aspect as inferior and regarded with contempt. The archetypal masculine is often projected on to other men when gay men feel that their own masculinity has been denied and impugned. The psychological work of individuation would require the owning and validation of these aspects of the personality, bringing them into a more mature relationship within the self. This would in turn enable the individual to form more intimate and satisfying relationships with others.

Clinical Example

Warring between Anima and Animus

Mr and Mrs A, a couple in their late thirties, referred themselves to me for help with a sexual problem, namely Mr A's impotence. They presented as clearly an angry couple, although each was also clearly struggling to be 'adult', nice and reasonable. Mr A's non-interest in sex had dogged their ten-year marriage, although Mrs A pointed out bitterly that it had not stopped him being repeatedly unfaithful to her when he went on business trips. (I pondered on why she always took him back.) They had a two-year-old son whom they described as angelic but 'demanding' of their attention and time. Both had high-powered jobs, stressful and also demanding: his in business, hers in academia. She had taken time out from her work to look after their son. She wanted another baby, after which she planned to return to work. It was obvious that much was being expected of me by both of them. During this first interview I felt under intense pressure to 'perform' and 'deliver the goods'. They claimed that they had tried everything. It became apparent that somehow or other they both 'arranged' to avoid sex while consciously claiming to want it. From me they wanted medical advice, suggestions, homework, perhaps even pills to cure the problem. Physically they were a handsome couple; she blonde and pretty, he dark and good looking.

They were afraid of intimacy at a deep level. What were the fears due to? His mother, to whom he was very attached, had run off with another man when he was fourteen years old. She was an exciting, vivacious woman, while his father was dull and boring, though reliable. He could understand why his mother had run away and he did not blame her (I wondered whether Mrs A envied, consciously or unconsciously, this sexy mother).

Mrs A described herself as being closer to her father than to her mother, who had spent time in a mental hospital. There had always been a question about her sanity. Father was described as quiet and hard working, building up his own business. He was very proud of his daughter's academic achievements. (I mused on the fact that there were two dull fathers and two unstable mothers in Mr and Mrs A's background.)

During their early courtship Mrs A had seemed the more confident one. She had seduced him and was very pleased that she had 'won' the best-looking man in her year. He liked her because she was pretty and lively. Sex had been all right in the early years of marriage, when she took the initiative, but he continued to remain passive and she was tired now of doing all the work. She wanted change. He did not seem very bothered. In the transference he seemed to experience me as the exciting sexual mother enjoying the talk about sex. She was coldly analytical, asking penetrating questions as if she would bore into me. She seemed to regard his penis as a 'thing' that should be made to work by the doctor – me. She was devoted to their son but found his needs overwhelming, although she seemed to exacerbate them so that he could not be without her (for example, she often slept in his room). Thus I came to see how she was projecting her needs and dependency into him, as if having already given up on the possibility of finding sustenance from her husband, while at the same time he experienced her as overwhelming and intrusive, and found sexual satisfaction outside of a committed intimate relationship.

Comment

Neither partner could identify with the same-sex parent: for her, it would be akin to risking identification with a mad mother; for him, the risk would be of becoming dull and boring. His mother seemed to be identified for him with the anima, incestuously exciting and seductive, but eventually betraying him. He identified with his mother by having sexual affairs but always betraying and abandoning the women he slept with, speaking of them quite callously. Thus he appeared to be punishing his mother vicariously through these affairs.

Though bitter about the affairs, Mrs A knew at some level that he would never abandon her for another woman. She identified with her father's positive animus image, resolute, loyal, using her intelligence in what appeared to be a rather cold and analytic way. She enjoyed her position as father's favourite, triumphing over her 'mad' mother. She had 'won' the oedipal battle, but it was a pyrrhic victory.

As a couple, Mr and Mrs A both longed for and avoided sexual intimacy because they shared an unconscious phantasy that thereby incestuous, dangerous feelings would be released. Neither carried within themselves a good internal couple capable of enjoyable intercourse.

When she had seduced him, he had been reassured that he was desirable, but it also meant that by her taking the responsibility for their sexuality, he was freed from incestuous guilt feelings. Her ability to seduce him confirmed her power but did not reassure her that she was desirable. If he were to give her that assurance of desirability, he feared, unconsciously, that he would lose her. Neither was comfortable or secure with their sexual identity. She was identified with her animus in both a positive (successful academic) and negative (opinionated, argumentative) way. He was more identified with his anima in a negative way – moody, sulky, capricious. Both overvalued the masculine and devalued and attacked the feminine: she more openly; he surreptitiously.

Why had they stayed together? He knew she would never betray him. She knew that although he might be sexually unfaithful he would never abandon her. Both had been abandoned by one parent, and so they would neither abandon their child. Intellectually they had much in common; 'intercourse' at that level was allowed and enjoyable. However, they were also stuck with apparently no room for change. There was thus no real *coniunctio*.

In the therapy I was attacked and denigrated but expected to perform. She wanted to battle with me and occasionally I found it hard to resist, as when she demanded to know what kind of doctor I was and my training. He would lull me into a false sense of security with his seductive charm but then subtly denigrate me, as when he reassured me that I must be trying to do my best with them. What did I represent for them – the dull, boring, worthy father, or the mad/sexy mother, unable to have good intercourse?

Mrs A attacked and provoked me unconsciously in an attempt to find in me her own mad and abandoning mother. Mr A, also at an unconscious level, alternately flirted and attempted to seduce me, while ignoring or deprecating everything I said, in an attempt to find in me his sexually exciting but reprehensible mother. They attempted thereby in their different ways to cause a split in me. Likewise, they were contemptuous of and attacked the me who was both the sympathetic, loving mother and the thinking, concerned father.

What did I do? I survived, I did not abandon them, reject them or go mad. I did not stop thinking. I struggled to maintain the possibility of ongoing intercourse between an internal couple, a father and mother, and be neither seduced nor destroyed by either. They in turn allowed themselves to become attached to me, never missing sessions, and were eventually able to internalise my interpretations and introject me as a figure capable of having a good internal *coniunctio*. This drama happened at an unconscious level.

As they began to trust me they began to trust each other. She visibly softened, he became more attentive. Sex was resumed secretly and shyly. They were able to let go some of their anger and developed an increased capacity to acknowledge my contribution before they ended therapy. Mrs A later wrote to tell me she was pregnant. Their daughter was named Zoë (the Greek word for life).

Conclusion

Jung's concepts of anima and animus, the contrasexual aspects in the psyche, risk being dismissed by postmodernist critiques as stereotypical and culture-bound. Nevertheless, in considering them as archetypes within the psyche, unknowable except through personifications in myths, legends, art, literature and via projection on to others, a deeper, richer understanding of the male and female psyche is possible. They contribute importantly to understanding the relationships between the sexes and with the same sex. Indeed, such understanding can benefit not only the individual (especially in the task of individuation) but also the couple, whether hetero- or homosexual, throwing light on why some relationships work and others do not. This can assist in conceiving the structure and content of therapeutic intervention. Over and above these contributions, there may be real benefit for society as a whole in changing stereotypes and stereotypical behaviours.

Acknowledgements

I would like to thank Mr and Mrs A for their permission to describe our work together.

References

Appighanesi, L. and Forrester, J. (1992) *Freud's Women*. London: Weidenfeld and Nicolson.
Benjamin, M.J. (1990) *The Bonds of Love*. London: Virago.
Carotenuto, A. (1984) *A Secret Symmetry*. London: Routledge and Kegan Paul.
Christopher, E. (1987) *Sexuality and Birth Control in Community Work*, 2nd edition. London: Tavistock.
Colman, W. (1995) 'Cross-gender identifications in heterosexual couples', *British Journal of Psychotherapy*, 11(4).

Dunne, C. (1989) *Behold Woman: A Jungian Approach to Feminist Theology.* Wilmette, IL: Chiron Publications.

Durden-Smith, J. and de Simone, D. (1983) *Sex and the Brain.* London: Pan.

Frosh, S. (1994) *Sexual Difference: Masculinity and Psychoanalysis.* London: Routledge and Kegan Paul.

The Freud–Jung Letters (1974) *The Correspondence between Sigmund Freud and C.J. Jung*, ed. William McGuire. London: Hogarth.

Gee, H. (1995) 'The archetypal themes in Ucello's painting *St. George and the Dragon*', *Harvest*, 41(1), London: C.J. Jung Analytical Psychology Club.

Gordon, R. (1993) *Bridges.* London: Karnac.

Grinnel, R. (1973) *Alchemy in a Modern Woman: A Study in the Contrasexual Archetype.* Dallas, TX: Spring.

Hillman, J. (1985) *Anima: An Anatomy of a Personified Notion.* Dallas, TX: Spring.

Hopcke, R. (1989a) *A Guided Tour of the Collected Works of C.G. Jung.* Boston, MA and London: Shambala.

Hopcke, R. (1989b) *Jung, Jungians and Homosexuality.* Boston, MA: Shambala.

Johnson, R. (1989) *He.* New York: Harper and Row.

Jung, C.G. (1963) *Memories, Dreams, Reflections.* New York: Pantheon.

Kast, V. (1984) *The Nature of Loving.* Wilmette, IL: Chiron Publications.

Neumann, E. (1949) *The Origins and History of Consciousness.* London: Karnac.

Neumann, E. (1955) *The Great Mother.* Princeton, NJ: Bollinger Foundation.

Rowan, J. (1987) *The Horned God.* London: Routledge.

Samuels, A. (1989) *The Plural Psyche.* London: Routledge and Kegan Paul.

Samuels, A., Shorter, B. and Plaut, A. (1986) *A Critical Dictionary of Jungian Analysis.* London: Routledge and Kegan Paul.

Sayers, J. (1982) *Biological Politics – Feminist and Anti-Feminist Perspectives.* London: Tavistock.

Shuttle, P. and Redgrove, P. (1986) *The Wise Wound: Menstruation and Everyman.* London: Paladin.

Stoller, R. (1968) *Sex and Gender.* Vol. 1. Maresfield Reprints, London.

Tatham, P. (1992) *The Making of Maleness.* London: Karnac.

Whitmont, E.C. (1969) *The Symbolic Quest.* New York: Putnams.

Zinkin, L. (1992) 'Anima and animus: an interpersonal view', in N. Schwartz-Salant and M. Stein (eds) *Gender and Soul in Psychotherapy.* Wilmette, IL: Chiron Publications.

Suggested Reading

Kast, V. (1984) *The Nature of Loving.* Wilmette, IL: Chiron Publications.

Schwartz-Salant, N. and Stein, M. (eds) (1992) *Gender and Soul in Psychotherapy.* Wilmette, IL: Chiron Publications.

Stevens, A. (1990) *On Jung.* London: Routledge and Kegan Paul.

Part II
Jungian Thought and the Collective

4

Modern Western Society –
The Making of Myth and Meaning

Helen Morgan

Introduction

According to Lévi-Strauss (1983), myth is a means by which the mind can imitate itself as an object *and* act as a reflection of the universe of which the mind is a part. In the struggle to find meaning, individuals, groups and cultures need to tell stories about themselves. These stories are contingent, relative and constructed. They emerge at particular moments to convey a latent message that has significance for the times in which they are evoked. They can be thought of as emerging as a transcendent function of and between the psyche and the social. Having arisen from and been taken on by the collective, the myth, in turn, affects both the social and the individual psyche, thus forming a new state of affairs and a new dialectic. Therefore, the question as to whether the chosen myths are 'objectively true' is of less interest than the subjective truth they hold for those who tell them and for those to whom they are told. Furthermore, having considered why one myth rather than another has been tacitly accepted as 'truth' by a group, it is worth wondering how that particular story has played its part in creating a new culture and set of social conditions.

Whilst he accepted the validity of the theories which Freud saw as encapsulated in the myth of Oedipus, Jung challenged its primacy and developed his theory of the collective unconscious and deep archetypal structures which could be known indirectly through a pantheon of myths that any culture tells itself. In this chapter I will argue that it was the myth of Oedipus, and then that of Narcissus, which resonated with the modern age and which led to a wider acceptance of Freud's theories than those of Jung. However, I will also put the case for the limitations of this myth and the dead-end it has led us into in this postmodern age. I suggest that Jungian thought offers a route out of this impasse.

Modernity

Western society, based in the monotheistic religions of Judaeo-Christianity, held at its centre in the pre-modern era the existence of an external, omniscient and omnipotent 'God the Father', creator of all things and arbiter of law and morality. The Church provided the Christian world with the overarching construct for defining the individual's place in that world. It was essentially a projective culture where ultimate power, knowledge and creativity were located in a supreme being that defined and determined the laws of nature. Man (more significantly than woman) was seen as a separate, superior creation of God, designed to manage and keep his place in the greater order of things, somewhere between the animals and the angels. A similar hierarchy within society prevailed: 'the rich man in his castle, the poor man at his gate, God made them high and lowly, and ordered their estate'. Things may not have been bright and beautiful for all, but the individual's place in society was ordained and to be borne. It was a patriarchal society where secular power was held by the aristocracy and passed from father to son, whilst spiritual authority passed from father to father.

By the end of the nineteenth century, huge upheavals in every branch of knowledge were taking place. In science there was the discovery of radioactivity, the development of a new model of the atom, and the theory of relativity. The new genetics and the theories of evolution revolutionised our view of the order of things and our place in it. The second wave of the Industrial Revolution included the development of the internal combustion engine, electricity, the automobile, the telephone and new synthetic materials. The fields of entertainment and the media saw the beginnings of mass circulation of newspapers, of radio-wave transmission and the first movie theatre. The foundations were laid for an explosion of scientific developments which confronted man's perception of the world, of nature and of his (and eventually her) place within it. The implications for the previous order of political, social and philosophical thought were shattering.

The remaining gaps in knowledge were closing fast towards what was perceived to be the inevitable end point where we could, and would, know all there was to know. Whilst not yet at the imagined goal of understanding all, its very possibility meant that God's authority was threatened by the potential omniscience of humankind. It was merely a matter of time and of better measurement before we would be tucking into all the apples from the tree of knowledge. And if man could know the mind of God, what was to prevent him from also assuming the other attributes of ultimate power and creativity? This was a brazen and dangerous endeavour. If humankind was to take it on, then a new science of humanity was needed, and a new myth that might give such hubris meaning.

Oedipus as Modernity's Myth

Whilst some of the concepts of the emerging study of human psychology were not new – the notion of the unconscious being already familiar, particularly within German philosophy – it was Freud who captured the central ground and was to become modernity's psychologist-in-chief. Freud offered a huge body of work and a system of thought that was to have profound implications for the way we have come to view ourselves. By insisting on the existence and primacy of infantile sexuality, and by locating desire within the family, he was both revolutionary and conservative. At the heart of his thinking he placed the myth of Oedipus, and it was this choice that encapsulated and gave meaning to the nature of the times. Borrowed from the Greeks, it tells of the son's overthrow of the father, and of its terrible consequences. It is a myth that dramatises the excitements of triumph, but also the terrors of punishment when the patriarchy is overthrown. James Hillman writes:

> In choosing the Oedipus myth, Freud told us less which myth was the psyche's essence than that the *essence of psyche is myth*, that our work is mythic and ritual, that psychology is ultimately mythology, the study of the stories of the soul ... But the story he chose to tell has left behind cursed issues: father-murder, wars of generations, unsolved incest longings and incestuous entanglements in both relationships and ideas, the distortion of the feminine in the Jocasta mold, the anima as an intellectual riddle with a monster's body, and destruction everywhere – suicide, blight and sterility, hanging, blinding – descending to future generations. Is this our myth? If it is, then how can we go from it to 'psychological creativity'? (Hillman 1972, p. 17; original emphasis)

Whilst Hillman and others criticise this choice of myth and see its impact on our understanding of ourselves as, at best, unfortunate, there remains the question of *why* this particular myth took such a hold in modernity? The features central to the story of Oedipus are the unconscious nature of the main players, the destruction of the father by the son, the marriage of the son to the mother and the dire fate that transpires. As the age struggled against the old patriarchy and saw changes in the role of women, as it found new knowledge and new consciousness, the awesomeness of the endeavour resonated in the unconscious. What excitement! What terrors! Given the events of the twentieth century – two world wars, the Holocaust, the development of nuclear weapons, the alienation experienced in industrial societies and the fall-out for the developing nations – it may be that the myth was accurate in its forecast of doom. One might say that, in comparison, Oedipus got off lightly.

Yet, if this is indeed our myth, then Hillman's question still remains: how do we go from it to psychological creativity?

The Project of Modernity

One way of looking at the tragedy of Oedipus with its prophecy of doom for those who challenge the patriarch is to see it as a compensation for the conscious attitude that prevailed. Indeed, the myth tells us that it is unconsciousness and ignorance that lead to disaster. The modernist endeavour, rooted in the Enlightenment, was one of moving further into the light of consciousness and rationality. The further we can travel down the road to 'objective truth', the closer we should come to the creation of a just and good society.

Supposedly freed from the shackles of the Commandments and of the past, there developed at the heart of modernity the notion of the Grand Idea. This was the emancipatory project central to which was the notion of progress as a linear and vertical process leading towards the perfect society, to Utopia:

> modern legislators and modern thinkers ... earnestly believed that the void left by the now extinct or ineffective moral supervision of the Church can and ought to be filled with a carefully and harmonized set of rational rules; that *reason* can do what *belief* was doing no more; that with their eyes wide open and passions put to rest, men can regulate their mutual relationships no less, and perhaps more and better (in a more 'civilized', 'peaceful', 'rational' manner) than at a time when they were 'blinded' by faith and when their untamed and undomesticated feelings ran wild. (Bauman 1993, p. 6; original emphasis)

In formulating his structure of the psyche, Freud portrays the id as the location of repressed desires, the source of the 'untamed and undomesticated feelings' which always threatened to break free and run wild. The original objectives of these desires – both sexual and murderous – were the parents. Acting in opposition to such intentions was the superego, which itself was seen as 'civilisation' transmitted via the parents. The ego is the location of consciousness struggling to manage the opposing pressures from the other, unconscious aspects of the psyche. Since both id and superego are heavily determined by the original family scenario, the psyche, despite all its attempts to break free, remains in the Freudian frame, chained to its personal early history.

In the pre-modern world, the fate of the individual was determined by the social context, class, gender, race, and so on, into which he or she was born. In modernity's project, the individual was to be emancipated from such restrictions and freed into an ideal state of true autonomy and creativity of the self. The problems inherent in such an endeavour lay not only in the conflicts between this ideal and the demands of capitalism, but in the turmoil with which the individual would have to struggle, the heavy requirement for stable identity to manage such demands. The theories of Freud and the myth of Oedipus were no longer sufficient for this state of affairs and psychoanalysis was required to develop further.

The Object Relations School

Object relations theory was a development within psychoanalysis pioneered by Klein, Winnicott, Bion and others, from the 1940s onwards. Whilst these theorists take us back beyond the relation between the child and the father to the earlier years of the infant and the mother, this stage is described as 'pre-oedipal', thereby retaining loyalty to both Freud and Oedipus.

In object relations theory, it is the primary relationship between the baby and the mother that is seen as the formative dynamic. In the ideal (or good enough) situation, the mother provides a stable setting which can contain and make sense of the infant's rage and attack as aspects of the so-called paranoid-schizoid position. The child projects unwanted, unbearable initial experiences externally into the mother who holds and manages them until the infant is able to re-introject them in a tolerable form. The child, for whom the container of these unhappy experiences is herself a depressed or unstable mother, has no way of developing the secure sense of self necessary for achieving the depressive position whereby the infant recognises its mother as containing both good and bad, positive and negative aspects. This is seen as a prerequisite for the child to hold and manage its own loving and aggressive feelings and thus to form a stable and whole sense of its self. From this stability of identity, the individual can then develop a capacity for concern, empathy, relationships, and a moral standpoint.

This shift in emphasis places the development of the individual in a position of considerable vulnerability, less to the place of the father within the social context into which he or she is born than to the emotional state of the mother. In the turmoil of the ever-changing upheaval of modernity, a stable self becomes paramount as a refuge from the uncertainties of the age. It becomes the location of identity and of creative activity. The early conditions required for its development are shouldered primarily by the mother who herself exists in turbulent times. It is contingent. The ideal of social progress requires that each generation improves on the previous one. Yet object relations theory tell us that the development of the next generation is dependent on the mother, who is also grappling with the complexities of the age, having inherited the unresolved problems of the previous generations. If a stream cannot rise higher than its source, then there is at best stasis, and at worst, a downward spiral.

The Myth of Narcissus

According to object relations theory, if born to an unstable, depressed or confused mother, the infant has little chance of developing his or her own stable 'true self', with a sense of identity and a capacity to make relationships with others. Instead, the adult will suffer from a sense of smallness and terror as he or she struggles with an uncertain modern world. Compensating for this inferiority, the individual will develop notions of grandiosity, turning his or her love back on him- or herself and unable to relate to others.

Into the foreground comes a different myth from the Greeks, that of Narcissus. Narcissus, a beautiful youth but incapable of returning love, of engaging in relationship, is cursed by an avenging and unrequited maiden that he should come to feel what it was to love and meet no return of affection. He comes to drink at a pool and falls in love with his own image. He remains pining for the love of this unresponsive, reflected beauty, until he fades away into death. Echo, the feminine principle, is left helpless, her love unmet, capable only of echoing her lover's words.

Modernity's project leaves the individual open to the chill winds of change, but also to a world full of possibility, what Frosh (1991) calls the 'thrills and spills' of the age. Here there is a place for creativity and an evolutionary, even revolutionary, endeavour. Here we have the potential for a political project and hope. However, if such a project is to succeed, without the strictures of a given order, the individual requires a stable self that can achieve the possibilities of the imagination and manage the uncertainties inherent in the situation. The prize is the excitement of the creative, the threat is of emptiness and despair. In modernity there is faith in progress and rationality, optimism concerning the future and a belief in an absolute and objective knowledge in all fields of human enquiry. The tragedy of the story of Narcissus is that in his failure to be in relationship with others, he is overtaken with his inflated sense of self and can only gaze lovingly into his own reflection, broken as it is by the waters, and Echo can only stand by with her mournful repetitiveness. Both are isolated and locked into death.

Postmodernity

It is perhaps ironic that the hard sciences, the developments which had been instrumental in the conception of modernity's social project, had long since given up any hope of absolute knowledge, and understood the inherent impossibility of separating the observing subject from the observed. As the notion of the subjectivity of knowledge, the requirement for deconstruction of previously accepted 'truths' and the part played by language in our 'knowing', seeped through into other areas of study, the belief in the modern project began to crumble. Whilst the concept of postmodernity is fiercely debated and confusingly portrayed, I am taking this disillusionment with the idea of absolute knowledge and of progress through rationality as a generally accepted feature relevant to this discussion.

It is the *disbelief* in such a possibility that is *post-modern* – 'post' not in the 'chronological' sense (not in the sense of displacing and replacing modernity, of being born only at the moment when modernity ends or fades away, of rendering the modern view impossible once it comes into its own) but in the sense of implying (in the form of conclusion, or mere pre-monition) that the long and earnest efforts of modernity have been misguided, undertaken under false pretences and bound to – sooner or later – run their course; that, in other words, it is modernity itself that will demonstrate (if it has not demonstrated yet) and demonstrate beyond reasonable doubt, its impossibility, the vanity of its hopes and the waste-fulness of its works. (Bauman 1993, p. 10; original emphasis)

Another fatality of this disillusionment seems to be the very concept of the 'true self' which has been perceived by some as an illusion, a defence. Everything is superficial, a glittering array of shards reflecting our own fragmented selves. There is no depth or centre, nothing to hold on to whilst on the rollercoaster of contemporary urban life.

This belief in the possible existence of a self is a central component of the mode of modernist reasoning – it is precisely this image and its potential for development which is called into question by what has come to be termed post-modernism. (Frosh 1991, p. 21)

On the one hand, we have created a world where we appear to be controllers of the universe where everything seems possible. On the other, we feel ourselves to be impotent, and even the 'self' that is supposed to be in control is in question. Jung notes the irony in humanity's challenge to become Lord of All, only to find ourselves slave to the machines we have created. 'Finally, to add comedy to tragedy, this lord of the elements, this universal arbiter, hugs to his bosom notions which stamp his dignity as worthless and turn his autonomy into an absurdity' (Jung 1958, p. 41).

Returning to Hillman's question of how we go from the oedipal myth to 'psychological creativity', it would seem that we are no better off with the new myth of Narcissus. From gazing upwards and outwards to God the Father, we then turned to face the father as patriarch. Having out-stared him, the gaze fell on mother. Now, it seems, we are left on our own, unrelated and scanning the mirror for the love we crave. Even this is shattered and we have only a glittering kaleidoscope of surface images offering little meaning. We are now told, in this postmodernist age, that the very idea of the 'true self' of which so much has been required, is itself a myth, an illusion and a defence against the verity of our existence which is emptiness, meaninglessness, the void.

A Map of the Freudian Psyche

It was Freudian theory that came to dominate analytic thinking, academia and the popular understanding of psychology. Whilst the reasons for this are complex, I have argued that a major factor was the resonance of his chosen myth with the times. A society that was taking on one God, through the discovery of one truth, to form one ideal, wanted one mythic tragedy and could not be doing with the messiness of the pantheon of gods. Furthermore, it needed a myth that spoke of the perils inherent in the project of the time – that of the overthrow of the father. From this position, with hindsight, it is perhaps inevitable that the twentieth century has unfolded as it has, and that psychoanalysis as the science of the internal world has moved alongside accordingly. These are powerful theories which affect as well as explain the *Zeitgeist*.

Jung's model of the psyche, since developed by contemporary Jungians, differs from that of Freud and post-Freudian thought in some fundamental ways. In order to illustrate this difference, I intend to build a map. Like all maps, it is a metaphor, a way of describing something in a way that might help. Like all maps, once drawn it is instantly flawed. By drawing the map in this way rather than another, choices are made concerning what is put in and, most importantly, what is left out.

The metaphor or image I am using to think about the Freudian model of the psyche is of an iceberg; not because it is frozen, but because it is a floating mass. The area above the surface of the sea is analogous to the conscious aspects of the psyche, including the ego. All analytic theories have as a central tenet this concept that consciousness is only one aspect of the whole, that 'what we see is not all we get'. Below the surface of the water lies an area, greater in mass, which is unconscious. Surface activity is, to a large extent, determined by this area, so that a conscious determination to behave in a certain manner can be overridden by unconscious drives compelling a behaviour that is 'irrational' and possibly causing symptoms (see Figure 4.1).

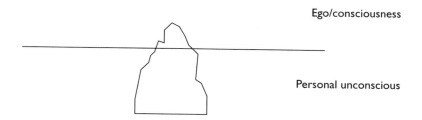

Figure 4.1

In this model, the individual psyche is perceived to be a discrete entity, weighty no doubt, but still afloat and profoundly susceptible to the movements of the waters and of the weather within which it exists. It should be noted that the theory places the drives and instincts as substantial determinants in the shape and form of the psyche, and these are located in our humanity, in our animal nature which we all share. Nevertheless, these are dynamics which we inherit at birth, and there is no voice in this model that speaks of connectedness between individuals that continues at a deep human level as we develop from birth onwards. We are born with certain tendencies such as the death instinct, an aggressive drive, envy, the oedipal urge, and so on, but once born, the mediation and development of these instinctual desires are contingent on the immediate environment – father and/or mother – in which we find ourselves. In this model, the psyche has a bottom, and what is contained in the area beneath the surface, the unconscious, is limited to the repression of drives which, due to the circumstances of early development, have become unacceptable.

On this map, we can depict what takes place at a social and cultural level as the atmosphere, climate or weather that exists above sea level and which affects, and is affected by, the nature of the islands of individuality. Whereas in pre-modern times, this climate was relatively stable and fixed, where the sphere of influence was limited to the village or the town, and where changes were slow and minimal, modernity meant a seismic shift in weather patterns. The development in global communications through the media has meant that events on the other side of the planet are relayed immediately into our living rooms. We are required to engage with not only the upheavals in our neighbourhood, but with those across the world. As consumers, we are tempted daily with an ever-changing array of possibilities and of outlets for the best and the worst in us. Not only do things seem to change at a rapid rate, we are constantly being told about it. At the same time as we are told by politicians, press and retailers that we are democratic citizens with the power to affect the world in everything we do and everything we buy, we experience events that we are powerless to alter. We are both continuously connected to the entire human race, and profoundly detached. (Figure 4.2.)

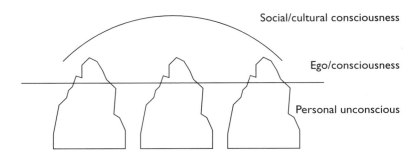

Social/cultural consciousness

Ego/consciousness

Personal unconscious

Figure 4.2

Because the iceberg floats, having no anchorage at sub-oceanic levels, it is subjected to the turbulence of these climatic conditions. Its steadiness or otherwise is dependent on its own weightiness. How well we individually manage the complexities and uncertainties of contemporary life depends on the strength of the ego which, in turn, is dependent on the dynamics of our early lives. Whether the focus is a classical Freudian one or that of the object relations school, the primitive familial scene is paramount.

Here I am not seeking to question the significance or 'truth' of this work; rather, I am asking, is that all? Can our humanity be reduced only to the peculiarities of the developmental forces that shaped us? And as long as we say that this is the psychological truth as far as it goes, does it matter? Should we be seeking for truths concerning areas beyond this construct, outside of the psychological enquiry – in religion, in the esoteric, in the political? I argue that it does matter, and that the dominance of this theory and of its two myths has led us up a cul-de-sac and serves to restrict and limit what Castoriadis calls 'the radical imagination at the core of the psyche' (Castoriadis 1994). It is a theory that locates the 'problem' and salvation *only* in the individual. Whilst there is an important acknowledgement of the power of the personal unconscious and the conscious ego's puniness in relation to the dark internal forces, that is all we are allowed. This places the struggling ego under immense pressure and severs it from any larger, internal source that may be creative. It cuts us off from each other.

A Map of the Jungian Psyche

The central distinction between Jungian thought and that of the Freudians and post-Freudians, is that, whereas in the latter case the psyche is limited to the conscious and the personal unconscious, for Jungians it extends further below into an archaic foundation of humanity which connects each to the other. This deep layer of connection is what is referred to as the collective unconscious. It relates to an *unus mundus* where the physical and the psychic are rooted within one deep structure. It is the realm of the archetypal forms (see Figure 4.3).

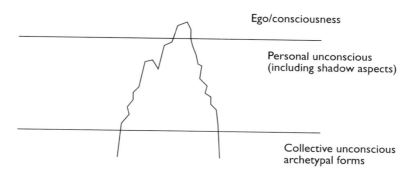

Figure 4.3

In this model, the layer between the conscious ego and the collective unconscious depicts the personal unconscious. Within this exists the personal shadow, those aspects of the self that are unacceptable to the conscious ego. However, it is not only the receptacle for negative, destructive elements, but, because of its connection to the collective unconscious, it contains within it the potential for creativity and imagination. It is a resource for, as well as a danger to, the ego.

In the process towards individuation, it is the relationship between these layers which is key. Ideally there should exist a semi-permeable membrane between each layer. If the dividing line is too rigid it becomes a barrier of defence, and we are cut off from deep aspects of ourselves which are not yet conscious. However, should the line become too weak or thin then the ego is in danger of being flooded by, or identifying with, the unconscious, whether personal and/or collective.

Because the collective unconscious is identical for all humans, it is the layer which connects us each to the other at the profoundest level. Therefore, when we develop the map to consider the complexities that arise between individuals in social settings, the following emerges (see Figure 4.4).

The concept of the shadow can be useful when considering behaviour at a social as well as at an individual level. Any object, once lit sufficiently for it to be seen, will cast a shadow. The larger the object and the stronger the light, the greater and denser the shadow. This means that any action has its dark side,

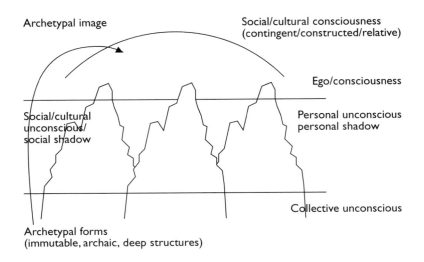

Figure 4.4

and that the 'purest' of intentions may lead to the greatest dangers. Perhaps the most terrible evidence of this in the twentieth century was the Holocaust. When we are intent on a project of cleansing and purification, we cannot contemplate the dark and the dirty within ourselves, and so will seek and find a common enemy to provide a receptacle for the projection of the shadow. Then, the evidence suggests, we are capable of the foulest of deeds.

This concept challenges the very possibility of modernity's project, of the Grand Idea, and leaves us socially with a paradox. The necessity of hope requires a vision of Utopia, a way of living together, a political system for which we can strive. However, the brighter the vision, the darker the shadow potential. If properly read, the Jungian view insists that our humanity is contained in this paradox. It refuses to allow us the escape route of illusion that we are, or ever can be, shadow-free. Indeed, it is this very fallacy that can cause the greatest harm. In the process of individuation, the project for the individual and for society is not the banishment of the shadow, not its transformation into light, but its acceptance and integration.

The realm above the surface of the water is also affected by the deep structures of the archetypes. Culture is a human creation, and the foundation of human experience, the archetypes, have a way of determining not merely individual behaviour, but also beliefs, attitudes and myths common to any culture. Whilst the archetypes cannot be known directly, they can be expressed and experienced through the archetypal image. All cultures will have, indeed they may be said to be constituted of, archetypal images. These are the commonly accepted symbols, myths or 'truths' of any particular time whereby socialisation becomes the initiation of the individual into that common acceptance which, in turn, plays a significant part in determining individual identity.

It is important to distinguish between the *archetypal structure* and the *archetypal image*. It is a confusion Jung himself made when he wrote with the apparent authority of the archetype on matters of social issues such as race and gender. Because the archetypal image is filtered through the cultural screen and perceived and reinforced by the whole of the individual psyche, it is susceptible to the vicissitudes of personal and cultural shadow aspects of which we are, by definition, unaware. Whereas the archetypes are immutable, archaic deep structures, the archetypal image is contingent and changeable. In the traditional, 'pre-modern' world, communication of these images was through myths, stories, literature and the arts generally, and those works that captured something of the archetypal were those that persisted across generations.

The archetypes cannot be known directly but can only be articulated through symbols or images. Such articulation will change according to the media of the day. In an essentially oral, stable culture, their expression was through spoken stories peopled by the heroes of the times. The forms of communication available to us today, and the constantly changing popular culture of which the media is a part, means that the archetypes are imaged in forms that erupt from and into that culture and then disappear as speedily. Music and movie stars, television soaps, films ... their form may be transient but they express something profound and collective.

Archetypal structures are not essential 'truths' so much as potentialities that can be unfolded into and through the image. Oedipus then can be regarded as an image of one archetypal potential amongst a whole pantheon. Lacan (1987) and some feminist psychoanalytic thinkers have attempted to return the myth to its original symbolic function, as a signifier, rather than the signified, calling it 'the name of the father' rather than the father himself. Deleuze and Guattari suggest that 'Jung is ... entirely correct in saying that the Oedipus complex signifies something altogether different from itself, and that in the Oedipal relation the mother is also the earth and incest is an infinite renaissance' (Deleuze and Guattari 1984, p. 162).

Whereas an image can articulate only one aspect of the potentiality, the archetypal structures themselves are multifaceted and amoral. The image can be grasped whereas the structure is unknowable. The human tendency is to conflate the two, to see the signifier as the signified and to become in awe of the image. This externalises and literalises the archetype. It also minimises the power of the archetypal potential. This limits the ways in which what Jung calls the religious instinct finds expression. The search for depth and meaning is easily trivialised into the quick fix, the cathartic moment, the self-help culture. As Hillman states:

For today, the myths which we have inherited, although necessary, are no longer adequate. Today the 'unconscious' is no longer a monster but a house pet, taken for granted, or a house god, worshipped with little rites of dream journals, symptom interpretation, and guilt-stimulating and guilt-allaying techniques. (Hillman 1972, p. 57)

Conclusion

It is noticeable how references to Jungian concepts are appearing in a wide variety of arenas in contemporary thought. The danger is that they are used, along with aspects of other psychological, philosophical and religious frameworks, to form a sort of 'pick-and-mix' conglomerate of shiny trinkets. This way we can avoid the hard work of facing the complexities of the personal psyche, making it instead into a 'house pet'. We can pay lip-service to the notion of the shadow without understanding its power or its tenacity in the unconscious. And we can be dazzled by the archetypal image and believe that we are knowing the archetype itself. All gives us the illusion of having become the God that we aspire to within the project of modernity. In fact, we are merely following Narcissus to the pool-side.

Jungian thought offers a framework for conceptualising a rootedness in our biology that continues to connect us to a deep collective layer beyond the peculiarities of our own individual development. It speaks of a plurality, a pantheon of gods, which reside within the deepest layers of the human psyche with which the individual ego is in relationship through the cultural myths of the day. It does not externalise responsibility, but neither does it leave the individual ego isolated from the internal resources of the unconscious of the collective. It is a framework that holds us to our humanity, however inhumane the times appear to be, and which gives us a form of linkage with each other, but also with what has gone before and, therefore, into a future.

References

Bauman, Z. (1993) *Postmodern Ethics*. Oxford: Blackwell.
Castoriadis, C. (1994) *Psychoanlysis and Politics, Speculations after Freud. Psychoanalysis, Philosophy and Culture*. London: Routledge.
Deleuze, G. and Guattari, F. (1984) *Anti-Oedipus, Capitalism and Schizophrenia*. London: Athlone Press.
Frosh, S. (1991) *Identity Crisis. Modernity, Psychoanalysis and the Self*. London: Macmillan.
Hillman, J. (1972) *The Myth of Analysis*. New York: Harper Perennial.
Jung, C.G. (1958) *The Undiscovered Self*. London: Routledge and Kegan Paul.
Lacan, J. (1987) *The Four Fundamental Concepts of Psycho-analysis*. London: Peregrine Books.
Lévi-Strauss, C. (1983) *Mythologies*. New York: Hill and Wang.

5

Racism in the Shadow of Jung – The Myth of White Supremacy

Stephen Gross

Introduction

I shall begin with two definitions of racism by contemporary authors and analytical practitioners which will provide an anchorage for what is to follow. The first is by Andrew Samuels, the second by Michael Vannoy Adams.
Samuels says:

> According to most definitions, racism involves dividing human kind into distinct and hierarchically gradeable groups on the basis of characteristics of biology and quasi biology. A racist is therefore someone who believes that people of a particular race, colour or origin are inherently inferior, so that their identity, culture, self-esteem, views and feelings are of less value and may be treated as less important than those groups believed to be superior. (Samuels 1993, p. 309)

Vannoy Adams states:

> I define racism to be any categorisation of peoples on the basis of physical characteristics (such as skin colour) that are indicative of putatively signif-icant psychological differences, *whether these ostensible differences are positive or negative, honorific or defamatory.* (Vannoy Adams 1997, p. 20: original emphasis)

The essential difference between the two is that Samuels' definition is predicated on the notion of a hierarchy of racial groups, whilst for Vannoy Adams it is merely the association of physical characteristics with any significant psychological differences. As this chapter is subtitled 'The Myth of White Supremacy' it would seem that the former definition of racism is the one that will confirm my argument. I think, in addition, it is important to hold in mind Stephen Frosh's reminder that

> racism is a social-psychological complex engendered at the level of social and political relations but also sustained and experienced deep in the individual psyche. (Frosh 1997, p. 224)

Running through this chapter are at least two major questions. The first question concerns the relationship between Jung the man and his ideas. This is everywhere a difficult question, if not one that is impossible to answer satisfactorily, but it is a vital one to consider; in particular, in relation to the sensitive issue of racism. The second question concerns the issues raised when considering Jung's ideas relating to racism within a contemporary moral, intellectual and political context.

It is commonly recognised that the early poems of T.S. Eliot contain undisguised anti-Semitic imagery which is stark and vicious. Eliot has come to be regarded as one of the greatest and most original poetic voices of the twentieth century and a highly celebrated and influential literary critic. His reputation some thirty years after his death and seventy years after the writing of these verses remains essentially intact, certainly until 1996 with the publication of Anthony Julius' book, *T.S. Eliot: Anti-Semitism and Literary Form* (1996).

Eliot's well known anti-Semitism expressed unashamedly throughout his life seemed not to have significantly undermined his standing as a literary influence within contemporary culture, although it may have demeaned him as a moral being.

In parallel fashion, Carl Jung, whilst branded by his harshest critics as an anti-Semite and a racist, has attained a similarly towering authority within his own field, the study of the human psyche. However, unlike Eliot, Jung's reputation both as a moral being and more significantly as a theorist and researcher has been progressively undermined by such accusations. Those of us adhering to a Jungian perspective are having to grapple with some unpalatable and discomforting questions in order that we may free ourselves from an uncritical dependency, both psychological and intellectual, which has been an all too common tendency of many of those within the Jungian school over the years.

However, the objective of this chapter is not to put Jung in the dock in order to pass moral judgement upon him. Although some of the evidence will be considered, its purpose will be to assess the contribution made by Jung to our understanding of racism, both at the collective and the individual level, through some of his principal concepts. Much has been said of Jung's anti-Semitism as something separate from his supposed racist thinking. I intend, however, to treat it as one particular expression of racist sentiment and practice. Our obligation is not to rehabilitate Jung in the light of contemporary attitudes towards racism but to best utilise the most creative of his ideas in order to enhance our understanding of this phenomenon, irrespective of where this leaves his reputation.

Jung's Contribution

Jung's notion of the collective unconscious together with that of individuation (the psychological process by which a person becomes him- or herself, whole and indivisible, differentiated from others and the collective but recognising his or her connection with them), the twin concepts on which is founded his entire theoretical edifice, were considered by him to have distinguished the primitive from the civilised human psyche. At the collective or primitive levels of the psyche, which constitute the ground of the conscious mind of each of us, is to be found the repository of humanity's psychic heritage and the seat of the archetypes which carry all our experiential potentialities. It is here that we find absolutely no trace of the individual but only that of collective relationships. This is what anthropologist Lévy-Bruhl called *participation mystique* in his 1926 publication *How Natives Think*, in which the subject cannot clearly distinguish himself from the object but is bound to it by a direct relationship which amounts to a partial identity. This primitive, or as Jung would also state, prehistoric human is undifferentiated, that is, the thinking and feeling functions are concrete, they are always related to sensations, since the four functions – thinking, feeling, intuition and sensations – have not yet separated out. Jung's assumption was that 'the prehistoric human' as a metaphor for primitive states of mind does not think in the sense of making differentiations.

Whilst distilling some of the most seminal of Jung's ideas in the previous paragraph I am also highlighting those key tenets of this thought on which Farhad Dalal, in a controversial paper written in 1988, bases his accusation that Jung's thought was racist in its very essence. Dalal condemns Jung on the grounds that he had written extensively that all the non-European races, particularly the African, remained at the primitive level of psychic development, and in so doing he equated the modern black with the prehistoric human, the modern black consciousness with the white unconscious and the modern black with the white child. In doing so, Dalal argued, Jung has lumped all blacks together, ignoring the differing social and historical experiences of both individuals and groups.

A pivotal feature of postmodernist thought is its refutation of both essentialism and universalism, particularly in relation to human identity. Most pertinently, this position is fiercely upheld by black writers such as bell hooks with regard to the experience of blacks. Her powerful critique

> challenges colonial imperialist paradigms of black identity which represents blackness one-dimensionally in ways that reinforce and sustain white supremacy. This discourse created the idea of the 'primitive' and promoted the notion of an 'authentic' experience, seeing as 'natural' those expressions of black life which conformed to a pre-existing pattern or stereotype. Abandoning essentialist notions would be a serious challenge to racism. (hooks 1996, p. 118)

As stated above, it is not my intention here to defend Jung the individual against charges of personal racism which may or may not be upheld by historical and biographical evidence, but rather to consider to what extent some of these key ideas, which would appear to be so productive in their application to our understanding of racism in our own times, are themselves tainted by inherent racist assumptions of which Jung would not have been aware. It is after all only as a result of the horrors of the Holocaust that we have come to offer a coherent conceptual formulation to the reality of racism, both as a form of social and political action as well as a virulent psychological constellation.

A first line of defence against accusations of racism on Jung's part would be that rather than being in themselves ideas which are essentially flawed – specifically, in this instance, by racist assumptions – the problem lies only in their particular application to non-European, and especially black African, peoples. Ideas that had been conceived and developed independently were then perhaps rather crudely and mechanically applied to non-European societies merely as a means of illustration rather than as irrefutable evidence of their validity.

For all the undoubted brilliance and originality of this thinking, Jung was, like lesser mortals, inescapably a man of his time. Visiting as he did Africa and India in 1920 and in the 1930s, he could not help but see tribal and feudal societies through the perspective of a sophisticated and cultured European. His Eurocentrism would no doubt have been significantly reinforced by his own personal experience as the son of a Lutheran minister growing up at the turn of the century in the land-locked ultra-conservative society of Switzerland. Is it any wonder, therefore, that from our own politically enlightened standpoint at the very end of the twentieth century we might judge Jung's interpretation of the black man's psyche as fundamentally patronising and racist? However, as well as reflecting inevitably the cultural and political prejudices of his time and personal history, I suspect that Jung was also guilty of projecting aspects of his own shadow (I shall consider this term in more detail later) into these black peoples; especially, perhaps, infantile and emotive aspects which he had failed to integrate successfully into his own conscious mind.

Nevertheless, it is when we come up against the term 'white supremacist' in this application to the very foundation of Jung's thought that it appears most vulnerable to the damning accusations of racism. I will look at the ideas of two writers who have considered the question of Jung's racism in some depth. The first is the Jungian analyst James Hillman, who provides the most profound as well as eloquent example of how contemporary Jungian thought is seriously engaged with the issue of its own implicit racism. The other is the black psychiatrist and revolutionary Frantz Fanon (1925–1961) who was familiar with the work of Jung.

An eminent representative of the archetypal school of Jungian analysis, Hillman (1986) claims that Western culture is white supremacist and that such a position is fundamental to Western society's linguistic roots and is affirmed in its major texts, thereby determining the structures of Western perception. Similar expressions of white supremacy can be found in the belief and value systems of black Africans who have been particularly subjected to white influence through colonisation. Hillman then makes the crucial assertion that the fantasy of supremacy is archetypally inherent in whiteness itself, and, named first, white is paired with black as its opposite. For Hillman it is the *a priori* nature of the supremacy of white that establishes black as its opposite and inferior rather than its difference. In other words, in a different category of thought it is not that black is inherently inferior to white, but that it is merely different. It is only because white carries a necessary sense of supremacy that it needs to find an opposite to sustain itself and so chose black for that purpose. Difference does not necessitate competition, contradiction nor opposition.

According to Hillman, only white possesses this built-in supremacy which annihilates its shades and admits no shadow. It casts out its own white shadow, seeing it in black not because black and white are unevenly opposed, but simply because it is archetypally given for whiteness to imagine in oppositions. The supremacy of white, he contends, depends on 'oppositional imagining'. When the perception of white entails a simultaneous perception of black then we have projections, since neither white nor black can be thought of as possessing attributes of the other projections. This logic of opposites preserves white from its own shadow aspects. Hillman enjoins us to give up the opposites in order to move beyond white supremacy.

Hillman goes on to draw our attention to the vital significance of Jung's turning to alchemy at the time of his Eranos lectures of 1935 and 1936 – which marked, he believed, a return to the coloured soul and the coloured world and, with the alchemical appreciation of colour, recognises the shadow within any hue. Alchemy thus provided Jung with a very different version of the supremacy of white. It is a work against whiteness even whilst striving to attain it. Its way of resolving opposites is by *'desubstantiating the principle of opposition itself'* (Hillman 1986, p. 50; emphasis added). Thus, says Hillman, the problem becomes resolved because now it does not arise.

The combination of Hillman's postmodernist critique of language and his sympathetic evaluation of Jung's alchemical research has enabled him to conceive of the possibility of overcoming the white supremacist foundation of European/African culture, which of course includes analytical psychology as a system of thought. I shall return to Hillman when I come to consider the shadow.

Frantz Fanon, to whom I shall turn in more detail later in relation to the shadow, is important as a black writer who integrates both political and psychological analysis in his exposure of the white suprematism so criticised by Hillman. Fanon claimed (1986) that what was regarded as the black soul was nothing more than the creation of white people who remain sealed in their own whiteness. The black man is a victim of white civilisation. He regarded it as a fact that white people consider themselves superior to the black and that those of them who adore the Negro (this was the term used by Fanon) were as 'sick' as those who reviled the Negro. Here he aptly reminds us that the commonly encountered idealisation of the ethnic other is likely to emanate from a repressed antipathy. He sees the European as possessing a fixed concept of the Negro, and, like bell hooks, reminds us that Negro experience is not a whole as there is 'not simply one Negro, rather there are Negroes' (Fanon 1986, p. 35).

In returning to Jung, it is important to recognise that his perspective was of a symbolic nature and that the primitive African and other black and ethnic groups to which he refers as 'natives' or 'primitives' represent for him the primitive aspect or level of the civilised European psyche which he felt so passionately had lost touch with its collective matrix. It is at the primitive level that the vital source of humankind's creative potential and its capacity for myth and symbol formation can be found. This forms the central thesis of his influential *Modern Man in Search of a Soul* (Jung 1933). Jung admired and sought out 'primitive' peoples because he believed that they had retained this living connection to the psychic roots of the species which Western people had lost. He wrote in *Memories, Dreams, Reflections* that

> The predominately [sic] rationalistic European finds much that is human alien to him, and he prides himself on this without realising that this rationality is won at the expense of his vitality and the primitive part of his personality is condemned to a more or less underground existence. (Jung 1963, p. 273)

And, from the same book:

> Out of sheer envy we are obliged to smile at the Indians' naiveté and to plume ourselves on our cleverness; for otherwise we would discover how impoverished and down at heel we are. Knowledge does not enrich us; it removes us more and more from the mythic world in which we were at home by right of birth. (Jung 1963, p. 281)

These two extracts are important in any assessment we might want to make of Jung's racist attitudes, as they express his disgust at what we might now term 'cultural imperialism'.

> What we from our point of view call colonisation, missions to the heathen, spread of civilisation, etc. has another face – the face of a bird of prey seeking with cruel intentness for distant quarry – a face worthy of a race of pirates and highwaymen. All the eagles and other predatory creatures that adorn our coats of arms seem to me apt psychological representations of our true nature. (Jung 1963, p. 277)

It could be said that Jung's own attitude towards black non-European people was highly complex, composed at a deep unconscious level of the unreconciled oppositions and tensions that shaped his own personality, as well as reflecting his overarching purpose in tracing the historical evolution of the human psyche. According to Fanon, however:

> Jung was an innovator: he wanted to go back to the childhood of the world, but he made a remarkable mistake. *He went back only to the childhood of Europe.* (Fanon 1986, p. 190; emphasis added)

Whilst no doubt expressing elements of his own shadow projections which we would now choose to regard as racist in their manifest form, it can also be seen as Jung's profound regard for the purity and integrity of the primitive psyche as well as for the culture and religions of the East, of Africa and of pre-colonial North America. Such understanding may, however, take another twist by regarding Jung's attitude as an idealisation or a form of splitting in which he denigrates white rationalistic Christian consciousness whilst celebrating the black primitive unconscious.

Whilst it is important here to recognise Jung's alleged anti-Semitism as one example of his putative racism, the purpose, as stated earlier, is not to consider the validity of such allegations, but to see what can be learned about contemporary racism as a sociopolitical and psychological phenomenon by looking closely at the underlying assumptions of his 'anti-Semitic' utterances.

Although in his personal life Jung does not seem to have displayed any evidence of anti-Semitism, it was whilst speaking in an official capacity as a psychologist that he rendered himself vulnerable to serious accusation. It was during the 1930s, when he was president of the German-based General Medical Society for Psychotherapy, that he wrote about differing racial psychologies. At that time he made crude generalisations about Jewish culture and psychology. One such telling example comes from his 1934 paper 'The state of psychotherapy today', when he wrote:

> The Jew who is something of a nomad has never yet created a cultural form of his own and as far as we can see never will, since all his instincts and talents require a more or less civilised nation to act as host for their development. (*CW* 10, para. 354)

The key concept in this portentous claim is that of *nation*. Samuels, in *The Political Psyche* (1993), suggests that it was Jung's misguided attempt to establish a psychology, using his considerable authority to legitimise ideas of innate psychological differences between nations, that led inexorably to his fall into racist and anti-Semitic theorising. Jung believed that a nation developed its own uniqueness through a combination of culture and land, that is, through its own territory with which it established a special relationship. This tendentious and all too simple concept of the nation as a psychological entity was for Jung seriously compromised by the existence of the Jews, who, lacking a chthonic relation to the earth, and without national and cultural forms of their own, had to depend on a host nation. In other words, he was claiming for the Jewish people parasitic status.

Necessary to Jung's classification of psychological differences between nations is the notion of complementarity whereby the self-definition and identity of one nation is dependent upon its perceiving in others those features or characteristics which it does not itself possess, or at least believes itself not to possess. This idea provides a vital link to our understanding of racism in our own time. What Jung has here theorised is the identification of the other, the 'not-I' or, speaking of nations, the 'not-us', into whom we can project all of those undesirable, unpalatable aspects of ourselves which we have denied integration into our own consciousness and from which we seek to free ourselves. It is to this aspect of the self designated by Jung as the *shadow*, a major archetype to which I now wish to turn. However, just before doing so, it is perhaps worth noting the significance for Jung that identity plays in the psychology of individuals and nations alike, in contrast to recent post-structuralist thinking. Here identity is regarded as something unstable, decentred and elusive. Such psychological processes as complementarity to which we are compelled in order to sustain a secure and stable sense of ourselves are reassuring but fundamentally false.

The Shadow

Jung's concept of the shadow provides a vital link between Jung the man and the understanding of the shocking and virulent racism that so pervades our times, at both individual subjective levels and at the political level, as an instrument of oppression and control.

Many writers – from the classical Greeks, to Shakespeare in the Elizabethan age, to Doris Lessing in our own time – have explored this dark subterranean side of human nature, whilst some – such as Dostoyevsky and Joseph Conrad – have devoted their entire literary output to its exploration.

Paying due respect to Freud, Jung acknowledged his revolutionary insights into the dimension within the human psyche between the light and the dark side. As early as 1912, before his break with Freud, Zweig and Abrams inform us that 'Jung was talking of the shadow side of the psyche to characterise not recognised desires and repressed portions of the personality' (Zweig and Abrams 1991, p. 3). They go on to say that

> By 1917 in his essay On the Psychology of the Unconscious, Jung was speaking of the personal shadow as *the other* in us, the unconscious personality of the same sex, the reprehensible *inferior* (the key term in the earlier definition of racism), the other that embarrasses or shames us. 'By shadow I mean the negative side of the personality, the sum of all those unpleasant qualities we like to hide, together with the insufficiently developed functions and the content of the personal unconscious.' (Zweig and Abrams 1991, p. 3)

For Jung, however, the shadow is negative *only from the point of view of consciousness*, and this marks a radical departure from Freud, who insisted that the dark side of the human psyche was totally immoral and incompatible with our conscious personality. Jung believed that, potentially, the shadow contained values of the highest morality. This most closely approaches what Freud saw as the repressed. In contrast to Freud's view, Jung's concept of the shadow is like an *inferior* personality that has its own content – thoughts, images and value judgements – that are parallel to the superior conscious personality. By 1945, he was referring to the shadow as simply 'the thing a person has no wish to be' (*CW* 16, para. 470). As Samuels, Shorter and Plaut remark in the *Critical Dictionary of Jungian Analysis*:

> In this simple statement is subsumed the many-sided and repeated references to shadow as the negative side of the personality, the sum of all the unpleasant qualities one wants to kick, the inferior, worthless and primitive side of man's nature, the 'other' person in one, one's own dark side. (Samuels et al. 1986, p. 138)

This may very well describe the way that Jung's own shadow projection influenced his perception of non-Europeans, particularly the black-skinned, grounded, as his view of the world was, within a white supremacist matrix. It is possible that his own more overly racist attitudes were defended against by his tendency somewhat to extol the purity and integrity of the black psyche.

In current Jungian thought the shadow is considered to be that part of the unconscious mind that is closest to consciousness, though not accepted by it. Because it is contrary to our chosen conscious attitude, the shadow personality is denied expression and so breaks off into a separate splinter personality in the unconscious where it is insulated from exposure and recognition by consciousness, thereby compensating for the one-sided identification we make with what our consciousness deems acceptable.

Given that the shadow is an archetype, its contents are powerful and marked by affect; compelling, possessive and autonomous and therefore capable of startling and even overwhelming the well ordered ego. Like all psychic content capable of breaking through into consciousness, they appear in projection. When that consciousness is in a threatened or doubtful condition the shadow often manifests as a strong irrational projection upon one's neighbour. When one's sense of identity either as an individual or as part of a collective is seriously challenged, then a certain psychic dynamic becomes constellated whereby the conscious mind, threatened as it feels itself to be from without, but really unable to tolerate the powerfully activated internal shadow content, must now urgently find a way of ejecting these unwelcome and unmanageable affects, and so expels them, into a suitable other. This is the scapegoat, found to carry the shadow projections. In identifying these processes Jung threw considerable light on our understanding not only of personal hatred but of the collective prejudices and acts of cruelty and barbarism that have so scarred the twentieth century.

It is instructive to return to Hillman to consider the shadow within the context of the white supremacist mentality which, he avers so persuasively, has underpinned all Western psychological theorising. In his paper 'Notes on white supremacy', Hillman (1986) maintains that white casts its own white shadow. The shadow of white may be white, but it is still shadow. It is only white that has this built-in supremacy which annihilates its shades. It does not admit to shadow and thus it rejects distinct forms. He goes on to observe that Jung's notion of shadow, like that of the unconscious, emerges from out of what he calls the white tropes or affinities. Repression, projection and the unconscious together are taken to be fundamental laws of psychology. However, they remain so only within the tropes of their origins, which for Jung are the white North, the Christian West and modern Western Christian history.

Though serving the aim of self-correction, the ideas of shadow and unconscious maintain the theory of opposites, thereby locating consciousness with light, bright and day. The shadow then resides in this 'white' consciousness and, contrary to common assumption, is not only projected out into black. There is for Hillman always, and by its nature, shadow within light and, similarly, light within shadow.

Writing as a black psychiatrist with an acute political awareness into what we have now come to identify as shadow projection, Frantz Fanon, in the language of a black revolutionary thinker, seems to dovetail with the ideas of James Hillman. In *Black Skin, White Masks* (1986), Fanon maintained that the collective unconscious was not dependent on the Jungian idea of a collective heredity but was rather the consequence of a cultural imposition. What he termed 'the myth of the bad nigger' was, he claimed, an aspect of that collective unconscious, and, remembering Jung's remark that he had returned only to the childhood of Europe, this collective realm of the psyche was that of the white European. Fanon claimed that in Europe the black man was the symbol of evil and ugliness, standing for the bad side of the human personality and responsible for all the strife and conflict that arises between humans. He was the embodiment of raw sexual instinct and the representation of an unbridled genital potency. Hillman also noted how the Jew has been used by white European culture to carry its shadow projections, and, though free from the sexual projections that have so oppressed blacks, both Negro and Jew have stood for Evil in the white European psyche.

Fanon effectively raises a searing challenge to Jung's central ideas on the psyche of the black man by claiming that the Negro came to be embodied, in contradiction to his sinful attributes, as the 'childhood of the world', representing innocence, ingenuousness and spontaneity. For white European society, founded as it was on myths of liberalism, education, progress and civilisation, the Negro, for Fanon, had become the scapegoat.

The Scapegoat

I turn now to the notion of the scapegoat, so essential to our understanding of racism, first reviewing some of the ideas of Sylvia Brinton Perera.

Perera, a Jungian writer of the archetypal school, claims that the search for a scapegoat relieves a society of its relationship to what she terms the transpersonal dimension of life. In Jungian terms, scapegoating appears to be a means of denying the shadow of both God and humankind. That which we consider to be at variance with our ego ideal or with our idea of the perfection of God, we repress and banish to the realms of the unconscious. Those who identify with the scapegoat, she continues, identify with the unwelcome shadow qualities which leave them feeling inferior, rejected and guilty, and responsible for more than their personal share of shadow, for the scapegoats function effectively as caretakers of those sins for which the majority of their society cannot themselves assume conscious responsibility. Like Fanon, she notes that women as well as minority groups have carried the collective shadow in Western consciousness. The scapegoat serves the community by

> returning evil to its archetypal source through sacrifice, carrying back to the gods a burden too great for the human collective to bear. (Perera 1986, p. 98)

Perera emphasises collective psychological processes regarding that aspect of the shadow that is culturally relative which, when made conscious and resolved, can be reintegrated, thereby enriching the collective. Because groups retain their shared sense of identity by uniting against an adversary, and projecting on to that adversary their own intolerable parts, it is only when the scapegoated individual can see his or her own experience as meaningfully related to an image of what Perera calls the transpersonal, that this individual identified as a scapegoat might attain the degree of self-acceptance necessary for an autonomous and creative life.

Jerome Bernstein is a Jungian writer who has applied his thinking to a particular sociopolitical event, the Los Angeles riots of 1992, which was fundamentally an issue about racism in contemporary American society. He begins by quoting the German sculptress Kathe Kollwitz who died in 1945.

> Although death and devil are portrayed as dark and black, this particular association with colour block is Western, not archetypal and not universal. (Kollwitz, cited in Bernstein 1992, p. 152)

Bernstein informs us that in Western culture, skin colour is the greatest determinant of shadow projection on a collective level. The darker the skin, the greater the shadow projection, and the greater the degree of discrimination. The association of dark/black with death/evil is a purely Western phenomenon, neither universal nor archetypal. He goes on to support this claim by asserting that in many African cultures dark and evil are portrayed as white, with the characteristics chosen to represent the shadow invariably being the very opposite of the external characteristics of the group. The scapegoat is the permanent outcast of society who cannot be assimilated by the dominant culture, his or her role being to carry society's sins and thus to be expelled on that society's account.

From an archetypal perspective Bernstein's Jungian argument proceeds thus: both oppressor and oppressed are victims of a complex psychological process; shadow projections take place in the absence of a conscious capacity to hold or to contain these projected qualities, so they continue to predominate at both an individual and a collective level.

In archetypal terms the scapegoat dynamic is only one half of a more comprehensive ritual. In ancient times the scapegoat ritual was a symbolic act which was followed by a conscious collective sacrifice, a sin offering. Without such a sin offering the community (both individually and collectively) would not take conscious responsibility for the grievances and offences it had committed, and so the cycle of projection and identification would continue without resolution or redemption.

Referring to the 1992 riots in Los Angeles, Bernstein affirms the need for a collective, conscious sacrifice – a sin offering – that would seek to *resymbolise* the archetypal scapegoat dynamic that had been literalised in American society.

If in ancient times reclaiming of the shadow was dependent upon a symbolic act such as a sin offering, what must we do, need to do, in our own times if we are to reclaim our own shadow from its objects of projection? Bernstein identifies five stages in this process from Jung's writing.

1. The person initially is convinced that what he or she sees in the other is in fact the reality.
2. Gradually, a recognition emerges of a differentiation between the other as he or she really is, and the projected image; a process which may be facilitated by dreams or other psychological events.
3. Some kind of assessment or judgement is made of this discovery.
4. A conclusion is reached that what was felt previously about the other was either illusory or erroneous.
5. A conscious exploration of the sources and origins of the projection takes place which will include both collective as well as personal determinants.

When this process is accomplished, it can then be claimed that the shadow, or at least those aspects of it that were previously projected, has been successfully reintegrated into consciousness.

Conclusion

If racism can be understood primarily as a shadow phenomenon, at both an individual as well as a collective or societal level, then this process of shadow integration will play a most significant part in its eventual eradication from tomorrow's world. It remains, however, a tall order. We do not surrender our shadow so easily.

Julian Lousada offers a salutary warning to all of us who are committed to working towards the elimination of racism. He states:

> There are, it seems to me, two traumas associated with racism. The first is the appalling inhumanity that is perpetrated in its name. The second is the recognition of the failure of the 'natural' caring/humanitarian instincts, and of thinking, to be victorious over this evil. We should not underestimate the anxiety that attends the recognition of these traumas. In its extreme form this anxiety can produce an obsequious guilt which undertakes reparation (towards the oppressed object) regardless of the price. What this recognition of a profoundly negative force fundamentally challenges is the comfort of optimism; the back to basics idea that we are all inherently decent and that evil and hatred belong to others. Being able to tolerate renunciation of this idea and the capacity to live in the presence of our positive and destructive thoughts and instincts is the only basis on which the commitment to change can survive without recourse to fundamentalism. (Lousada 1997, p. 34)

Despite his own personal failings and moral shortcomings – for he, too, carried and cast his own shadow – Jung's work as both theorist and clinician has established a richly generative foundation for an understanding of racism that disfigures our own times at all levels of individual and collective life.

Jungian clinicians, like therapists and analysts of all other schools, need to confront the reality of racism within the consulting room as well as outside in society at large. Like any individual therapeutic relationship, analytical psychotherapy as an institutionalised body of theory and practice offers a particular microcosmic embodiment of the underlying intellectual and moral value systems of the larger society and the cultural context within which it exists.

The patient enters the consulting room with his or her racial prejudices, but so does the therapist, of course. These are very rarely confronted in analytical work. To date, they remain very much part of psychotherapy's shadow, because they are far too dangerous and frightening to integrate. Here the unconscious phantasy may be that, if given conscious recognition, the very foundation of the psychoanalytical and psychotherapeutic tradition would be destroyed to the extent that it rests on the premise of white suprematism.

However, now that this shadow aspect of analytical psychotherapy has been identified, there can be no turning back, no return to denial and repression. After all, increasingly, though still at a depressingly slow rate, black patients are coming to consult white therapists and, albeit even more slowly, more black therapists are taking on work with white patients. If serious and effective therapeutic work is to take place, it will become progressively more difficult for issues of race and racism to be avoided in the consulting room.

The debate within the psychotherapy profession as to how to work with this issue has really only just begun. One of the most honest and helpful suggestions to emerge so far comes from my Jungian colleague Helen Morgan, who, in discussing the relationship between a white therapist and a black patient, suggests four possible approaches that the therapist might adopt; the fourth being the one she advocates, which

> recognises that racism will effect the relationship between us. That there is a power differential inherent in that relationship over and above the power relationship which both exists and is perceived to exist between any therapist and any patient. Elaboration and exploration of the reality of this differential may provide an important means of access to the transference. (Morgan 1998, p. 52)

Jungian thought has provided us with some vital theoretical tools for making sense of racism. However, unless we can mobilise the moral courage and psychological determination necessary to utilise these in confronting our own deepest held racist feelings and phantasies, then we will only succeed in colluding in the perpetuation of racism in society at large, both at home and across the globe.

References

bell hooks (1996) 'Post-modern blackness', in W. Truett Anderson (ed.) *The Fontana Post Modernism Reader*. London: Fontana.

Bernstein, J. (1992) 'Penetrating the archetypal dilemma of racism', *Psychological Perspectives*, 27, Los Angeles: C.G. Jung Institute of LA.

Dalal, F. (1988) 'Jung: a racist', *British Journal of Psychotherapy*, 4(3).

Fanon, F. (1986) *Black Skin, White Masks*. London: Pluto Press.

Frosh, S. (1997) *For and Against Psychoanalysis*. London: Routledge and Kegan Paul.

Hillman, J. (1986) 'Notes on white supremacy. Essaying as archetypal account of historical events', *Spring Publications*, 29: 56.

Julius, A. (1996) *T.S. Eliot: Anti-Semitism and Literary Form*. Cambridge: Cambridge University Press.

Jung, C.G. (1933) *Modern Man in Search of a Soul*. London: Routledge and Kegan Paul, 1978.

Jung, C.G. (1963) *Memories, Dreams, Reflections*. London: Fontana, 1979.

Lévy-Bruhl, C. (1926) 'How nations think', in A. Bullock and R.B. Woodings (eds), *The Fontana Dictionary of Modern Thinkers*. London: Fontana.

Lousada, J. (1997) 'The hidden history of an idea: the difficulties of adapting anti-racism', in E. Smith (ed.), *Integrity and Change: Mental Health in the Market Place*. London: Routledge and Kegan Paul.

Morgan, H. (1998) 'Between fear and blindness: the white therapist and the black patient', *Journal of the British Association of Psychotherapists*, 3(34).

Perera, S.B. (1986) *The Scapegoat Complex: Towards a Mythology of Shadow and Guilt*. Toronto: Inner City Books.

Samuels, A. (1993) *The Political Psyche*. London: Routledge and Kegan Paul.

Samuels, A., Shorter, B. and Plaut, F. (1986) *A Critical Dictionary of Jungian Analysis*. London: Routledge and Kegan Paul.

Vannoy Adams, M. (1997) 'Jung and racism', *Self and Society*, 25(1), Stroud: Association for Humanistic Psychology.

Zweig, C. and Abrams, J. (1991) 'Introduction', in Zweig and Abrams (eds) *Meeting the Shadow: The Hidden Power of the Dark Side of Human Nature*. New York: G.P. Putnam's Sons.

Suggested Reading:

Fanon, F. (1986) *Black Skin, White Masks*. London: Pluto Press.

Hillman, J. (1986) 'Notes on white supremacy. Essaying as archetypal account of historical events', *Spring Publications*, 29: 56.

Jung, C.G. (1963) *Memories, Dreams, Reflections*. London: Fontana, 1979.

6

Warring Opposites

Ann Kutek

The deeper we delve in search of these causes the more of them we discover, and each single cause or series of causes appears to us equally valid in itself, and equally false by its insignificance compared to the magnitude of the event itself.

Leo Tolstoy, *War and Peace*

Jung lived through two world wars, in the quiet eye of the storm, which Switzerland shared as part of its Germanic patrimony. He wrote about warring before the Second World War and in its aftermath, in a country where at least three distinct linguistic groups have managed to confine their 'warring' to the political plane for hundreds of years. It has been noted elsewhere in this volume that his views in this context have been judged as open to attack. This chapter is an attempt to synthesise through glimpses drawn from history, anthropology, current events and mythology, what the understanding of analytical psychology could contribute to the study of conflict in international relations. The grounds for this intervention were spelled out clearly in Anthony Stevens' *The Roots of War*, now regrettably out of print, and they were that most studies of war share three major shortcomings: they ignore the unconscious, they rely too much on rationalising political behaviour and they eschew the biological nature of humans. He explains, 'Jungian psychology is well placed to rectify these deficiencies in the literature of war, for its cultural and intellectual contribution has been largely compensatory to the contributions of other disciplines' and, 'since analytical psychology concerns itself with the polar oppositions of life, their resolution and transcendence, it is an appropriate discipline to apply to the study of war and peace' (Stevens 1989, pp. vii–ix).

However, it may be noted with surprise that, in the current Jungian literature, with the exception of American contributions on the issue of nuclear destruction, there is little in English on the subject of international conflict or the significance of war. In the *Journal of Analytical Psychology* there is one reference dating from the 1960s which addresses the threat of nuclear war. Among Jungian writers, only Stevens (1989) has produced a volume devoted to the origins of war, and Redfearn (1992) examined the pervasive fear of apocalyptic destruction from the perspective of a psychotherapist. More recently, Papadopoulos (1998) has reported on his work with Bosnian refugees, relating it to the nature of destructiveness. There is a coherent theme in all these Jung-inspired writings, which could be considered, with benefit, in a broader discourse, but which it continually fails to achieve. In summary, it is that 'real warfare and particularly nuclear warfare, allows the personal conflict to be avoided or by-passed in the grand cosmic or international scenario in which the fantasy is made real. Moral impoverishment is the price of this outer enactment' (Redfearn 1992).

Is it the case that the state of war is as axiomatic as the state of peace? Is there any choice in the avoidance of war, or is it that, as happens in families, explosive and overtly destructive behaviour is 'sent elsewhere' to be played out? From a European perspective, the First World War was the war to end all wars; yet the state of conflict was unfinished and erupted again in the 1930s in Spain and then in earnest from 1938 through the agency of Germany, with the *Anschluss* of Czechoslovakia and Austria and the invasion of Poland a year later. Since the close of the Second World War, the world has seen few days free from armed conflict. Wars have been prosecuted in other zones, particularly in the 'majority' world, until Bosnia, Kosovo and Albania, where centuries-old scores and unfinished business after the fall of the Ottoman Empire have broken out once again.

We appear to owe our development as a species to warring. Stevens comments on this apparent paradox:

> War so disturbed the ancient ecological balance that it made civilisations possible and then proceeded to destroy them. Civilisation resulted from breaking through the normal constraints of homeostasis, but the *enantio-dromia* was not thereby prevented; it was merely delayed. (Stevens 1989, p. 69)[1]

Both Freud and Jung were preoccupied with conflict. In 1917, Freud wrote:

> it is precisely the minor differences between people who are otherwise alike that form the basis of feelings of strangeness and hostility between them ... it would be tempting to pursue this idea and to derive from this 'narcissism

of minor differences' the hostility which in every human relation we see fighting against feelings of fellowship and overpowering the commandment that all men should love one another. (Freud 1917, p. 272)

Whereas this extract dwells on the minute physiological differences between the sexes, in *Group Psychology and the Analysis of the Ego* (1921), he moved on to group differences, pointing out that in close relationships emotions of hostility and suspicion compete with feelings of kinship. The same phenomenon is observable between human groups and nations:

> Of two neighbouring towns each is the other's most jealous rival; every little canton looks down upon the others with contempt. Closely related races keep one another at arm's length; the South German cannot endure the North German, the English casts every kind of aspersion upon the Scot ...We are no longer astonished that greater differences should lead to an almost insuperable repugnance, such as the Gallic people feel for the German, the Aryan for the Semite and the white races for the coloured. (Freud 1929, p. 305)

Author and philosopher Michael Ignatieff has visited scenes of conflict during the 1990s in Bosnia, Croatia, Rwanda, Burundi, Angola and Afghanistan, and has written an incisive analysis of contemporary ethnic war and the modern conscience. *The Warrior's Honor* (1998) examines the ubiquity of the television camera, the evolution of war from the business of a regular soldiery to that of irregulars, with the often simultaneous arrival of compassion in the guise of non-governmental organisations, and delves into the psychoanalytic interpretation of conflict. Finally, he considers memory and 'moral healing'. He contends that

> there is nothing in our natures that makes ethnic or racial conflict unavoidable. The idea that different races and ethnic groups can co-exist in peace and even goodwill is not a hopeless illusion ... When individuals live in stable states – even poor ones – they do not need to rush to the protection of the group. It is the disintegration of states, and the Hobbesian fear that results, that produces ethnic fragmentation and war. (Ignatieff 1998, p. 7)

By contrast, in Plato's view, 'only the dead know the end of war', Certainly, our presumption, on a state level, is that war is still a possibility, for we dare not dismantle our 'defence capabilities'. A cynic could say that at most we can delay a state of war, because it cannot be averted indefinitely. The Truth and Reconciliation Commission in South Africa, and the Oslo, Dayton and Good Friday Agreements, are attempts to avoid major conflict, transcend traditional enmities and promote their transformation into cooperation. Equally important have been the conscience-searching fora; most notably the Pugwash conferences formed by Nobel laureate, Joseph Rotblat and others (1993) in response to the Manhattan Project and the consequences of Hiroshima and Nagasaki. In a post-Cold War world and in the light of the failed Rambouillet talks of early 1999, the paradoxical aspects of conflict remain.

As is often the case, Carl Jung's insights find their realisation after some delay in other disciplines. Mary Kaldor's *New and Old Wars* (1999), a striking analysis of organised violence in a global era, captures the newly emerging features of war in a way which coheres with a Jungian perspective without specifically mentioning analytical psychology. Her central argument is that during the past two decades, a new kind of organised violence has developed, especially in Africa and Eastern Europe, as one aspect of the current globalised era. She terms it 'new war'. It involves the blurring of distinctions between war, organised crime, violence undertaken by privately organised groups for private purposes, and large-scale violations of human rights. Such conflicts, of which Bosnia Herzegovina is a case in point, are at once marked by apparently opposite propensities. She observes: '[the] process of intensifying interconnectedness is a contradictory process involving both integration and fragmentation, homogenization and diversification, globalization and localization' (Kaldor 1999, p. 3).

In Jungian terms, conflict or war is a limiting case of the *coniunctio oppositorum*, a symbol drawn from the alchemical procedure whereby unlike substances are combined to produce a third, a synthesis, whose final goal is the 'philosopher's stone'. Significantly, this process was represented in alchemical texts as the sexual union of a king and queen resulting in the birth of a son. For Jung, this stood for the dynamics of *transformation* and renewal in the psyche. As should become apparent in what follows, the warring of opposites has always been inextricably bound with sexuality and regeneration. Indeed, the actual shape and use of contemporary weaponry inescapably resembles human genitalia and the act of murderous penetration, often accompanied by the ritual rape of women in contrast to 'good intercourse'.

Jung wrote about his forebodings of the Second World War and its aftermath (see, for example, *CW* 10). Compared to military historians, sociologists, poets and philosophers, contemporary depth psychologists remain marginal to the predicaments of Sudan, Rwanda, Bosnia and now Kosovo. In a sense, the subject is too big and overwhelming. It is beyond the province of individual concerns, belonging more to the preoccupations of group analysts and systems thinkers. However, a common observance of rigid divisions in language and conceptualisation seldom allows historians, let alone politicians and strategists, to reach for formulations about archetypal propensities, transcendence or personality types in their consideration of war. Nevertheless, from the hidden context of the analytic consulting room, there emerge testimonies of lost parents, lost childhoods or war-related losses and unconsoled grief.

Even if the fulcrum of international conflict, barring Northern Ireland, has moved from British shores, it has been endemically reported in British newspapers, on television and radio and the advertisements which beg for alms for those injured and rendered destitute by war, which are routinely put through letterboxes. Equally ubiquitous is the availability of virtual war in computer software games which invade the minds of Western youth at least. Many people have some vestigial connections with conflict, whether through migration; or photos in a family album; or discarded gas-mask bags, trench coats or other utilitarian army surplus stored in a corner of the attic. Very few people cannot recall the strains of a military tune or anti-war song, or bring to mind the colour and vibrancy of a military pageant.

Then there are the less visible signs: the silent arms trade, and the threat of annihilation. There are also the more inchoate difficulties of people who carry through their lives the war traumas of their forebears. Finally, there are actual memories, depictions in art and literature, narratives and those archetypal images of war which inhabit each of us. Such is the ubiquity of warring that it emerges on the football field and the terraces, at the Olympic games and in the methods employed to gain advantage, and as a topic for the Reith Lectures on BBC Radio 4 (see Keegan 1998). Moreover, in our lifetime, we have lived through the Cold War, a state of permanent threat of total annihilation whose manifestations occur in the 'hot' conflicts which flare up in different spheres of influence far from the seats of power and producers of weaponry.

Britain's Mental Health in the First World War and Second World War

Paradoxically, just as developments in science and technology owe a direct debt to armaments and war systems, so developments in psychiatry and psychotherapy can be traced to war casualties and their military doctors. Joanna Bourke, an economic and social historian who has studied what happened to men and their bodies in the Great War, demonstrates that the lessons from that war were instrumental in the growth of psychiatry as a discipline. She highlights (Bourke 1996) that the Tavistock Clinic, established in 1920, 'was one of the first clinics in Britain for out-patients requiring psychotherapy, as a direct result of the experiences of Hugh Creighton-Miller in treating neurasthenic servicemen'. A graphic illustration of their problems appears in *Regeneration* (1991), part of a fictional trilogy by Pat Barker depicting the horrors of the Great War, in which the character of Rivers is based on an authentic doctor of that time.

Although the neurological understanding of nervous disorders continued to dominate, the First World War had resulted in a wider knowledge and acceptance in Britain of certain aspects of depth psychological and psycho-analytic theory, resulting in the founding of the British Psychoanalytical Society soon after the war. Furthermore, there was great hope that the insights of military medicine would be transferred to civilian life, although there were deficits as well. In 1917, the *Lancet* reported the great interest that had been created for new ways of treating men with nervous disorders:

> we have repeatedly drawn attention to the inferior position we occupy amongst nations in our attitude to psychiatry. But the war is changing things. The problem of 'shell shock' and other new more mysterious illnesses, they are the every day problems of nervous breakdown. (Bourke 1996, p. 123)

A few doctors argued that war had taught them that nervous disorders were essentially of mental origin and therefore required treatment by men trained in psychological theories, rather than by neurologists or asylum doctors.

The transfer of this knowledge to the civilian population was slow. Medical institutions remained essentially unshaken by the war – services were biased towards ex-servicemen and there was little long-term improvement in the facilities offered to civilians suffering from nervous disorders. Not until 1928 was the first psychologist employed in a psychiatric setting, at the Tavistock Clinic. Hostility towards psychoanalysis continued to dominate. Greater knowledge of Freudian ideas after the war did not benefit the mentally ill. Mental breakdown was considered shameful, vaguely associated in the public's mind with sexual deviance and moral degradation. As for the social standing of psychiatrists, war-time failed to improve it and they continued to earn less than physicians and to be regarded as inferiors. Although in 1922 the War Office's Committee of Inquiry into Shell Shock recommended that the Royal Army Medical Corps (RAMC) officers should be instructed in psychoneurosis, little was done to put this recommendation into practice.

Servicemen who had suffered as a result of their war-time experiences faced an additional threat: the denial of their existence. Shell shock did not end with the war. In 1929, the government granted more pensions for psychiatric illness than they had in the first four years immediately following the conflict. Hospitals dedicated to helping such men were kept short of funds and sufferers were discharged prematurely.

The rules and rituals governing malingering were widely feared. The cost of refusing to submit to military obedience or civil authority were high. In the context of war, the policing of the male body was more vigilant and infractions of the rules were more stringent. Archives opened in the mid 1990s at the Public Record Office in London shockingly reveal that some three hundred men were shot by the military for desertion or cowardice. Thousands more were subjected to physical punishments, of almost medieval cruelty, and exposed to the elements for days on end.

The balance between strike action and malingering shifted according to the power structures being opposed. In the armed forces, men were more liable to be forced to resort to individual, isolated acts of rebellion. The struggle between medical officers and psychiatrists over men suffering from neurasthenia did little to ease their plight or to improve the position of the mentally ill after the war. Despite the large number who did feign illness during periods of immense stress, it is still surprising that more men did not do so. As Major Fleming wrote in 1914, 'the men have realised the fact that it's safer to sit in a trench than to get out of it and run away'.

At the outbreak of the Second World War, a member of the RAMC complained that the British Army had made scarcely any provision for psychiatric help. It began 'with hospital treatment forbidden, with no plan for treatment of combat troops, no unit to provide such, no plans for training, no psychiatrist in combat divisions and not even a psychiatrist in the headquarters when war was declared' (Bourke 1996). Janet Oppenheim (1991) summarised the situation as follows: 'The Great War may have demonstrated beyond doubt that psychological aspects could by themselves, utterly disrupt the body's functions, but the lesson [had done] nothing to mitigate the certainty that nervous breakdown unmanned men' (p. 152). In 1947, William Munnings indicted the psychiatric profession for permitting the military 'to forget almost all of the lessons that we learnt in the last war'. There were notable exceptions, however. A number of military psychiatrists were able to impact on mental health. Tom Main, a senior officer and psychoanalyst, has written about the two Northfields experiments which took place in a Midlands military psychiatric hospital which was the site of groupwork initiatives by such notable practitioners as Michael Foulkes, Wilfred Bion and Harold Bridger which became the cradle of the now common concept of the 'therapeutic community' (Main 1989). The richness of thought and application which emanated from this group in the immediate post-war period, did not stay with the military. It was expelled and eventually nurtured thinking in civilian health provision and entered the recondite sphere of organisational consultancy. A creative line of thinking was suppressed by its originating institution, the army.

The Dawning of Globalisation

It was only with the British intervention in Bosnia in 1994 that psychiatric provision was dispatched with the troops. Until the change of government in 1997, hundreds of claims against the Ministry of Defence on account of 'Gulf

War syndrome' were utterly denied. Why this dogged opposition to recognise the mental as well as physical ravages of war? A clue may be found in the masking of attitudes to war casualties. When Alex King, the Victoria and Albert Museum historian (1999), recently reviewed the iconography of war memorials, he reported that in Germany, building memorials to the dead of the Great War got off to a slower start than in Britain or France. Perhaps deep local political divisions prevented this until the late 1920s, even if there was no lack of anti-war feeling in Germany at that time. It has been suggested that many memorials were only completed after the Nazis ended local democratic politics after 1933. In that case, a masking of the true nature of war took place and a nationalist cult of the dead developed instead. Jung's own published response to the cataclysm did not itself see the light of day until 1936, with the publication of his essay 'Wotan' (*CW* 10).

Significantly, in the case of Britain, it was not until 1996 that a plaque was placed in Westminster Abbey to commemorate the sacrifice of civilians who perished in the conflicts of this century. The key to these conundrums lies undoubtedly in the quasi-metaphysical status and honour ritually accorded by the establishment to the conduct of war. The warrior archetype, whether exemplified by an archaic memory of Sir Lancelot or his counterpart of recent times, General Sir Michael Rose, belongs to a caste apart and opens the gateway to understanding the *shadow* side of the psyche, whence emerge the extremes and chaos of conflict as well as the possibility of renewal and order.

The great military philosopher Clausewitz, writing in 1832, argued persuasively that war was an extension of foreign policy by other means. In his day, in the aftermath of the Napoleonic campaigns, the question of legitimacy did not arise. In our day, with the potential of nuclear annihilation, this question is forced upon us. Rapoport (1982) observes that 'pleading for war as an extension of foreign policy in a sense is a plea for its legitimacy'. President Clinton's retaliatory strikes in Sudan and Afghanistan after the bombings of two US embassies in East Africa, in spite of the simultaneous attacks and ridicule heaped on his personal sexual conduct, were a demonstration of his presumed legitimacy and an example of the notion that violence breeds even harsher violence as a means of reasserting dominance.

Thus, if all-out war in a nuclear age has become a political absurdity,

> much intellectual effort is devoted to theorising about limited wars, controlled escalation, the game of threats and self-terminating nuclear exchanges. This investment in intellectual effort seems motivated to a considerable degree by a determination to preserve the struggle for power as the theoretical bedrock of political reality. (Rapoport 1982, p. 412)

Herein lies a source of confusion between the nature of political reality and that of physical and psychological reality. Hence, taking for granted the struggle for power as the basis for political reality makes the philosophy of war 'realistic'. If war is perceived as a normal, albeit regrettable, stage in the relations between states or factions within states, as seen in Kosovo, then it behoves each state to become proficient in the 'art of war' and to pursue a 'just war' both as a moral end and as an efficacious means of combating what is perceived as a 'greater evil'. The problem is compounded when a state's authority figures have the opportunity to confound their personal psychological wounds with what are perceived to be the nation's wounds, and in turn project them on to and act them out in the public arena. The outcome is invariably the sacrifice of non-combatants, social disruption and trauma, which can linger in individuals and the collective psyche for generations.

At this juncture, the rules and rituals of what constitutes 'acceptable' war in most of the world has been thrown into doubt. Kaldor notes the intriguing *volte face* of ratios of war casualties. Until the last two decades, military casualties outnumbered civilians eight to one; this is now almost completely reversed – eight civilians die for each member of military personnel. There remains Clausewitz's concept of the 'People's War', which consists of the autonomous motivations of people on the spot, the efforts and sacrifices of the local populace resisting a foreign or remote invader, such as the peasantry taking up arms. While unarmed, a similar phenomenon occurred in Budapest and Warsaw in 1956, Prague in 1968 and 1989 and, in its armed form, this was witnessed recently in Kosovo, Sri Lanka, Sierra Leone, East Timor, Indonesia, Israel and Northern Ireland. Perhaps continuing the ruminations of Clausewitz on the aetiology of war may be the very thing that will put an end to the only wars which are still rationalised in the 'civilised' world, those of counter-insurgency, which are a continuation of policy by other means. If sufficient powerful political factors agreed that war is not a continuation of policy but a failure, then perhaps we could envision the end of it. If, as Kaldor argues, new wars are about identity politics and less about geopolitical or ideological aims, then there is a massive untapped political constituency – that of mothers, sisters, wives and daughters, who are not in touch with their power. Such a phantasy was depicted in antiquity by Aristophanes' play, *Lysistrata*, when the women refused sex to their warring menfolk until they ceased fighting. Contemporary women (and like-minded men) are not at the stage of reclaiming their assertive, reflective and containing functions.

In *The Political Psyche* (1993), the analytical psychologist Andrew Samuels poses a challenge to his peers: 'Can analytical psychology learn from its founder's experiences? I suggest that renewal will not occur until Jungians resolve their work of mourning for Jung. This will lead, eventually, to our giving him up.' He goes on to appeal to therapists of all persuasions to align themselves with the powerless, those who are abused in whatever way:

> We could contribute our limited but profound expertise to the achievement of their goals ... We could do this by using our therapeutic capacity to work with the inexpressible in a clarification of the psychological experience of being Jew, German, African American, homosexual, woman, man. We would assist such groups in getting behind the defensive stereotypes imposed by a threatened dominant culture as we explore the nature of difference itself. (Samuels 1993, p. 326)

Samuels considers that it would then be possible, through a pluralistic analysis, to infer a necessary competitive tension between being alike and being unalike. People may choose to ally themselves with a minority profile and tradition, or they may identify with a majority set of values. Whatever their own conscious (or unconscious) choice, they will also receive projections from everyone else around them. A dissonance between self-identification and projections from the outside may in some circumstances lead to deadly acting out of intolerance against difference, and this probably lies at the heart of the psychology of difference. Examining the role of the transcendent function in cultural and ethnic difference could yield the answer Ignatieff sought in his unsatisfied reading of Freud. The Eurocentric and absolutist castes of psychoanalysis and analytic psychology may need to be turned on their head and become lost in a branch of science long known as wisdom, of which, perhaps, we have only glimpses. Seeking to unravel the paradox of war may mean also having to resort to the semiotics of myth and metaphor.

Mythologies, Symbols and the 'Collective Unconscious'

In *The Origins of the Sacred* (1993), Dudley Young draws attention to the point that in Sanskrit the word for 'war' denotes the desire for more cattle. It connects with the ancient rational grounds for war, which included stealing property, females and territory. More irrational grounds, such as the desire to achieve the honour of meeting the gods, were achieved in the sacrificial spilling of one's own or another's blood. Young argues that it is the dynamic sphere of the Greek *pneuma*, or wind, and, by extension, the invisible world of the soul and divinity, which clarifies our atavistic and ambivalent attachment to war. In this paradoxical attitude dwells the archetypal figure of the 'trickster' who appears in mythology as Hermes, the giver and taker of things that change, like the wind. In turn, wind is linked to the other element it fans, that of fire, whose characteristics, both actual and symbolic, approximate to the swarm. Its power has been perceived as limitless, moving constantly without contour and yet thing-like and all-consuming. Its power to alter the processes of nature is essentially destructive, yet when harnessed it symbolises all that gives warmth to our sense of well-being. In comparison to the phenomenon of swarming, it becomes perhaps the principal manifestation of divinity for primitive man.

In times past, people believed that metals which had endured the rigours of fire had taken on their death and been hardened into immortality. Today, with the availability of scientific culture, fire arguably remains for many people the principal agent of transformation. Early humans who worshipped fire might be appalled by other contemporary manifestations of swarming; the buzzing metropolis, the cancers that swarm through our bodies, and nuclear reactors where lethal energy breeds from itself in a tight box. It is possible that we pay insufficient attention to the metaphorical and actual significance of swarming. Its power occurs in a myth, astonishingly consistent throughout the world, and well known to Native American peoples for instance. In the myth, the trickster is an obscene figure who seems to be rising from the depths of unconscious and polymorphous desire towards the light of human clarity and adult capacity for separateness and individuation. Somewhere between monster and child, this inchoate power is instinct combined with metamorphosis, and therefore without determinate shape. Among the Winnebago Sioux, the trickster is depicted by lengths of intestine wrapped around the body and an equally long penis, similarly wrapped. The figure is defined, encircled and controlled by two bloated appetites, for food and for sex. The two appetites give rise to a third, the appetite for killing and destruction which is partly symbolised by the penis as snake and as battering ram, but chiefly encapsulated by the anus, home of the fart and the turd, located at the end of the intestine. The trickster is intrigued by this aperture and tries to engage it in conversation. He uses various deceits to alter his contours and assume any shape to satisfy his desires.

The trickster is a preliminary sketch for the devil and inspires disorder. He has pretensions of being taken for a serious god of chaos, but in his anarchy there is laughter and even a few gifts for mankind – perhaps a representation of Prometheus. He brings with him some of the Dionysian spirit of Carnival – the temporary and permitted release from the constraints of civilisation and good order. In the trickster resides also the Shaman and the poet. The Sioux trickster myth described by Young (1993) stands as a metaphor for contemporary involvement with warring which would understand it in wholly rational terms, whereas it echoes the scenario of the native chief setting off to war after prolonged and illicit fornication. After the battle, the consequent unmaking of culture causes a regression that annuls all the differentiations that tradition and culture have achieved. Once beyond culture he is delivered back to nature, communes in its language and beastliness and becomes the target of tricks. He is caught between two worlds: bereft of animal instincts, but not yet refined by culture and law – hence the maelstrom of gargantuan appetites and lack of control.

The trickster saga is one of repeated monstrosity, excess, inversion and chaos. Yet, already in the primitive mind lie the seeds of astonishing insights into the evolution of imagination and human psychology. It also offers an extraordinarily lucid perception of the central role of deceit in the satisfaction and frustration of desire. In fantasy, the trickster would harness the power of the divinity, precisely the thing that cannot be grasped, and thus collapses repeatedly before re-emerging in ever-new guises (Young 1993).

Barbara Ehrenreich traces the roots of human violence to early predation-hunting in her illuminating book *Blood Rites* (1997). Her research shows that when humankind's survival depended on hunting, there were swarms and herds of animals. What evidence there is from artefacts and cave paintings show people necessarily in a defensive and sometimes offensive strategy of preying on animals which then succumb to them. Supporting evidence comes from Jared Diamond in his remarkable survey, *Guns, Germs and Steel* (1997). He shows that the stock of animals was eventually depleted after people had established dominance over them. The archaic goddess-fearing hunter gave way to a spear-wielding male likely to turn on his human foe. The early metaphysics of pre-Greek history depicts a powerful female who runs with wolves, menstruates and gives birth in blood to children and is then cast into darkness. Gradually, her job became to strip the prey of skin, cook the meat and bones and make clothes. As men took up farming and domesticating animals, she was made to stick to the weaving. The division of labour was absolute. Farming, states Diamond, enabled people to accommodate the parasites carried by creatures and helped them to develop immunity to germs – a huge advantage over peoples whose lifestyle was more precarious. Is this why *Homo sapiens* overtook the Neanderthals? It is, claims Diamond, what allowed Charles I of Spain to conquer Atahuallpa in South America and not the other way around. Raising crops, smelting metal, building settlements and establishing a social order were coupled with wandering and a predatory instinct, thereby setting the stage for intermittent incursions, capture and the continuation of the blood sacrifice.

Returning to more recent times, the mythological figure of the god Wotan emerges as an expression of the paradox of Germanic frustration and might. Jung wrote his essay 'Wotan' in 1936, with the perspective on the First World War and when neighbouring Germany was already in the thrall of national socialism. He characterises Wotan, an ancient deity of storm and frenzy, as a long-extinct volcano awakening to new activity in a 'civilised' country. He could be seen in many communal settings, this time somewhat shamefaced, in the meeting house of a religious sect of simple folk in Northern Germany, disguised as the figure of Christ sitting on a white horse. He is a restless wanderer who creates unrest and strife and works magic. Christianity relegated him to the role of devil. Since the Middle Ages, the role of restless wanderer was projected on to Jews and Gypsies by Christians in the same way as we often locate our unconscious psychic contents in other people. Jung hypothesised that the Wotan archetype is a better explanation of Nazism than the effect of economic, political or psychological factors. He attributes *Ergriffenheit*, or possession, by Wotan of the German people as the cause of the turmoil instigated by them.

The value of the Wotan myth as a parable lies not in the belief in any particular gods, but in the personifications it proposes of collective psychic forces which are psychotic. These have nothing to do with the conscious mind, from which they are dissociated. Our reluctance to accept this as a rational explanation has its roots, maintains Jung, in a persisting fear of metaphysics. The idea that anything could be real or true which does not come from the observable world is constantly rejected by the rational mind. The Wotan archetype is a plausible hypothesis for the state of humiliation and fury in which the Germans found themselves following the Treaty of Versailles. A parallel situation is detectable in the polarised position of the Serbian people in the 1990s who 'allow' themselves to be led by a reportedly deeply unhappy and flawed leader.

In Jung's account, the origins of the European disturber of peace originate in the wind that blows into Europe from Asia's vastness. He likens it to an elemental Dionysus breaking into Apollonian order. The rouser of the tempest, as characterised in 'Wotan', is discernible in the political confusion and spiritual upheaval 'he' has caused throughout history. The footprint of 'his' influence is firmly established in primordial types and images, the archetypes, which are innate in the unconscious of many races and exercise a direct influence upon them.

Are there or have there been peoples in whom chaos is burnt out? Perhaps this is true of the extinct Bushmen of the Kalahari, the actively dreaming native people of Australia, on the way to extinction, and the vestiges of native inhabitants of the Matto Grosso in Brazil or the mysterious Kogi of the High Sierra of Colombia who live in deliberate isolation and view the ills of the world as retribution for humankind's breach of honour to Mother Earth (Ereira 1990). In our time, examples might include conscientious objectors and religious communities such as the Quakers, Buddhists and the followers of Gandhi – always assuming that they are not projecting their split-off unconscious exploding selves into the rest of the community.

In the midst of any maelstrom may be found those who stand against the prevailing wind. Nechama Tec, a Holocaust survivor, studied Christian rescue of Jews in Nazi-occupied Poland. She concluded that they acted in the face of certain death to themselves and their families. They were all outsiders in a social sense. Some were anti-Semitic in attitude but, in their hierarchy of beliefs, either they denied the authority of the outside world and therefore the reality of risk, or they saw the preservation of life as being of paramount importance. They were mostly individuals acting in isolation, with the significant exception of religious communities – mainly Catholic nuns – who secreted thousands of Jewish children (Tec 1985).

How do rational adults become enthralled by a Wotan archetype? Jung asserts that because the behaviour of a race takes on its specific character from its underlying images, it becomes possible to speak of an archetypal force. By the archetypal effects on the collective life of a people, it reveals its nature. The archetype has what Jung calls a 'biology' of its own, independent of human nature. Only occasionally do individuals fall under the influence of this unconscious factor. When it is quiescent, awareness of it is no more than that of latent epilepsy. Thus, groups of people with extreme views can be viewed as 'mad' until they are swept into something more powerful. Such astonishing transformations are, in Jung's terms, the effect of the god of wind that 'bloweth where it listeth'. Opposition forces are the Christian *pneuma* and the miracle of understanding that is symbolised by Pentecost. Jung asserts

> Archetypes are like riverbeds which dry up when the life-giving water deserts them, but which it can fill again at any time ... The life of the individual as a member of society and particularly as subject of the state may be regulated like a canal, but the life of nations is a great rushing river which is utterly beyond human control ... (*CW* 10, para. 395)

The Shadow Feminine

The opposition of the sexes has mostly left women, except for archaic goddesses, out of the narratives and analyses of war. There have been luminous interventions from the likes of Florence Nightingale and Mary Seacole, resistance heroines, the Land Army and indispensable office staff in the Second World War who were female, but the theatre of war in general has been the preserve of men. Is it that women become hidden objects in mass conflict? Their access to the line of fire – though not bombs – and to glory has mostly been blocked; along with children, the old and sick, women are invariably the civilian part of the swarm.

If war is a perversion of order and of creative intercourse, there is a need to attend to the interactive relations between the sexes and their collusion in masking the actual nature of war. The outcome of women's struggle for equality of opportunity has spread to war and the right to bear arms, but as would-be males. Only acknowledgement and acceptance of the female's difference, integrity and sexuality helps to differentiate her from the roles of consort and mother. Women who attain a sense of self can act as a counter-weight to the 'unguided missile' of men and complement the fertile *coniunctio*. If woman remains in the collective shadow she has no option but to be part of warring chaos. Integral to Jung's idea of the *coniunctio* of opposites is its archetypal capacity to sustain difference and conflict in the outer world. It is symbolically manifested in the feminine capacity to contain and in the com-plementary roles expressed by the Buddha in relation to Mother Earth, by Christ in relation to the Church as Bride, or by humankind in relation to the Gaia principle. In practice, this means the risk of admitting women and 'female' perspectives into centres of power without the conditionality of accepting 'male' rules.

Although order, compassion and pacifism may be regarded as predomi-nantly feminine factors, they are nevertheless detectable to an extent in phases of all warring. It is pertinent to note here the strange phenomenon of persistent visions of a female figure urging reflection and prayer, identified as the Virgin Mary, who appeared to a mixed group of youngsters in the Yugoslav town of Medjugorje in the early 1980s, as if a foreboding of things to come were emerging from the collective unconscious. A Jungian might account for this by the notion of an unconscious compensatory archetype operating in the absence of a sense of being held after Tito's death. In war it may appear also as selfless sacrifice, the case of Father Kolbe[2] in Auschwitz, or mercy for the vanquished. The integration of unconscious and opposite contents in the face of implacable warring is what eventually brings about the opportunity of peace, resolution and order, equivalent to an individual's act of realisation. Such a window of peaceful opportunity may have been opened inadvertently in Northern Ireland with the appointment of an iconoclastic female Secretary of State, in the person of Mo Mowlem. Not only was she the first woman with responsibility to be appointed to this traditional male preserve; she entered into the fray accompanied by her own personal shadow of death in the form of cancer, and simultaneously enacted both her vulnerability and courage by casting off her wig in negotiation meetings (her hair having fallen out as a result of chemotherapy). Other women are assuming high-profile roles across the spectrum of international relations, with Margaret Thatcher and Madeleine Albright at one end and Sagato Ogata and Mary Robinson at the other. No less significant is the fact that women are agonising and writing about war.

As Carl Jung reminds us (*CW* 10), integrating opposites, or the process of transcendence and individuation, is a most difficult task which demands a high degree of ethical responsibility (see Hester Solomon's chapter on ethics, this volume). Few people are capable of such an achievement, and those that do constitute not the political but the moral leadership of mankind. Kaldor remarks that 'among the global class are members of transnational networks based on an exclusivist identity, while at the local level there are many courageous individuals who refuse the politics of particularism' (1999, p. 6). Jung explains that the survival, maintenance and development of civilisation depend on such individuals:

> The vast majority are incapable of integrating the forces of order ... Yet in the long run, it will prove to be the only way by which man's lamentable unconsciousness, childishness and weakness can be replaced by a future man who knows that he himself is the maker of his fate and that the state is his servant and not his master. (*CW* 10, paras 451–2)

Conclusion

The emergence of globalisation and the breakdown of traditional war rules and the inevitable herding of people has produced a combustible cocktail of mass dependence which renders people unstable, insecure and suggestible. The operation of the compensatory mechanism to overcome individual weakness and fear of obliteration gives way to hidden desires for power. Hitler floated to the surface as a willing vehicle of a new order. In Hitler, every German should have glimpsed his or her own shadow and his or her own worst danger. The remedy suggested by a Jungian reading is to set up an internal conflict in each man and woman; the task for each individual being to transcend the conflict rather than project it into an external context where it can join with other people's grievances. Mere external talk shops are insufficient. Jung contrasts the League of Nations – which was meant to have been a supra-national authority but which has been likened by some contemporary observers to a child in need of protection itself – with the unconscious life of nations rolling along unguided like a boulder rolling down a hill and only capable of being stopped by an obstacle larger than itself.

Archetypes begin to operate when individuals are confronted with situations which cannot be dealt with in any familiar or rational way. The 'possessed' in Germany, the reasonable men, went to great lengths to present their state of possession as less alarming by dressing it in conciliatory historical garb. Jung viewed Germans in the 1930s as victims. He alluded to the obverse of Wotan's character, as his ecstatic qualities which were to emerge later when the storm had abated. He reified him as a sort of unruly pet, who, though a rogue, was really lovable. This deceit, or trick, has earned him much criticism since. The tone of his essay 'The fight with the shadow' (*CW* 10), written after the end of the Second World War, is almost trivial as he grapples with the events of the previous decade and reduces his assessment of the perpetrators of the Holocaust and other ravages to a simplistic analogy with a mad patient.

The burden of this chapter has been to show that conflict and the state of warring are ingrained in us as a form of *coniunctio* in its diverse guises. It is possible to demonstrate that it is not only destructive, but can be transformative and creative. The challenge we now face includes the moral dilemma of exploiting unequal power and resources and entering upon war with its inevitable 'collateral damage'. This not only includes the destruction of human, civilian life, tradition and heritage, but also keeps the female half of humankind subjugated and stores for the future hidden psychological wounds which emerge in groups and individuals over decades. This cost appears to be omitted from consideration by the instigators of war.

At times of great change, such as economic instability or social disquiet associated with the crossing of a millennial time zone, disturbance in individuals may be heightened and the tendency to swarm may likewise increase. The drive to settle old scores may be unleashed. There are also ever-increasing opportunities for self-observation, but they are usually concentrated on the external. The alternative is for internal examination, internal to ourselves and to the groups of which we are members. The difficulty is in maintaining an individual perspective while forming part of a wider group.

Moreover, it seems that the rules of warring and engagement have altered: women and children now bear arms. Fighting is no longer the preserve of a disciplined or uniformed caste; instead, irregulars, aid workers and peace-keeping forces mingle as never before. The technological revolution ensures that the trickster's sphere of propaganda and spin have greater immediacy. Conflict as a source of energy continues to be paradoxical. Could we therefore harness it, as the splitting of the atom has been harnessed for peaceful purposes? Unless we practise both mediation and meditation and engage with the meaning of our dreams and nightmares, as part of the responsibility to individuate, our dangerous legacy to our children's children will be to swarm again.

Notes

1. *Enantiodromia* denotes the propensity of all polarised phenomena to go over to their opposite.
2. Father Maximilian Kolbe was a Franciscan missionary in Japan who, like many Catholic priests and other clergy liquidated in Nazi concentration camps, was incarcerated as a subversive. His final act was to volunteer to die in place of another Pole, who had been picked randomly by the SS during a camp purge.

References

Barker, P. (1991) *Regeneration*. London: Penguin.

Bourke, J. (1996) *Dismembering the Male – Men's Bodies, Britain and the Great War*. London: Reaktion Books.

Diamond, J. (1997) *Guns, Germs and Steel*. London: Jonathan Cape.

Ehrenreich, B. (1997) *Blood Rites – Origins and History of the Passions of War*. London: Virago.

Ereira, A. (1990) *The Heart of the World*. London: Jonathan Cape.

Fleming, Major (1914) 'Letters'; letter to 'Randolfo', 6 December, Imperial War Museum 90/28/1.

Freud, S. (1917) 'The taboo of sexuality', *Freud and Sexuality*. Penguin Freud Library, London, vol. 7.

Freud, S. (1921) *Group Psychology and the Analysis of the Ego*. Penguin Freud Library, London.

Freud, S. (1929) *Civilization and Its Discontents*. Penguin Freud Library, London, vol. 12.

Ignatieff, M. (1998) *The Warrior's Honor – Ethnic War and the Modern Conscience*. London: Chatto and Windus.

Kaldor, M. (1999) *New and Old Wars – Organized Violence in a Global Era*. Cambridge: Polity Press.

Keegan, J. (1998) *War and our World*. The Reith Lectures 1998. London: Hutchinson.

King, A. (1999) 'The Iconography of War Memorials', *Independent*, 18 February.

Main, T. (1989) 'The hospital as a therapeutic institution', in J. Johns (ed.), *The Ailment and Other Psychoanalytic Essays*. London: Free Association Books.

Oppenheim, J.C. (1991) *Shattered Nerves: Retreat and Depression in Victorian England*. New York: Oxford University Press.

Papadopoulos, R. (1998) 'Destructiveness, atrocities and healing: epistemological and clinical reflections', *Journal of Analytical Psychology*, 43(4): 455–77.

Rapoport, A. (1982) 'Editor's Introduction', in C. von Clausewitz, *On War*. London: Penguin.

Redfearn, J. (1992) *The Exploding Self – The Creative and Destructive Nucleus of the Personality*. Wilmette, IL: Chiron Publications.

Rotblat, J., Steinberger, J. and Balchandra, U. (eds) (1993) *A Nuclear-Weapon-Free World*. Boulder, CO: Westview Press.

Samuels, A. (1993) *The Political Psyche*. London: Routledge.

Stevens, A. (1989) *The Roots of War – A Jungian Perspective*. New York: Paragon House.

Tec, N. (1985) *When Light Pierced the Darkness – Christian Rescue of Jews in Nazi Occupied Poland*. New York: Oxford University Press.

von Clausewitz, C. (1832) *On War*. London: Penguin, 1982.

Young, D. (1993) *The Origins of the Sacred – The Ecstasies of Love and War*. London: Abacus.

Suggested Reading

Kaldor, M. (1999) *New and Old Wars – Organized Violence in a Global Era*. Cambridge: Polity Press (Chapters 3 and 4).

Redfearn, J. (1992) *The Exploding Self – The Creative and Destructive Nucleus of the Personality*. Wilmette, IL: Chiron Publications (Chapters 10, 13 and 14).

Stevens, A. (1989) *The Roots of War – A Jungian Perspective*. New York: Paragon House (Chapters 1, 7 and 8).

Part III
Jungian Thought and the New Sciences

7

The New Physics through a Jungian Perspective

Helen Morgan

Introduction

There has been a major revolution in science since the beginning of the twentieth century which has challenged the very basis of classical materialism and caused a fundamental re-examination of the traditional division between mind and matter. Many physicists are writing about this revolution, trying to tell us what an outdated paradigm the physics of Newton is, and urging us to give up on it and see what is going on in the thinking of some aspects of physics. They suggest we are moving towards a new paradigm where the old divisions no longer apply and which cross over previously separate disciplines.

One interface which seems to offer a potentially interesting and productive interaction is that between physics and depth psychology. In this chapter I will be exploring the parallels between some of the ideas of the new physics and those of Jungian thinking to see how together they may suggest ways for thinking about the relationship between mind and matter.

The New Physics

Throughout the twentieth century, science has been undergoing several revolutions at what Paul Davies calls the 'three ultimate frontiers of physics: the very small, the very large and the very complex' (Davies 1989). In 1905, Einstein presented his Special Theory of Relativity, which challenged some of the accepted ideas of cosmology, especially those of space and time. In 1927, the Quantum Theory, a theory of the very small, was presented at the Solway Conference and was to overthrow the laws of classical physics concerning atomic behaviour. In the 1960s, the major developments in computers enabled scientists to examine closely the complex world of real, as opposed to ideal, physical phenomena, and came to some surprising conclusions which have been, rather misleadingly, termed Chaos Theory.

At the end of the nineteenth century, physicists were sure that, apart from a few minor problems, they had discovered most of what we needed to know about the laws of physical reality. The investigation of these few remaining difficulties led to an entirely new set of paradigms that turned the old system upside down and led scientists along all sorts of unexpected paths. It was the end of the age of certainty. One could say that the twentieth century, in contrast, has been the age of uncertainty.

Of these three great theories: relativity, quantum and chaos, I intend to focus in this chapter on quantum theory. This is partly due to the limited space available, and partly because it is this theory which most completely challenges the classical assumptions about the physical world, and also offers interesting possibilities for links with Jungian thought. Indeed, one of its findings is that matter is somehow linked with consciousness and a way has to be found for understanding the relationship between the material world and psyche – matter and mind. Jung himself, although he met Einstein, was most profoundly affected by his involvement with Wolfgang Pauli (and vice versa), who was a major player in the development of quantum theory.

There are a number of difficulties in attempting an understanding of the theory for those who are not familiar with it. The first is the non-scientist's fear of the subject. Never before has science impinged on our lives to such an extent. Our days are touched by technology from beginning to end. We are used to not having a clue about how things work – we just hope they will. It is a small step from this to assuming we cannot understand the theories behind the technology. It seems an unfathomable world peopled by boffins and those who have undergone a lengthy, and essentially mathematical, initiation.

This perception is not helped by the fact that the articulation of the quantum theory seems to be moving deeper and deeper into maths, and ways of conceptualising or of symbolising the conclusions seem increasingly difficult to find. It is as if we are going beyond the limits of the human imagination. In the search for understanding, some physicists are ranging over territory which includes religion, philosophy and psychology.

Another difficulty lies in how profoundly we have internalised the classical, Newtonian assumptions about the way the physical world works. Included in these assumptions are those postulated by Descartes, that mind and matter are divided. It is important to appreciate what a tight grip these assumptions have in the West, and therefore how difficult it is to challenge the paradigm and allow the new to take hold.

The danger is that we can flip over into a position where anything goes, where we use the theory to 'prove' anything we like. Quantum theory does not 'prove' Jung to be right. But it just might, if considered in conjunction with Jungian thought, offer one sort of framework for the exploration of how mind and matter might be in relation to each other. As Mansfield warns:

> It would be poor scholarship and a disservice to both physics and depth psychology to make too many easy parallels and use them as a hunting licence for affirming all kinds of parapsychological phenomena. This is slippery ground. Tread with caution. (Mansfield and Spiegelman 1989, p. 19)

The Fundamental Assumptions of Classical Physics

Because much of this chapter will attempt to highlight how different quantum theory is from the classical paradigm, it is important first to be clear what this paradigm entails. Classical physics, founded on Newtonian mechanics, was the scientific description of the physical universe which dominated Western scientific thought from the eighteenth century until the beginning of the twentieth century. This system of thought can be characterised by certain fundamental assumptions:

- This Newtonian view of the physical world was essentially *mechanistic*, in that the universe was perceived as a giant clockwork machine, the movement of which was to be understood as the movement of the parts that make up the machine. The workings of a machine can be reduced and analysed in terms of its constituent parts.
- Whilst the different parts are not internally connected in any way, they do interact externally, either through direct contact or impact, or by a system of forces or fields. All motion can be understood in terms of these forces or fields, and therefore all motion has a cause. Whenever a body moved, it was always possible to determine what had caused the body's motion. *Cause and effect are always linked.*
- Bodies, therefore, can act upon each other, but only when they are sufficiently close to each other both spatially and temporally. Objects which exist apart from each other, separated by time and space, are independent of each other. This is the notion of *locality*, that is, objects must be local or proximate to each other in order to affect each other.
- If we know the position and the motion of a body, and we know the causes which act upon the body, we can predict its motion and position in the future. Everything, therefore, is *determined*, and our knowledge is only limited by the limitations of our instruments of measurement.

- There are two ways in which we can describe energy in motion: one as a particle and the other a wave. Energy must be *either* a wave *or* a particle.
- The workings of the machine and its parts exist as distinct from the human observer. Mind and matter are separate.

To a great extent, these assumptions have proved very useful in the development of scientific thought which underpinned the Industrial Revolution. For these assumptions were not considered as assumptions, but were rather thought of as 'known facts' about the world in which we lived. They seemed to fit our experience of the day-to-day world that we encounter, at the scale on which we operate. Yet it is these assumptions which have been blown apart by the developments of the new physics.

Quantum Theory

The quantum theory was first postulated in the 1920s and has continued to dominate scientific thinking ever since. It has proved to be a remarkably successful, yet persistently puzzling, theory of the fundaments of matter, explaining as it does the periodic table of the elements, the formation of molecules and chemical reactions, and DNA. It is also the theory that lies at the heart of the development of microchips and lasers. Yet its implications are profoundly disturbing to our most basic assumptions about the physical universe, violating all the laws of classical physics and seeming to take us way beyond the limits of our imagination into places that are often only possible to describe mathematically. Niels Bohr, one of the major architects of the theory, himself declared that 'anyone who is not shocked by quantum theory has not understood it'. But this is not an easy theory to 'understand', for it turns on its head the central paradigm in which the West is steeped. We have to try and suspend our usual ways of thinking and allow something new to happen.

The view of the atom at the early stages of the development of the quantum theory was of a central nucleus surrounded by electrons in different energy states (Figure 7.1). When an electron moves from a higher energy state to a lower one, it radiates energy in packets, or 'quanta'. When an electron absorbs a quanta of energy, it can move into a higher energy state within the atom. This exchange of discrete quanta of energy provides the bond between atoms, thus enabling the creation of molecules and the chemical elements of which all matter, organic and inorganic, is composed. It is these 'quantum leaps' which can cause energy to be emitted from an atom in the form of light quanta, or photons. It was when the question of whether light travelled as a wave or as particles was pursued, that the theory began to move into some very strange territory indeed.

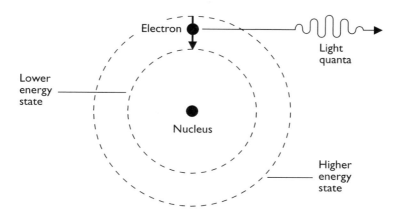

Figure 7.1 Bohr's model of the atom

Whether something is a wave or a particle is a basic question about its nature. The characteristics of the two are entirely different and mutually exclusive. By the end of the nineteenth century, there was a general consensus that light was a wave, yet there were certain pieces of experimental evidence that seemed to show that it was a particle. This anomaly was puzzling and the new quantum theory was applied, theoretically at first, and later experimentally, to solve the problem. To illustrate what arose from this work, the two-slit experiment is central in demonstrating just what an odd world we were beginning to move into.

The Two-Slit Experiment

To be clear about the fundamental differences between the way particles move as opposed to waves, imagine first that a stream of bullets are fired from a gun moving in an arc. In the line of fire we place a bulletproof screen with a hole in it and a series of bullet detectors on the other side. After a while, we find that the detector placed directly in line with the hole registers the largest proportion of bullets. Others close by register a few bullets that hit the edge of the hole as they go through and so 'bend' around the corner. If we now make a second hole in the screen, we detect an identical distribution on the other side of the second hole. Whether there is one hole, or two, or fifty, it makes no difference to the patterns we find on the other side of the wall opposite any particular hole (Figure 7.2).

Now consider a series of waves on a pond caused by a motor vibrating in the water. The waves spread out from the motor in circles. If we place a barrier across the pond with one small hole in it, the waves that reach the hole pass

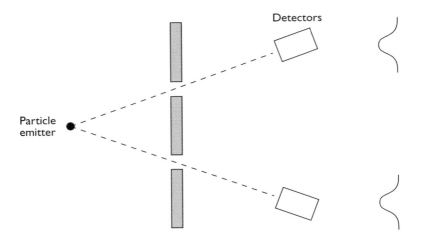

Figure 7.2 Particles travelling through two slits

through as a secondary wave. A detection screen that registers the peaks and troughs of the wave is placed beyond the barrier. If we make a second hole in the barrier, two secondary waves are formed at the holes. As these two waves spread out they 'interfere' with each other so that where two peaks meet, a high peak is formed; where two troughs meet, a deeper trough is formed; and where a peak meets a trough, they cancel each other out. On the screen we see this new 'interference pattern' registered as highs and lows. This pattern is one which can only be made by waves. Therefore, if the same experiment is done passing light through two slits in a screen and an interference pattern is recorded, then the conclusion must be that light travels as a wave (Figure 7.3).

In the experiment, a stream of photons is emitted from a source. In front of this source is a screen which has two slits, either of which can be closed. First, we open up only one slit and place a detector on the other side of the screen, and we find that it registers the arrival of particles in just the pattern we would expect from a stream of bullets. If we close that hole and open the other, the same pattern forms behind that slit. As with the bullets, if the photons are travelling as particles, we ought to find that having two slits makes no difference at all to what is happening behind the slit which is already open – we just double the same result. However, what in fact happens is that as soon as we open up the other slit, the particle distribution disappears and an inter-ference pattern is seen instead. This has to be because the photons are travelling as waves and therefore doing what only waves can do – which is to interfere with each other (Figures 7.4 and 7.5).

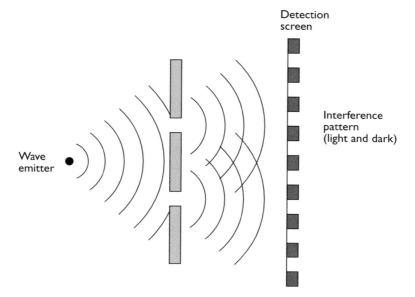

Figure 7.3 Waves travelling through two slits

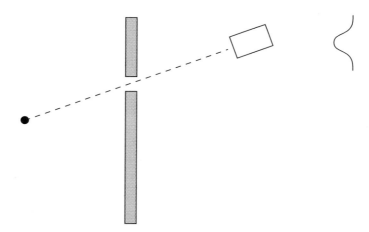

Figure 7.4 Light travelling through a single slit

If we slow the stream right down so only one photon is emitted at a time, the result is exactly the same. When there is one slit, we get a particle with no sign of a wave. When there are two slits, we get a wave, and there is no point in asking, 'Where is the particle?' We can try to fool the photon by setting the experiment up so that the second slit is opened (or closed) *after* the photon has

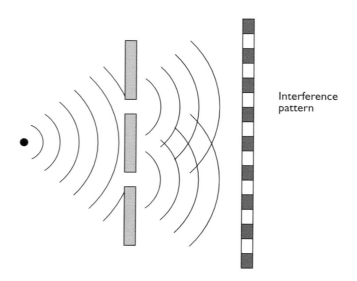

Interference pattern

Figure 7.5 Light travelling through double slits

left the emitter, but the photon still behaves according to the situation that exists at the moment when it passes through the slit or slits. As we persist in trying to catch the photon out, we open the two slits and place a detector at one of them. Then the photon shows itself as a particle and it is either there or not. Those that reach the slit where the detector is not, seem to 'know' that the other slit is being watched and behave accordingly, registering as particles when they reach the screen.

This is very strange. What it seems to mean is that, prior to detection, and while we are not looking, the photon keeps all of its options open. As soon as we look at it, however, it becomes a definite thing. A single photon, as it goes through one slit, 'knows' whether the other slit is open. If we try peeking at it on its way, it 'knows' we are doing so and becomes whatever it needs to be appropriate to the instant of our observation. It seems that it is not only the nature and behaviour of the photon which determines our result, but also the whole experimental set-up, the number of slits, the method of detection and the fact of being observed.

The classical question as to whether light was a wave or a particle now finds the unexpected answer that it is a wave *and* a particle. In fact this wave–particle duality is found whether one is considering photons, electrons, atoms, or any other quantum entity. All have a wave nature and a particle nature and we can never see both at the same time. If we set up an experiment in a certain way, we get a wave; set it up another way, and we get a particle.

Heisenberg, a colleague of Bohr, formulated the uncertainty principle in 1927 which states that we can never measure both the momentum (or velocity) *and* the position of a quantum object, such as an electron or a photon, at the same time. We can discover where an electron *is* but we cannot then know how fast, or to where, it is travelling. On the other hand, we can know its velocity and where its going, but then we lose all information about where it is. This principle placed uncertainty within the very fabric of the system we were seeking to pin down. It can no longer be thought of as merely a limitation in our capacity to measure, an irritating matter of ignorance, but an ontological impossibility. Complementary characteristics are mutually exclusive and yet both are necessary if we are to fully understand the nature of the object. They cannot be known simultaneously.

Shrödinger's Wave Equation

The conclusion reached by Bohr and others was that any atomic state was undefined and consisted only of probabilities until a measurement is made. A quantum object, such as a photon, can move in an indefinite number of paths. The existence of each path has a certain probability, although the probability of many will be very small. It is as if the wave nature of the travel is a wave of probability, a superposition of all possible states which defines the likelihood of finding the photon at any point at any time, and the photon travels along all possible paths until it is observed. The mathematical statement of this system of all possible states was described in 1925 by Shrödinger in his wave equation. This equation contains a wave function which describes this multitude of possibilities, all equally real and some mutually exclusive. All these possibilities exist until we observe what is happening. As soon as we place a detector in the situation, any quantum object – say, the photon or electron – 'decides' on just one of these possibilities and all the others seem to disappear. This act of observation seems to be what, in terms of quantum theory, 'collapses the wave function'.

This concept of human observation collapsing the wave function brings consciousness on to the stage of this odd theatre. Perhaps the most familiar way of trying to conceptualise this is the metaphor of Shrödinger's cat. This is a thought experiment where an imaginary cat is placed in a sealed, opaque box. Inside the box is a radioactive emitter which has a 50 per cent probability of one particle decaying every hour. Should a particle be emitted it will hit a contraption set up in the box, which will then release poisonous fumes and thus kill the cat. There is, therefore, a 50 per cent probability that, after an hour, the cat will be alive, and a 50 per cent probability that it will be dead. Because quantum theory states that all probabilities are real until the act of observation, after an hour, as long as no one has looked, the cat would be *neither* dead *nor* alive, but a mixture of the two states. It would be *both* alive *and* dead. However, when, and only when, someone lifts the lid of the box to find out what was happening, the wave function collapses, and the cat is found to be either definitely alive or definitely dead.

The EPR Paradox

The conclusions that quantum theorists were reaching seemed so incredible that many were having trouble accepting them. Einstein was especially troubled and so, with Podolsky and Rosen, set up an imaginary thought experiment to 'prove' that some of these conclusions were impossible, thereby challenging the theory itself. This experiment was termed the EPR (Einstein, Podolsky, Rosen) paradox.

Imagine two electrons which are emitted from the same atom so that their states are correlated. According to the laws of quantum physics, since two correlated electrons cannot be in the same energy state, these two must be spinning in different directions – say, 'spin up' and 'spin down' – but as they are unobserved at this stage, they form a single system of all possible states. The electrons are sent many miles in opposite directions and then one of them is observed and will be found to have either spin up or spin down. Quantum theory tells us that if one is spinning up, then the other must be spinning down, and vice versa. Thus, as soon as one electron's spin becomes fixed, then so must the other's – but in the opposite direction. Since the direction of the spin of one is entirely random and decided only at the point of observation, the other would have to 'know' which direction the observed photon was spinning in, and this 'knowledge' could only be conveyed at the very instant of measurement. Observation of one has to instantaneously collapse the probability wave of the other.

An analogy is to imagine a pair of twins who are separated at birth and one taken to live in London and one to Sydney. Years later we find that they have been called the same name, have married similar individuals and have followed the same careers – all of which might be explained by the original genetic correlation. But then we find that they have gone dancing at the same moment and, as they dance, when one raises her left arm, the other raises her right; when one turns in a clockwise direction, the other instantaneously spins anti-clockwise.

Einstein, Podolsky and Rosen put forward this paradox as a challenge to quantum theory as a whole. This, they said, was a logical conclusion of quantum theory and, since the consequences violated the laws of special relativity, the theory was impossible. It was impossible assuming two important suppositions: one was that nothing can travel faster than the speed of light, and the second was the independence of spatially distant objects.

That is, as nothing can travel faster than the speed of light, no means of communicating a message from one electron to the other was possible. And, assuming objects cannot act on each other at a distance, then one electron cannot instantaneously affect another when so far apart.

John Bell, in his theorem Bell's Inequality developed in the 1960s, demonstrated that the EPR paradox was, in fact, a theoretical possibility. Physical experiments have now been carried out which seem to uphold this strange conclusion, and the consequences, whilst now accepted by most, continue to be hotly debated. The first of the above assumptions, that nothing can travel faster than the speed of light, continues to be accepted. What has been severely challenged by this conclusion is the concept of the independence of spatially distant objects. The possibility is raised, at least at the quantum level, of objects which have once been connected, continuing to affect each other whatever the distance between them. This is described as 'non-locality', or what Einstein called 'spooky action at a distance'.

We now have a whole new description of physical reality which violates all the laws of classical physics. Quantum 'stuff' has wave–particle duality, where the wave aspect is thought to describe the superposition of all probabilities smeared out over space and time. Movement is random and not determined, and events are acausal. They are also non-localised in that quanta do not exist independently of each other but can interact whatever the distance between them. An atomistic, mechanistic view is contradicted and, instead, a holistic approach is required, including the thing observed, its context and the observer, for it is when it is observed that its state becomes defined. Consequently, human consciousness moves from being the classical nomad wandering around the physical universe, observing and recording as a separate, detached being, to one that takes on an interactive role. When we observe physical reality, whatever it tells us it is, depends on the questions we ask of it. From its conception, the quantum theory has revolutionised thinking in the scientific community. Physicists know it *works*, yet they still do not know what it *means*. In the search to understand, a startling revolution has taken place in science, leading some into an exploration of questions of consciousness, philosophy, religion and the paranormal.

The Psyche and the Physical

One difficulty in grasping the implications of these findings is that quantum theory describes how matter works at the atomic and subatomic level. The material we 'know' and are familiar with in our daily lives does not seem to behave like this. The rules of classical physics seem to do really rather well when we engage with 'stuff' at the human scale. Objects in this classical reality seem to behave in a way that is determined and causal, and where interactions are localised in both time and space.

In considering the relationship between mind and matter, Western 'rational' thinking followed Descartes in seeing the two as separate, with mind located in the physical matter of the brain. Consciousness could act upon the physical world by causing things to happen. Through experimentation we were able to observe the consequences of our interventions and formulate laws which could then be tested. However, all this was essentially localised in space, and mind was seen as fundamentally external to, and other than, physical matter. Anything more holistic was seen to belong to the realm of metaphysics or theology, where considerations of soul and God were located.

This relationship, which might still be said to apply at the level of the physical world we engage with on a day-to-day basis, might be conceptualised as a horizontal line between classical reality and the conscious mind (Figure 7.6).

Figure 7.6 The relationship between mind and matter

In a classical Cartesian model, the two ends of the line are perceived as fundamentally different. This is no spectrum but describes a relationship between the two whereby mind has to exist in the physical world by understanding its laws and manipulating matter through their application. Each clearly affects the other, but in a manner which is causal and localised.

Yet a classical analysis of the situation is also atomistic and mechanistic. Within this framework we can break matter down, reduce it to is parts, and then analyse these. If we follow this assumption when considering the book that you now hold in your hand, we can say that it is paper made of molecules, made of atoms, made of mainly empty space and subatomic particles including electrons. From developments in microphysics we also can understand that it is the quantum interactions between these electrons that allow the molecules to be formed, which can make up the paper that feels solid enough. As you read, light photons will be hitting the paper and being reflected to your eye. A series of connections transfer the pattern on your retina formed by this reflected light to your brain, where a most complex set of neuronal interactions will be at work. Every little bit of the physical reality around you and every little bit of the physical you, can be thought of in this way. As everything is made up of the subatomic that can be described by quantum theory, then the foundation of all matter has to be considered as being indeterminate, acausal and capable of non-localised action at a distance. In other words, it behaves in a manner almost diametrically opposed to the way our 'common sense' tells us the world is.

We now have a problem in conceptualising how these two realities – classical and quantum – are related one to the other. One tendency is to see the quantum reality as a 'special case' of the classical, a sort of breaking down of the 'normal' rules at the very small scale – that essentially everything in the universe behaves according to classical laws except for the very, very tiny, which moves to the beat of a different drum. Or, more accurately, that it moves to no beat at all, but just seems to follow a random, unpredictable path.

Some physicists, however, suggest that it is more appropriate to think of the classical, large-scale world as a 'special case' of the quantum reality. In this view, the quantum characteristics of indeterminacy, acausal and non-local interactions 'collapse' into the world of localised, determined and causal behaviour that we are more familiar with. It is possible, then, to think of a vertical line, or connection, between a deeper, underlying quantum reality which expresses itself in a classical reality at the level of the apparent (Figure 7.7).

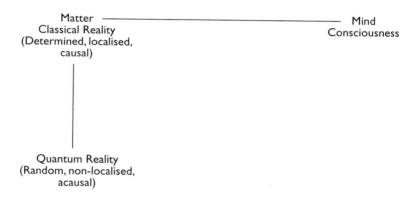

Figure 7.7 The connection between quantum reality and classical reality

Why and how this 'special case' arises, what the nature of this connection is, whether it is continuous or not, remains a puzzle which science is seeking to explore.

The findings of quantum theory to date also include the strange phenomenon of a seeming relationship between the conscious, observing mind and quantum reality. As illustrated by the two-slit experiment and the case of Shrödinger's cat, it seems that how we set up an experiment and how we observe; and, indeed, the very act of observation, alters reality itself. In the diagram we are building, we have to add another connecting line between the conscious mind and quantum reality (Figure 7.8).

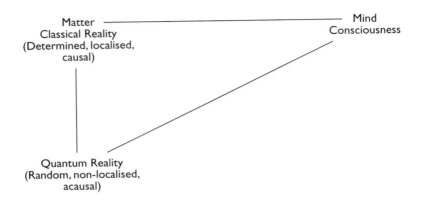

Figure 7.8 The connection between the conscious mind and quantum reality is added

The aspect of mind which has now been included is consciousness. Indeed, ever since the observer began to be a factor in the behaviour of quantum reality, the nature of consciousness has been seen as an appropriate and necessary subject of enquiry for scientists. Whilst physics has been groping to explore the unknown in matter, and been led into a consideration of psyche, so depth psychology has been feeling its way into the unknown in psyche which, largely through Jung, has raised questions about its connection to matter, for the psyche is viewed as comprising not just consciousness, but also the unconscious. For Jungians, this means not just the personal unconscious, but also the collective unconscious.

The concept of the personal unconscious is common to all analytical thinking. It assumes that the aspects of ourselves of which we are aware concerns only part of the whole psyche. The unconscious aspects of ourselves, by far the larger part, is quite literally unknown to us. What it comprises is largely dependent on our personal development, yet continues to act upon and affect us throughout our adult life. According to Jungian thought, the collective unconscious is an even deeper layer of the psyche which is common to all. The archetypes can be considered as organising principles or shapes which exist by virtue of our being human. Whilst these archetypal patterns may be mediated differently depending on the personal developmental experience of each individual, the overall shapes or patterns are the same for all humans.

The Concept of the *Unus Mundus*

The essential collectivity of this layer of archetypal experience means that each psyche is connected one with the other. However, Jung also postulated that the connection extends into the animal kingdom as a whole and so to matter itself. In 'Mysterium coniunctionis' (*CW* 14), he speaks of the *unus mundus* whereby we are each rooted in 'one world' at the level of the 'psychoid' which connects mind and matter in one universe.

On the diagram a fourth factor can be added which might offer a vital dimension when thinking about the dynamics of the system as a whole (Figure 7.9).

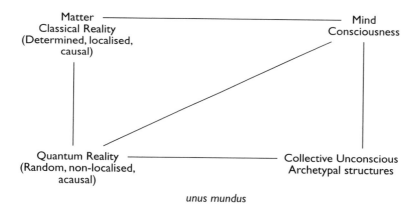

Figure 7.9 A fourth factor is added

It is possible to think of this *unus mundus* as a general reality which 'collapses' into consciousness as experienced by the individual. Consciousness, then, becomes a 'special case' of the collective unconscious. Whilst this strata cannot be known directly, its forms can emerge into awareness via the symbol and the archetypal image. Consciousness experiences such forms through an awareness of pattern which is perceived as *meaningful*. It is this capacity to recognise pattern and find meaning which may be the central characteristic when we contemplate the place of consciousness in the whole scenario.

By including all four elements in the diagram, and keeping to the difficulty of imagining the whole, we might prevent ourselves slipping back into a quasi-classicism by breaking the problem up into its constituent parts. It is tempting to see the left vertical line as the domain of the physicists, and the right as that of the psychologists. If we are to sustain the idea of the whole, it is the connections between the parts which become as important to explore as the parts themselves. As Jung says:

> This brings us a little nearer to understanding the mystery of psychophysi-cal parallelism, for we now know that a factor exists which mediates between the apparent incommensurability of body and psyche, giving matter a kind of 'psychic' faculty and the psyche a kind of 'materiality', by means of which the one can work on the other ... If we give due considera-tion to the facts of parapsychology, then the hypothesis of the psychic aspect must be extended beyond the sphere of biochemical processes to matter in general. In that case all reality would be grounded on an as yet unknown substrata possessing material and at the same time psychic qualities. (*CW* 10, para. 780)

There have been several attempts in science to imagine this 'unknown substrata'. Such explorations are in their infancy, each has its critics, and none can be thought of as the answer. As the questions have been formulated here, it seems useful to consider the ideas of David Bohm. In *Wholeness and the Implicate Order* (1980) he suggests that we could consider there to be an underlying *implicate order* within which, as the term implies, everything is *enfolded*. Bohm refers to the hologram as a model, in the way that any part of the hologram has the whole enfolded within it. The observable material world is an *explicate order*, which unfolds out of the implicate and where things and events have a specific location in time and space. The implicate order, and its unfolding, is dynamic. It is, according to Bohm, a *holomovement*:

> [E]verything is to be explained in terms of forms derived from this holo-movement. Though the full set of laws governing its totality is unknown (and, indeed, probably unknowable) nevertheless these laws are assumed to be such that from them may be abstracted relatively autonomous or sub-totalities of movement (e.g., fields, particles, etc.) having a certain recurrence and stability of their basic patterns of order and measure. Such sub-totalities may then be investigated, each in its own right, without our having first to know the full laws of the holomovement. (Bohm 1980, p. 178)

The criticism of these ideas is essentially that they suggest a 'hidden variable', a ghost in the machine, a force or field which determines how 'things' behave. This contradicts the findings of quantum theory which indicate that matter behaves in a random, acausal manner. However, it does provide a framework for imagining the manner of connection between what is hidden and what is apparent in the physical world, as well as the connection between what is hidden in both the physical and the psychic, for both can be seen as enfolded within the holomovement. There are also parallels with Jungian notions of the relationship between the archetypes of the collective unconscious and consciousness, and with the psychoid *unus mundus*.

When pondering on the relationship between mind and matter, the dominant view in the West has been the Cartesian division between the two. It is important to recognise that this view is deeply ingrained, for we can think we are moving away from it, but remain trapped. We may take a materialist position, locate mind in the brain and hence see mind as created by matter. Or we can take the idealist view that places mind as primary and capable of creating and altering matter. What we need is a way to see mind and matter as in relation to each other. If we follow Bohm and Jung, then the classical universe we experience and can observe and measure, is a particular unfolding into an explicate order. Consciousness may be seen as a particular unfolding of the collective unconscious into the explicate psyche. The collective unconscious is, like quantum reality, enfolded within the implicate order or the holomovement.

Returning to the diagram, we see that quantum theory describes, though it does not explain, the diagonal link between consciousness and quantum reality (Figure 7.10). We do not know how, but this link seems to be central in the unfolding into the explicate order we know as classical reality. The other connecting diagonal, between this explicate order and the collective unconscious, might offer a way of thinking about phenomena such as the

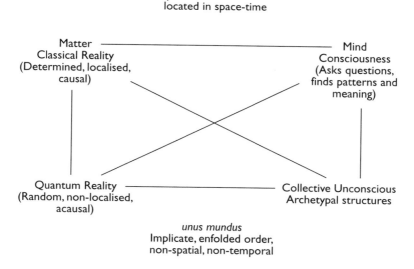

Figure 7.10 The linkages of quantum theory

paranormal and synchronicity. Whilst these areas remain dubious for many, and certainly need considering with a suitably critical eye, they are areas of enquiry which are increasingly being explored by science itself.

The *unus mundus* as conceptualised by Jung has parallels with Bohm's idea of the implicate order. The archetypal structures within the collective unconscious are not located in time or space. They are not manifest and cannot be known directly by the conscious mind, but they may be made explicit via the image. Jung stresses that archetypes are

> *forms without content* representing merely the possibility of a certain type of perception and action. When a situation occurs which corresponds to a given archetype, that archetype becomes activated. (*CW* 9i, para. 99)

This concept of something which describes possibilities has resonances with Shrödinger's wave function, which encapsulates the idea that the photon or electron, or whatever quantum entity, exists in a multitude of possibilities until it is observed. The archetype can be seen as a form – an implicate, enfolded set of potentialities – until something occurs at the conscious level which engages it. Perhaps this activation of the archetype, its appearance in a particular image or symbol, or its manifestation as neurosis, is similar to the collapse of the wave function by the observation by the conscious mind.

Conclusion

It is important to remember the acausal, indeterministic and random nature of quantum events. Electrons may move from one energy state to another in an entirely random way. There seems to be no invisible hand guiding them in any particular direction. This randomness is intellectually and emotionally hard to grasp because it means that, at the most fundamental level, there is no guiding light directing the show. Instead, we have a multitude of possibilities. It is tempting to fill this vacuum with an idea such as the archetypes, yet Jung himself was insistent that these represent psychic probabilities. If we can resist this temptation to reify the potential situation, a more interesting possibility arises. If, rather than causing events, either material or psychic, archetypes organise the events in such a way that the conscious mind can make meaning, then we have a possible framework for conceptualising the horizontal connection between psychic and physical phenomenon at the level of the psychoid, and between collective unconscious and consciousness.

The key word here is *meaning*. When discussing his thoughts on synchronicity, Jung stressed the acausal nature of the relationship between the inner psychic state and the external events which seem connected when these events are experienced as more than mere coincidences. It is not that the inner state *causes* the events to occur, or vice versa; rather, it is the meaning that consciousness finds in these occurrences that gives significance. It is what 'fixes' the event. If you think about a friend you have not seen for a long time and then that day you bump into another friend that you had not been thinking about, you make no connection between the thought and the event, for it has no meaning or connection for you. However, if you bump into the friend you *had* been thinking about, then the 'coincidence' will strike you. It will have a certain significance which you might even call synchronistic. The connection is noted by you; there is an experience of a perceived pattern that feels significant.

None of this explains what consciousness *is*, but it does focus on what consciousness *does* and the role its activity might play in the whole. Whilst a key characteristic of consciousness is that it is aware of itself and of the physical world, its essential position in the holistic dynamic may be to ask questions, for quantum theory tells us that it is how we set up the experiment and how we observe – in other words, what questions we ask of nature – that seem to affect the answer that nature gives us. The meaning we make of these answers determines what the next question will be. It is in consciousness that the psychic probability of the archetypal becomes located in time and space through the symbol. It becomes substantive and meaningful. This requires of consciousness a readiness to engage with the archetypal, to ask questions. It may be that the drive to enquire is not only an intrinsic aspect of the nature of the human mind, but also a central feature in the way in which the probabilities of quantum reality unfold into the material reality with which we can then engage.

References

Bohm, D. (1980) *Wholeness and the Implicate Order*. London: Routledge.
Davies, P. (1989) *The New Physics*. Cambridge: Cambridge University Press.
Mansfield, V. and Spiegelman, J.M. (1989) 'Quantum mechanics and Jungian psychology: building a bridge', *Journal of Analytical Psychology*, 34(1), January.

Suggested Reading

Davies, P. (1983) *God and the New Physics*. London: Penguin.
Gribbin, J. (1990) *In Search of Shrödinger's Cat*. London: Corgi.
Gribbin, J. (1995) *In Search of Shrödinger's Kittens*. London: Phoenix.
Johnson, G. (1995) *Fire in the Mind: Science, Faith and the Search for Order*. London: Viking.
McEvoy, J.P. and Zarate, O. (1996) *Quantum Theory for Beginners*. Cambridge: Icon Books.
Peat, F.D. (1987) *Synchronicity: The Bridge Between Matter and Mind*. New York: Bantam.
Zinkin, L. (1987) 'The hologram as a model for analytical psychology', *Journal of Analytical Psychology*, 32(1), January.
Zohar, D. (1990) *The Quantum Self*. London: Bloomsbury.

8
Recent Developments in the Neurosciences

Hester McFarland Solomon

[A]s in the case of Newtonian physics in relation to quantum physics, the limits of our conventional way of thinking are exposed under special conditions. Attempts to explain in causal terms the relationship between the brain and subjective consciousness create these special conditions ... The relationship ... is one of correlation, not one of cause and effect.

Solms (1997), 'What is consciousness?', pp. 700–1

Introduction

This chapter will seek to show how the archetypal and developmental analytic traditions can be correlated theoretically through an examination of the recent literature on the implications of early intersubjective exchanges, especially those between the infant and its mother, and their neurobiological correlates, the neural and biochemical consequences of such exchanges.

Traditionally, Jungian and psychoanalytic approaches to thinking about the self have been broadly conceived according to two separate, overarching perspectives. Jungian archetypal theory has understood the self as organised from birth to unfold according to universal, inherent deep structural patterns of experience that correspond more or less to the instinct-driven stages of the life cycle. This view was based on Jung's theory of the archetypes, the innate mental structures that organise much of our perception, emotion and behaviour throughout the whole of life. As the personal self passes through the various instinctually driven developmental stages from infancy through to maturation and death, its passage through this life cycle is charted and represented mentally via a number of archaic and typical images and symbols, drawing, for example, from the image of the Divine Child through to the image of an integrating mandala – from our beginning to our ending. On the other hand, the psychoanalytic developmental model offers a structural view of the self which is also instinct driven, with a greater emphasis on the organising principle of the psychosexual stages and the tripartite structural model of id–ego–superego, as charted by the structure of internal objects and their processes of formation, and the varieties of conscious and unconscious mental exchanges and ways of relating that inform the contents of the developing mind. Psychoanalytic theory has tended to focus on an understanding of the complex nature of the early developmental processes of the self, while Jungian analytic theory has focused on the rich area of creative and symbolic activity, and collective and cultural pursuits, that are especially relevant to the second half of life.

It takes only one imaginative step to perceive that each approach has roots firmly embedded in the other, and that to consider the infant without its organising (archetypal) mental foundations and processes, or archetypal processes without their infantile, primitive derivations and early relational vicissitudes, encourages a false and unhelpful dichotomy. Just as psychoanalyst Mark Solms has found it lamentable that 'Freudian metapsychology has become insulated from scientific progress [in the physical sciences] ... [as much as] contemporary cognitive scientists are hampered by a woefully inadequate acquaintance with the knowledge gained by psychoanalysts ... about the inner workings of the human mental apparatus from the viewpoint of subjectivity' (Solms 1997, pp. 701–2), so it is equally woeful that in many quarters the Jungian and Freudian analytic traditions have become so insulated from each other that they are unable to profit from the depth understandings each has achieved in respect of the self and its experience and perception of its internal and external reality.

Although Jung was mapping the imaginal contents of the psyche through his enquiry into the archetypal patterns and images that are the mental representations of the instincts, this does not mean that the imaginal contents of the psyche have a direct correspondance to the mind's neural substrate. To the extent that mental imagery corresponds to the biological, and therefore ultimately to the genetic, bases of the self, these internal images and figures can be understood to arise from the meaning the mind makes concerning the universal instinctual experiences in which the self participates. This is not to say that the neurological hardwiring of the self gives rise to specific mental images. The importance of the new psychoneurobiological research is that it provides morphogenetic evidence of the impact of the universal patterns of the meaningful affective relationship between infant and caregiver that influence the processes underlying the growth and development of the infant's brain. To the extent that archetypal imagery is implicated in these mental representations, there is a direct link between this research and archetypal theory. It is important to reiterate, of course, that no rationale is being offered here for positing the neurobiological basis of archetypal imagery or of the archetypes themselves. It is the instincts that derive from neurobiological and neuro-chemical sources, and it is the instincts that give rise to the archetypal components of the psyche. In this respect, it is interesting to note that, as early as 1905, Freud addressed a similar distinction between the explanatory principles of cause-and-effect and those of correlation when he emphasised that, in arranging the facts of psychopathology philosophically, he was 'making no attempt to proclaim that the cells and nerve fibres, or the systems of neurones which are taking their place to-day, are these psychical paths, even though it would have to be possible in some manner which cannot yet be indicated to represent such paths by organic elements in the nervous system' (Freud 1905, cited in Solms 1997, p. 702).

Another crucial point of convergence between the findings of the new neu-robiology and Jungian theory and practice concerns the advances in Jungian thinking regarding the understanding of early states and processes of mind. Once the post-Jungian developmental school, through the work of Michael Fordham and his colleagues in London, amplified by the rich field of infant observation studies, grounded the understanding of the bases of mental life in the early internal experiences of the real child, it was possible to link theoret-icaly the archetypal roots of the psychic functioning of the real child to information arising from clinical practice that included transference and counter-transference phenomena and the symbolic activity of the psyche in transformation (see Solomon 1997). Thus it was possible to conceive of an integrated matrix consisting of traditional archetypal Jungian psychology and what had until then remained within the purview of the psychoanalytic study of the early mind that could lead on to further theoretical integrations. We are currently in a position to elaborate the understanding of this archetypal/devel-opmental self. A particularly fertile area of future research involves recent findings from the new field of psychoneurobiology.

Psychoneurobiology and the Intersubjective Perspective

Recently, and particularly within the last decade, research into the develop-ment of the brain of the neonate has pointed to the crucial role of the nature and quality of the affective interactions between infant and mother. These interactions trigger the unfolding of the biochemical and neurobiological processes that underpin the maturation of the cortical and subcortical structures of the infant's brain *post partum*. These neural structures are respon-sible for the self's capacity for eventual self-regulation, underpinning the social, affective and cognitive development and identity of the self. What has emerged is that the two major brain growth spurts which occur during the first two years of life are dependent on what psychoneurobiology researcher Allan Schore calls 'the system of reciprocal mutual influences' (Schore 1996, p. 60) within the infant–mother dyad.

During the first growth spurt, at about ten to twelve months, the finely tuned reciprocal patterns of interactions between the infant and mother/caregiver ensure appropriate amounts of neurochemical production via the generation of optimal levels of arousal, leading to the infant's eventual attainment of the first early capacity for self-regulation of affect. The mother uses her ability to appraise and match through finely attuned responses the infant's internal states, and the infant learns to initiate through its 'spontaneous gestures' (Winnicott 1960, p. 145ff.), especially through eye contact, physical movements, sounds and cries, the regulatory responses of its mother. The second spurt of neural development, at around eighteen months, is preceded by a period of dramatic change in the infant–caregiver patterns of relating, with a direct impact on the production of related neurochemical substances. As the child becomes increasingly self-motivated, driven by curiosity and the uninhibited pleasures in respect of its own internal body and psychic experiences, the mother takes on an increasingly socialising role, restricting uninhibited freedoms and pleasures and thereby inducing feelings of shame and humiliation. These unexpected inhibiting responses from the one who had been experienced as a finely (narcissistically) attuned caregiver give rise in the child to states of physiological and psychological distress which are not immediately resolved by previous patterns of dyadic attunement. A shift from high to low arousal states in the form of a shame reaction is activated and persists until repair and recovery can again be attained through carefully timed reattunements. In a thorough and detailed analysis of current neurobiological and psychological research findings, Schore demonstrates that 'these experiences trigger specific psychobiological patterns of hormones and neurotransmitters, and the resultant biochemical alterations of brain biochemistry influence the experience-dependent final maturation of the orbitofrontal cortex' (Schore 1996, p. 72).

Schore's contributions (1994, 1996) have been especially valuable in pointing out that 'the self-organization of the developing brain occurs in the context of a relationship with another self, another brain ... [who thus acts] as an external psychobiological regulator of the "experience-dependent" growth of the infant's nervous system' (Schore 1996, p. 60). In other words, the formation of the attachment bond between infant and caregiver gives rise to experiences which shape 'the maturation of structural connections within the cortical and subcortical limbic areas that come to mediate socioaffective functions' (Schore 1996, p. 60). This is a skin-to-skin, brain-to-brain (in particular, right-hemisphere-to-right-hemisphere) model of psychological development, in which the quality of attunement between mother and infant, which both members of the dyad play an active role in creating, is as crucial to the infant's ongoing neural development (as supported by its own bio-chemical processes), as it is to its psychological development. To the extent that the infant contributes actively in these exchanges, the infant directly par-ticipates in the formation of its own neural structures. This has important implications for the theoretical understanding of the nature of the self and of object relationships, as well as for clinical treatment techniques when the 'system of reciprocal mutual influences' has led to pathogenic rather than adaptive results, when exchanges in the early dyadic functioning have led to things going wrong.

This evidence of the mutuality of exchanges leading to the growth of the infant's brain at the neural and biochemical levels provides hard data that has direct relevance to the findings from analytic and developmental studies, including infant research and clinical reports of work with children and adult patients, concerning the critical interactive role of infant and mother in ensuring a stable and secure foundation for the self to develop and grow. For example, in the closely associated field of developmental psychology, Daniel Stern (1985) has been at the forefront in mapping the impact of the varieties of attunement responses, or their failures, that form the basis for the psy-chosocial development of the infant through the relationship with its earliest caregivers. The concept Stern calls 'RIGs' – repeated representations of dyadic infant–mother interactions – denotes generalised patterns created through the interactions in the early dyad. These constitute the basic units of the core self, integrating the multiple experiences the infant has with its caregiver into an internalised affective pattern that is fully established preverbally. Stern's devel-opmental work has close affinities with Schore's psychoneurobiological findings concerning the system of reciprocal mutual influences.

Furthermore, in the early days of his investigations regarding questions of analytic technique, Jung gave a clear indication of his appreciation of the importance of the analyst's own capacity to be subjectively responsive to the impact of the relationship with the patient (*CW* 16, para. 163). Since that earlier time there had been a relative dearth of work relating to the importance of the real relationship between the two partners in the analytic dyad, in particular regarding the crucial role of the analyst's subjective responses to the patient. However, recently there has been a spate of analytically oriented pub-lications concerning various aspects of what is being called intersubjectivity and the interactive field (for example, see the work of Aron (1996), Kumin (1996) and Stein (1995)). In a recent in-depth study, psychoanalytical marital psychotherapist James Fisher (1999) closely examined the vicissitudes of dyadic relating in respect of marital couples. Fisher usefully distinguishes between narcissistic and genuine forms of object relating, which he sees as a fundamental human tension characterised by ongoing oscillations between the two states. Indeed, in Chapter 12 of this volume, I attempt to show how the capacity to attain an ethical attitude is predicated on the quality of early intersubjective exchanges. Recently there has been a marked increase in interest in the conditions and effects of the analytic relationship on both partners, examining the impact of intersubjective states on each member in the analytic dyad.

In this connection we should observe that Schore bases his analysis of the therapeutic implications of the two-stage model of neural growth in the infant on the principles of attachment theory as applied to adult psychotherapeutic treatment (Bowlby 1969). Although this is clearly a worthwhile clinical pursuit, it has, nevertheless, kept Schore's enquiry to some degree, but not wholly, separate from many of the intricacies of psychoanalytic theory; in particular, the detailed understanding of those subtle intersubjective and often pre-verbal communications that are called projections, identifications and projective identifications, involved in the laying down of internal worlds and their transformations across the life cycle. This separation is not necessary, in the same sense that Solms (1997) found that the parcelling of the psychoanalytic and neuroscientific enquiries was wasteful of human knowledge, and can be bridged theoretically and clinically through acts of translation, such as that attempted in this chapter.

For example, there is a common link that can be clearly identified between attachment theory and archetypal psychology in the importance the two traditions have placed on the work of the first ethologists (for example, Tinbergen 1951, Lorenz 1977). Ethologists demonstrated the crucial role of the first attachment object in the ongoing development of the self. It is the first attachment figure that triggers the onset of developmental processes, the quality of which informs the next cycle of development and the nature of the self's identity, including its capacity for relating (see Solomon 1991, for a discussion of this connection). The notion of 'critical periods' for the emergence of self-regulating systems via the influence of various attachment modalities is common to ethology, clinical psychology, depth – including archetypal – psychology and the complex processes at work in the psycho-neurobiological development of the infant. This in turn has implications for psychotherapeutic theory and technique.

The Two-stage Developmental Model

The two stages of the model proposed by Schore correspond roughly to the first and second years *post partum*, and are differentiated according to the type and quality of attunement required from the caregiver to ensure the infant's optimal development. In the first phase, the development of 'mutually attuned synchronized interactions is fundamental' (Schore 1996, p. 61). The mother and infant are delicately matched and resonate with each other, each transforming the other's emotional and physical states for optimum pleasure and receptivity. Stern (1985) has called this 'vitality' or 'crescendo' affects, components of overall 'affect attunement'. The mother's very presence and the quality of her interactions with the infant ensure that

> the mother is not only acting as a modulator of the child's current affective state, she is also regulating the infant's production of neurohormones and hormones that influence the activation of gene-action systems that program the structural growth of brain regions [specifically of the right hemisphere orbital pre-frontal cortex and limbic systems] essential to the future socioemotional development of the child. (Schore 1996, p. 61)

The maturation of this brain area is more or less completed at the end of the first year of life and is predicated on the fine-tuned responses between mother and infant which ensure that the infant has internalised basic self-regulating physiological and psychological mechanisms at the core self level by this time.

In the second stage, there is a significant change in the relationship between infant and caregiver, who now increasingly takes on the role of an agent of prohibition and socialisation, arousing generally more negative, as opposed to generally more positive, feelings within the infant. Shame inducement and the tension and negotiation around the restoration of positive affect, mean that the regulation of attunement exchanges becomes more complex, problematic and stressful. Different neurochemical, hormonal changes and neurobiological growth spurts in the frontolimbic and orbitofrontal cortex accompany these behavioural affective developments, culminating in the structural changes in the brain of the growing infant during the neural growth spurt of the last half of the second year (Schore 1996, pp. 71–2). Through these two critical stages of neural growth, with their cognitive and emotional correlates, the patterns of affect regulation are laid down as the core foundations of the self.

Psychotherapeutic Implications of the Brain–Brain Model

The two-stage developmental and interactive model as outlined by Schore has implications for analytical theory and clinical treatment techniques in a number of ways. Schore argues that if those socioaffective, attunement exchanges that would lead to optimal neural development in the first two years of life have not occurred, then real functional deficits will result, leading to variations in self and attachment pathologies. Moreover, these exchanges need to arise at two critical periods in infancy when changes at the biochemical and neurobiological levels occur which underpin important changes at the psychological level, thus shaping the emerging self's capacity for self-regulation at both the physiological and psychological levels of functioning (Schore 1996, p. 75). Early forming psychopathology is a 'disorder of attachment [which] manifests itself as failures of self and/or interactional regulation' (Grotstein, cited in Schore 1996, p. 80). In archetypal terms, this would include the activation in a dyadic setting of archetypal potentials that may not be adequately 'humanised' by optimal attunement exchanges. Instead, they remain unmitigated in their power to polarise affects, thus impairing the capacity for self and interpersonal regulation.

On the other hand, within a treatment context, affects that were hitherto not triggered developmentally or regulated interactively within an attachment framework might be thought of as unactivated potentials that require an appropriate analytic setting in which to unfold, including variations in the quality of the practitioner's responses to the patient appropriate to the level of functioning that might trigger their activation. This notion may at first glance appear to be advocating a similar approach to the erstwhile advocacy that the analyst should provide the patient with 'a corrective emotional experience', that is, as a corrective to transference expectations (Alexander 1961). However, this latter notion fell from favour when some practitioners took it to mean that the analyst could and should seek to provide a compensatory, often a parenting, experience via some concrete enactment (perhaps, to take a hypothetical example, offering a cup of tea when the patient was reliving painful memories of lack of parental sources of nourishment). This approach was criticised for having deteriorated into concrete enactments, and having become detached from symbolic meaning and analytic understanding.

The two-stage developmental model advocated by Schore suggests a different treatment technique. Starting from the idea that structural deficits at the neurobiological level result from early failures in dyadic regulation, an alternative view is provided regarding the inclination to understand negative events in the consulting room solely in terms of different forms of unconsciously motivated attacks on analysis, such as negative therapeutic reaction, unconscious resistance, disavowal, and so on. Instead, the understanding based on the two-stage developmental model would revolve around identifying functional deficits and provide optimal conditions for neurochemical and neurobiological correction via appropriate interactive attunements in the analytic relationship. This would include the provision of different types of empathic care through monitoring and moderating excessive or limited arousal states. These are the states which originally have led to the creation of a 'growth-inhibiting environment that produces immature, physiologically undifferentiated orbitofrontal affect regulatory systems' (Schore 1996, p. 82). Schore offers a long list of such 'empathy disorders' (Trevarthen and Aitken, cited in Schore 1996, p. 83), including autism, schizophrenia, mania, unipolar depression, phobic states, post-traumatic stress disorder, drug addiction, and borderline and psychopathic personality disorders (Schore 1996, p. 83), all of which belong to the territory of depth analytical work.

Crucial to this therapeutic understanding is the central role of the analyst's involvement in the patient's processes, his or her personal capacity to be involved subjectively, such that optimal attunement interactions with the patient can occur. It follows that there is a need for greater emphasis on the overall quality and variations within the analytic relationship than generally has hitherto been allocated in analytic training, which tends to stress the vicissitudes of the transference/counter-transference relationship as essentially a function of the patient's inner world. The implication of the input from the neurobiological perspective concerns the need to factor in the importance of appropriate empathic responses of the analyst. Along with other right-hemisphere-to-right-hemisphere interactions, such as non-verbal psychobiological attunement processes, mirroring and patterning of the subtle transferential and counter-transferential visceral–somatic responses between patient and analyst, this picture points to the necessary inclusion within a thoughtful treatment modality of the analyst's spontaneous, subjectively attuned responses to the patient.

The two-stage psychoneurobiolgoical developmental model implies that the analyst may need to participate differently at different stages in the patient's development, as well as according to the variations in the psychopathologies of different patients. This may include the tone, quality and import of the analyst's responses to the patient's mental and physiological states.

Theoretical Implications

The major theoretical implications of recent psychoneurobiological findings tracking the two-stage maturation of the corticolimbic system of the neonate over two years *post partum* concerns the capacity of that neural system to reproduce, or internalise, working models of patterns of affect regulation arising from the interactive relationship between the infant and its caregiver. These begin with a pre-symbolic sensorimotor capacity, similar to Daniel Stern's concept of vitalising attunements, which would also include Fordham's idea (1985) of the patterns of deintegration and reintegration, through to a symbolic representation in which more complex interactions incorporating negative but reparable experiences are possible. These are seen to happen via the self's expectation that a transformation of a dissonant state to a more comfortable one will occur, an expectation based on experience of things having gone well enough. This has implications for the explanation of the development of the self at the teleological level, but in fact it is a process that happens equally at the biochemical level, thus producing neurological correlates that may have archetypal representations. Thus, at various levels of self-functioning, there are powerful contributions to the ongoing developmental drive of the self, the foundational core of which is seen to be achieved by experience-dependent dyadic interactions via 'a system of reciprocal mutual influences'. Complex, finely attuned right-brain-to-right-brain interactions between infant and caregiver have as their later interpersonal correlates the subtle, interactive and often unconscious processes so elegantly schematised by Jung ('The psychology of the transference', *CW* 16) as an intersubjective matrix, and subsequently developed psychoanalytically in terms of the subtle projective and introjective processes especially encountered in transference/counter-transference phenomena.

A further important implication of this is the idea that the imprinting of the model of self-regulation depends on the quality of the interaction with, and internalisation of, the mother's cortical activity. The mother's internalisation of an appropriate pattern of attunement responses will depend on her own experience of the *post partum* two-stage developmental process via reciprocal mutual influences in her childhood. Hence the importance of generational models in understanding psychopathology cannot be disregarded. The relative balance of excitatory–inhibitory processes which eventually result in the enduring quality of the self have a direct bearing on archetypal theory as providing an explanation of the derivation of mental correlates of instinctual development and how these are then mediated by real experiences. Because the experience-dependent nature of brain development in the neonate, based on mutual affect regulation, is interactive and causes similar development in the caregiver, archetypal potentials unfold in each member of the dyad.

Thus, those psychobiological and interactive states of mind underlying affect, cognition, behaviour and bodily functioning point to the Jungian model of the deep structural bases of dynamic mental functioning, linking instinct and mental representation via archetypal images. We have considered the implications of this for psychotherapeutic treatment requiring involvement of the therapist in the patient's inner processes. This is a brain–brain treatment, especially important in evoking 'hot moments', those enactments and adjustments to them which can subsequently be internalised, encoded and replace the prevailing, more defensive or pathological patterns. The integration of neurobiological and psychological perspectives is essential to achieving a deeper understanding of adult affective and behavioural dysfunction, understood as the result of early failures in interactive and therefore archetypal regulation.

Conclusion

In this short chapter, I have sought to demonstrate that we are now in a position to synthesise archetypal theory, the ethological bases of attachment theory, psychoanalytic object relations theory, and Jungian developmental theory, all of which can now be hard-grounded in the skin-to-skin, brain-to-brain neurobiological interconnectedness between the infant and its primary caregiver. This in turn may provide a holistic account of the primary self and its unfolding processes, which includes the absolute importance in terms of neurobiological development of the quality of the earliest interactions between self and other.

In that intimate space created between the infant and mother, which psychoneurobiologist Allan Schore (1996) has called 'the system of reciprocal mutual influences' and psychoanalyst Kenneth Wright (1991) has called 'the positively amplifying circuit mutually affirming both partners', successive stages in the formation of neurobiological structures that underpin those developmental achievements in psychological functioning, linked with states of self-identity and intersubjectivity, are forged. Thus can we link the current neurobiological and depth psychological understanding of development.

References

Alexander, F. (1961) 'Unexplored areas in psychoanalytic theory and treatment', in *The Scope of Psychoanalysis. Papers of Franz Alexander*. New York: Basic Books, pp. 319–35.
Aron, L. (1996) *A Meeting of Minds: Mutuality in Psychoanalysis*. Hillsdale, NJ: Analytic Press.
Bowlby, J. (1969) *Attachment and Loss. Volume 1: Attachment*. London: Hogarth and the Institute of Psycho-Analysis.
Fisher, J. (1999) *The Uninvited Guest: Emerging from Narcissism towards Marriage in Psychoanalytic Therapy with Couples*. London: Karnac.
Fordham, M. (1985) *Explorations into the Self*. Library of Analytical Psychology, vol. 7. London: Academic Press.
Kumin, I. (1996) *Pre-Object Relatedness*. New York: Guilford Press.
Lorenz, K. (1977) *Behind the Mirror: A Search for a Natural History of Human Knowledge*. London: Methuen.
Schore, A. (1994) *Affect Regulation and the Origin of the Self*. Hillsdale, NJ: Lawrence Erlbaum.
Schore, A. (1996) 'The experience-dependent maturation of a regulatory system in the orbital prefrontal cortex and the origin of developmental psychopathology', *Development and Psychopathology*, 8: 59–87.
Solomon, H.M. (1991) 'Archetypal psychology and object relations theory: history and communalities', *Journal of Analytical Psychology*, 36(3): 306.

Solomon, H.M. (1997) 'The developmental school', in P. Young-Eisendrath and T. Dawson (eds), *The Cambridge Companion to Jung*. Cambridge: Cambridge University Press.

Solms, M. (1997) 'What is consciousness?', *Journal of the American Psychoanalytic Association*, 45(3): 681–703.

Stein, M. (ed.) (1995) *The Interactive Field in Analysis*. Wilmette, IL: Chiron Publications.

Stern, D. (1985) *The Interpersonal World of the Infant*. New York: Basic.

Tinbergen, N. (1951) *The Study of Instinct*. London: Oxford University Press.

Winnicott, D.W. (1960) 'Ego distortion in terms of true and false self', in *The Maturational Processes and the Facilitating Environment*. London: Hogarth, 1972.

Wright, K. (1991) *Vision and Separation: Between Mother and Baby*. Northvale, NJ: Jason Aronson.

Suggested Reading

Jung, C.G. (1946) 'The psychology of the transference', *CW* 16.

Schore, A. (1994) *Affect Regulation and the Origin of the Self*. Hillsdale, NJ: Lawrence Erlbaum.

Solomon, H.M. (1997) 'The developmental school', in P. Young-Eisendrath and T. Dawson (eds), *The Cambridge Companion to Jung*. Cambridge: Cambridge University Press.

9
Creative Life in a Scientific World

Michael Simpson

Introduction

In 1916 Jung argued that creative fantasy is a 'psychic function that has its roots in the conscious and the unconscious alike', and is the 'creative matrix of everything that has made progress possible for humanity' (*CW* 7, para. 490). Redfearn defined the true end of analysis as 'the attainment of an adequate knowledge of the methods whereby a fruitful contact with the unconscious can be maintained' (Redfearn 1977, p. 132).

This chapter looks at the opportunities for creativity in our lives and work that can open up as we relate to the unconscious, described by Jung as 'not this thing or that; it is the Unknown as it immediately affects us' (*CW* 8, between paras 130 and 131, p. 68). Bright (1997), referring particularly to Jung's (1955) paper on 'Synchronicity: an acausal connecting principle' (*CW* 8, paras 816–997) discusses how the transcendent function (*CW* 8, paras 131–93) is activated in what Jung describes as situations which 'have as their common characteristic an element of "impossibility"' (*CW* 8, para. 847), involving meaningful coincidence, fantasy or dream. Out of what may be at times an unbearable conflict between the opposites involved in such experiences (*CW* 8, para. 189), 'psychic non-ego', or the 'objective psyche' (*CW* 18, para. 1720, and next section), activates the transcendent function to prompt in us an image or symbol which might offer the ego a way through to a new level of functioning. This is a way of referring to the leavening work of creative spirit. Samuels et al. (1986, p. 150) state that Jung considered the transcendent function to be the most significant factor in psychological processes, bridging the gulf between the unconscious and consciousness. The symbol produced helps one to bear the conflict, without succumbing to the destructive tendency to be pulled out of it onto just one side (Jung offers an example of this in his work on a dream in *CW 7*, paras 121–40).

In 'The spirit Mercurius' Jung (*CW 13*, paras 239–303) presents and amplifies the fairy tale 'The spirit in the bottle' (Grimm and Grimm 1983, pp. 458–62), as portraying 'the spiritual adventure of a blind and unawakened human being'. In the story, a spirit was released from a bottle by the son of a poor woodcutter. At once huge, the spirit said: 'Whoso releases me, him I must strangle.' But the woodcutter's son kept his head, remembered the tiny containing bottle, and challenged the spirit to go back in, saying: 'I must first know that you really were shut up in that little bottle, and that you are the right spirit.' Fortunately, the spirit was so full of himself that he fell for the trick. He then pleaded piteously to be released for a second time: 'I will do you no harm, but will reward you richly.' On releasing the spirit again, the lad now more consciously used his judgement in deciding to trust to his luck. Because he himself is in the 'right spirit' to participate in a containing relationship with the spirit, the inert glass bottle can be discarded. Then he becomes a healer who can also turn iron into silver, a transforming agent.

Jung ended his paper on Mercurius, 'that two-faced god', by writing that 'every spiritual truth gradually turns into something material, becoming no more than a tool in the hand of man. In consequence, man can hardly avoid seeing himself ... as a creator, with boundless possibilities at his command' (*CW 13*, para. 302). This applies to the two-edged gift of modern science, which lets us materialise ideas to both life-saving and devastating effect. Writing in 1942 (*CW 13*, para. 303), Jung alludes to Nazi Germany, referring to Mercurius as one 'who could have brought light, becomes the father of lies whose voice in our time, supported by press and radio, ... leads untold millions to ruin'. More recently, Symington (1994, p. 52) wrote of the spiritual passion, almost divorced from instinctual humanity, behind the scientific and technical logic of Hitler's 'Final Solution'. In Woodman's (1993, p. 82) words: 'Disembodied spirit is just as tyrannical toward the soul as is unintegrated instinct.' The question for us is whether we are awake enough to take responsibility for our relationship with the spirit of our scientific world.

I was a research scientist for thirty-two years, and I love the openness of science's findings, which can in principle be checked and confirmed by anyone with access to the relevant publications, appropriate apparatus, and technical training. Candace Pert (1998) writes of the pain and passion of living out such love. I am now a psychotherapist trained as a Jungian, and I love my profession's commitment to putting the truth of the patient's experience first, so that nothing – no scientific theory, clinical theory, or religious dogma – comes between him or her and his or her own mysterious being (*CW 12*, para. 32; *CW 18*, para. 6). I would be poorer, and quite possibly dead, without today's scientific technology and without having been in analysis, which respectively may have saved me from rabies and too-open madness.

As an average scientist and analysand I have had my '1 per cent inspiration' of genius, perhaps one new creative idea every other year of each activity. This chapter is written in gratitude for such moments, and the hope that others will have such luck. The remaining '99 per cent perspiration' involves in my case 'minute particulars', like looking into the faces and faeces of between fifty and ninety monkeys daily for twenty-five years, or remembering (or sometimes not remembering) my typical 'hello' as a patient arrives for a session, attending to my counter-transference as I remember or realise that I have forgotten and am challenged for having done so, at the same time trying to eschew the dictates of memory and desire (Bion 1970), all the while deciding what, if anything, to do next.

This chapter is also written out of my growing feeling that the Western scientific and technological attitude is no more able to see beyond its own ken and ability than it was in when Jung wrote about Mercurius, so that we can still read that the answers of science 'contain everything there is' (Humphrey 1995, p. 37). Something so uncontained and boundless can become as intimidating as the spirit out of the bottle. Thus I want to approach science in the spirit of the woodcutter's son, who might say that our knowledge and understanding remain incomplete, so that our ignorance must extend to not yet knowing whether we will ever be able to know everything.

I write also out of my hatred of the ways science can be used in the service of power. Writing in March 1999 in Britain, I see how close Britain, its scientists and its government are to being pocketed by 'biotech' companies seeking to monopolise genetic modification and the pharmaceutical industry. With half an eye, we, the media-consuming public, are perhaps waking to half a sense that what we see of the results of the science involved is muffled and confused. As we become more disillusioned with science as we perceive it via the media, we become less willing and able to remember how science tests findings and hypotheses, and thus more easily fobbed off by those explanations that are quoted in press releases. In its collaboration with big business (Ho 1998), science becomes 'bad' in the worst way of no longer being open for all to see. Such abuse is hateful, whether in the name of profit tomorrow or of fascism in Germany fifty or sixty years ago.

This chapter makes for bumpy reading, because it goes where the tensions between knowing and not knowing, between being open and being hidden or occult, are greatest. Of course, creative science and psychotherapy need their secret protected spaces, but the spaces need to be protected in the name of love, not of profit and power. Research science and psychotherapy work on the edge of the unknown, where things are secret, because partly hidden from us. In so far as they are poorly understood human activities, they use and are at the mercy of processes that seem to work partly by hit and miss, for good or evil, like magic. My thesis is that true creativity begins when we come to the end of our scientific and magical resources.

The Objective Psyche

Jung's term 'the objective psyche' for the unconscious (*CW* 10, paras 312–15), or the unknown as it immediately affects us, is useful because it stands for a view of the unconscious as more than a personal repository of retrievable memories (*CW* 7, para. 103, note 4), with some of its contents possibly coming from elsewhere, from the collective psyche. An 'objective' view is usually taken to be independent of and outside the viewpoint of the viewer: it gives us all the same mile, however long any one of us may find it on a particular day. As 'psychic non-ego', the objective psyche gives each of us, as if from outside, our unmediated and immediate experience (*CW* 8, para. 421; *CW* 11, para. 769; *CW* 12, para. 51). But, because we are inside this psychically given world, we have no 'archimedian point' (*CW* 17, paras 163, 164) outside the psyche from which to take an 'objective' view of what psyche is giving us, and how it is doing so. At times it is given with all the numinous living autonomy and seemingly absolute authority of an inspiration, dream, angel, spirit, God or devil.[1]

In contrast, our ordinary conscious world is very much a mediated one; for example, by shared language and shared conventions embodied in the arts and sciences. Thus science has agreed objective and explicit standards by which to measure distances, or for repeating the experiments in the new physics (see Chapter 7, this volume, by Helen Morgan) and parapsychology (see below) which so challenge our current workaday standards and conventions, forcing us to look at their underpinnings and reminding us that science is the product of the psyche (Bloom 1987, p. 200) as much as vice versa.

Whether we are research scientists or psychotherapists, we are drawn – liking it or not, and knowing it or not – into doing metaphysics. In his 1925 lectures on 'Science in the Modern World', Whitehead (1960, p. 23) described how physics had shaken our understanding of science to its foundations in space, time and causation, and reminded us how, in taking causation for granted, scientists had 'remained blandly indifferent to' David Hume's argument (1739–1740;[2] see also Whitehead 1960, p. 22) that we have nothing but a metaphysical belief or faith (Collingwood 1940) on which to ground the belief in causation that has so enabled us as scientists and technologists. In this context it is notable that there is no entry for 'cause' in Chamber's 1991 science and technology dictionary (Walker 1991, p. 142).

In the materialist and positivist world of much of the twentieth century, 'metaphysics' has often seemed 'irrelevant', like human body products, not allowed to hang messily around the openings between what we can and cannot see. Jung's 'transgression, as inevitable as it was suspect' (*CW* 8 para. 421) led him to see 'metaphysical claims and assertions as mental phenomena' and to regard them 'as statements about the mind ... that derive ultimately from certain unconscious dispositions' (*CW* 11, para. 760). Stevens (1982), Pauli (in Jung and Pauli 1955) and Lorenz (1977) extend this argument; Lorenz doing so along the lines that our particular unconscious views of space, time and causation had survival value for our mobile hunting and hunted ancestors.

For Jung (*CW* 11, para. 459), metaphysical statements, especially dogmatic ones, are archetypal statements, and archetypes are metaphysical because they transcend consciousness (*CW* 18, para. 1229). Jung argues that a materialist is a metaphysician *malgré lui*, and that 'matter' is just as much an archetypal symbol as 'God' (*CW* 11, para. 763), and as ultimately inscrutable as 'mind' (*CW* 8, para. 650).

Archetypes are regarded by Jung as 'fragments of' the objective psyche (*CW* 7, para. 184). Archetypes are seen as factors which interact with conscious-ness to produce statements (including metaphysical ones), dream images and fantasy images, including those arising in active imagination (*CW* 8, para. 403). But archetypes are regarded as irrepresentable as such, and grounded, together with spirit and instinct (discussion in *CW* 8, para. 420), in the psychoid unconscious (*CW* 8, para. 417), which is the irrepresentable place where matter and psyche are ultimately the same (*CW* 8, para. 418).

Because they are metaphysical, Jung's statements about the irrepresentable unconscious of the objective psyche or collective unconscious (*CW* 7, para. 103, note 4) cannot be verified scientifically (*CW* 8, para. 417). Indeed, '[p]sychology is doomed to cancel itself out as a science and therein precisely it reaches its scientific goal' (*CW* 8, para. 429; see also *CW* 7, para. 493). It is thus doomed to position us in the 'impossible' places, inviting us to face the unknown with as much unknowingness as we can bear, and as much empirical knowledge of instinctual and archetypal material as we can muster. There, with the help of the transcendent function, we may find a creative symbol that releases us into what is, 'at bottom, a purely experiential process in which hit and miss, interpretation and error, theory and speculation, doctor and patient, form ... a coming together – and at the same time are symptoms of a certain process or run of events' (*CW* 8, para. 421).

*   *   *

I now turn to a presentation of some relatively recent findings about psi (a neutral term for all ESP (extra-sensory perception)-type and psychokinetic phenomena). *As a scientist*, I believe that many of these findings are now due for serious attention. But I am also aware that until we have a widely accepted framework of scientific principles to accommodate them, the results will seem questionable to many. Others, of course, may easily welcome them as support for their own ideas about body–mind connections. My own guess is that if we can bear the conflicts as we try to accommodate the new findings and the new physics, we may – with the help of the transcendent function, and if we do not first lay waste to our planet as well as our capacity for reflective thought (Bloom 1987) – come to some new view about matter and psyche, to surprise us all. Meanwhile, how such a surprise might affect our understanding of the objective psyche as formulated by Jung remains an open question, which I discuss below.

As a *working analyst and therapist*, I have two more points to make. First, when we follow John Keats into his impossible state of 'negative capability' where we can be 'in uncertainties, mysteries, doubts, without any irritable reaching after fact and reason' (quoted in Bion 1970, p. 125), we are invited to enable meaningful work when we eschew manipulative techniques, whether or not we yet have a widely acceptable scientific understanding of them. From this point of view, science, whether or not it embraces psi, might seem irrelevant. In so far as the symbolic approach 'works' for our patients, the idea of the objective psyche finds its most persuasive outcomes in the consulting room, and my thesis might comfortably skip forward to the section of this chapter headed 'Symbolic Approaches'.

Second, however, enabling the patient to work in an impossible stuck place demands technique and knowledge from the analyst. The idea that the conscious and unconscious attitudes of patient and analyst subtly interweave and affect each other is, in my view, uncomfortably reinforced by the parapsychological experiments and the new physics, as is the consequent demand of the analyst for a still and open attitude. For the sake of this, conscious and disciplined technique, informed by what we can know of all fields of science, must be paramount.

Parapsychological Experiments and the New Physics

Accounts of parapsychological phenomena are given in publications by Broughton (1991) and Eysenck and Sargent (1993). Both books are comprehensively researched and referenced introductions by people who can think rigorously and scientifically. Radin's recent and comparable book (1997) is written out of his deep feeling for the science of these past 150 years. His graphically illustrated statistical re-analyses confirm J.B. Rhine's results with tossed dice (Radin 1997, pp. 134–8), as well as ESP card tests (including Rhine's) conducted between 1882 and 1939 (Radin 1997, pp. 96–8). Jung referred to Rhine's results (in *CW* 8, paras 837, 975–81, for example). When references in this section are not given for particular experiments, they are to be found in Broughton (1991) and Eysenck and Sargent (1993).

Eysenck and Sargent (1993, p. 175) wrote: 'Human beings do seem to use sensory abilities beyond their "conventional" senses. They do seem to influence distant events and objects through will alone.' Such phenomena challenge conventional materialistic views of science and have invited rigorous challenges from sceptics, who continue to spur parapsychologists on to improve apparatus and statistical techniques, so that the analyses of Honorton's 'Ganzfeld' experiments (described below) owe much to his confrontation by and cooperation with the sceptic Honorton (see Broughton 1991, pp. 282–8). Of especial value for all life sciences has been the role of parapsychologists in developing statistical methods whereby results from similar studies, including those separately failing to achieve statistical significance, can be grouped for more powerful meta-analyses (Eysenck and Sargent 1993, pp. 179–82; Radin 1997, Chapters 4 and 5). Thus combining the results from thirty-nine Ganzfeld studies suggests odds of about a trillion to one against their being due to chance (Broughton 1991, p. 288).

Some parapsychologists and physicists are working actively on possible meeting points between parapsychology and quantum mechanics. Broughton (1991) and Eysenck and Sargent discuss some of this work thoughtfully and at length, commenting 'At times, theories and models in sub-atomic physics are so Alice-in-Wonderland that telepathy seems almost banal by comparison' (Eysenck and Sargent 1993, p. 136).

For example, the two-slit experiment (for this and other examples of findings in the new physics, see Chapter 7 by Helen Morgan, this volume) suggests that we participate in producing the observations of quantum mechanics. Thus the conscious act of making an experimental observation can influence the random events in the apparatus directly.

The role of conscious acts of observation of irrepresentable random events in physics experiments seems to parallel Jung's view of the role of consciousness in producing archetypal images in collaboration with the objective psyche, and Jung's concept of the psychoid unconscious seems well fitted to sub-atomic activity. Nearly sixty years ago Jung wrote: 'If research could only advance far enough, therefore, we should arrive at an ultimate agreement between physical and psychological concepts' (*CW* 9ii, para. 413).

Some physicists, however, believe that measurement 'just happens' and is not capable of deeper analysis: 'no further understanding beyond this point' (Eysenck and Sargent 1993, p. 139), or perhaps: 'things become irrepresentable beyond this point'. Other physicists (see, for example, Walker 1987) and parapsychologists (for example, Helmut Schmidt's experiments on 'retropsychokinesis') are actively working on the role of consciousness in observation. The belief that deeper understanding is always possible is a vital prerogative of the research scientist; and anyway it is metaphysical nonsense to believe that we could ever define some 'point' between what can and cannot be known or represented (see also Williams' (1963) argument that the personal and collective 'layers' of the unconscious (*CW 7*, para. 103) are indivisible).

Below I describe examples of four kinds of experiment in psi, to allow us to look at their special challenges to our thinking about the objective psyche, as well as science. There are now many statistically significant replications of each of these. However, we must be particularly wary of experiments in psi, especially new ones, for not all will have been subjected to rigorous scientific scrutiny by peer review, nor will they have been tested for replicability.

Some Experiments in Parapsychology

In a Ganzfeld experiment, a 'sender' views a randomly selected target picture. A 'receiver', after spending thirty minutes in a relaxed state, is asked to decide which of four pictures the sender was looking at. In another version, the receiver reports on the images he or she experiences during the session, and independent judges are asked to match his or her report with four pictures, one being the picture that was looked at by the sender.

'Ganzfeld' refers to a formal technique of 'quieting' normal sensory mechanisms to encourage an inward-looking mental orientation, by using opaque half-ping-pong balls to diffuse the light reaching the subject's eyes, and playing 'white' masking noise. Typically, ordinary receivers with no special gifts in psi can pick the sender's picture on 35 per cent of occasions, rather than the expected 25 per cent chance proportion. Gifted subjects, like Malcom Bessent, could do much better. He could also incorporate into precognitive dreams 'experiences' to be arranged for him by the experimenters a day later. Such experiments suggest that current and future events in a distant mind can affect another mind, without any known connecting sensory mediation between them.

Because they are easier to manage, 'micro-psychokinesis', or micro-PK experiments predominate over macro-PK studies, such as Rhine's dice-throwing experiments, or the observations on people able to move large objects without touching them. In a typical micro-PK apparatus, particles, released by radioactive decay at random time intervals, affect a device so that any one of four light-bulbs lights up briefly. Subjects are asked to concentrate on making one of the bulbs light up more often than on 25 per cent of the occasions to be expected by chance. Subjects can produce small but statistically highly significant biases. Thus it seems that a mind can bias events involving large objects or sub-atomic events without the operation of any known causal mechanism.

In experiments on blind PK, a subject is asked to wish for the 'right' outcome. This has been secretly chosen in advance by the experimenter. In an experiment with dice, the experimenter might have chosen a six as an outcome. The unknowing subjects are nevertheless able to produce the 'right' outcome for the experimenter significantly more often than would be expected by chance. Thus they are able to produce a material effect for someone else even when they are not conscious of what he or she wants.

In another experiment, subjects do not even know that there is any right outcome, whether for the experimenter or for themselves. All they know is that they have been asked to track a slowly moving target. As they do so they quickly discover that they are stuck doing an extremely boring task for what they believe to be a pre-agreed time. However, the experimenter has so arranged the apparatus that PK activity by the subjects can let them escape before then. They prove able to escape early nearly three times as often (20 per cent) as would be expected by chance (7.2%). PK responses, in the service of 'needs' like escaping or making the die fall the 'right' side up, are called psi-mediated instrumental responses (PMIRs). Thus in the escape task, even though the subject is unaware that the set-up allows a way out, his or her unconscious seems to 'know' how to affect the electronic processes inside the apparatus. Stanford (1990) comprehensively reviews such studies.

The implications of such a finding for creative inspiration and for our views of biology are potentially momentous: the objective psyche could 'give', or at least intimate to us, the structure of some aspect of our world, such as the tetravalent carbon atom (see, for example, Jung's discussions in *CW* 9ii, paras 411–12; *CW* 12, paras 327–8), or the ring structure of benzene, as given to Kekulé in a dream image of snakes biting their tails. For us, as well as other creatures, the objective psyche may also enable us to discover adaptive ways through extreme and seemingly impossible dangerous situations. More common are experiences of intuition, in which we 'find that' what one might call a 'book angel' from the objective psyche has led us to pick up just the book we needed, or another kind of angel has made us take our less habitual road home, and thereby avoid an unforeseen hazard. More often than we know, we may go unscathed and unaware where angels fear to tread.

The Roles of Ego and Conscious Wishing in Objective Psyche

Blind intuition in the service of needs is only one way in which objective psyche may operate. In contrast, some healers, characterised by Stratton (1996, p. 26) as 'power healers', can work very consciously towards specific goals (see Dossey 1993, for a more differentiated discussion of healing). For example, Broughton (1991, p. 329) and Eysenck and Sargent (1993, p. 116) describe Braud's (1990) work on subjects' ability to slow the haemolysis of their own red blood cells, drawn and held in hypotonic saline solutions. That people can protect their blood in this way suggests a protective PK effect, perhaps on the cell walls of the red blood corpuscles.

Our minds seem to be acting directly on our bodies when we use visualisation procedures for staying well (see, for example, Naparstek 1995), or for healing ourselves or others (for example, Achterberg 1985). In one instance, a consultant told a critically ill patient with irreparably damaged heart muscle that his heart had a 'wholesome gallop'. Against all expectations the man rallied, surmising that his heart must have a lot of kick in it (Achterberg 1985, p. 79). Thus so-called placebos may alter the images or expectancy that people have about their state of health, and thereby cause profound physiological change (Achterberg 1985, p. 4). Achterbeg and Lawlis (1987, p. 87) quote Jung's 'Psychology and alchemy' (*CW* 12, para. 400): 'The place or the medium of realization is neither mind nor matter, but that intermediate realm of subtle reality which can be adequately only expressed by the symbol.'

Against 'power healing', Stratton (1996, p. 26) contrasts 'empowered healing', where the healer encourages the person to be healed to initiate their own healing; for example, by inventing their own visualisations (see examples in Achterberg and Lawlis 1987, pp. 88–108). This contrast seems to be paralleled by that between classical hypnotic suggestions of particular outcomes and the autohypnotic procedures pioneered by Milton Erickson (see Erickson 1980, Yapko 1990, Sheehan 1995). Following Erickson, one conveys to the patient (or oneself) that his or her (or one's own) unconscious knows how to achieve some outcome, which is not necessarily visualised.

A similar contrast can be found in approaches to prayer, in which the ego seems involved to varying degrees. At one extreme, it is clearly directed ('take up thy bed and walk'), and at the opposite, surrendered in a place of 'unknowing': 'Let go and let God', from Meister Eckehart, or 'Thy faith hath made thee whole', or 'Thy will be done', or 'As long as you know you are praying, you are not praying properly', from Steindl-Rast, cited by Dossey (1993, p. 86). In between comes 'make me good, but not yet'.

If, as the parapsychology experiments suggest, we are 'members one of another' in the objective psyche, then we can also direct harm consciously, or project it unconsciously. In his paper entitled 'Phantasy effects that which it represents', the psychoanalyst Neville Symington (1985) considers that unconscious phantasies can have effects that 'muffle and throttle development'. For him, to 'effect' means to bring about something in the social environment. Thus an obliging and helpful but narcissistic man 'murdered' the individual feelings of his family and was told by his twenty-one-year-old son that he had destroyed his life (Symington 1985), and a twenty-year-old daughter's chronic fatigue syndrome could be seen in part as an effect of her family's wish that she had never been born (Simpson 1997). Von Franz (1986, p. 76) warns us that if we must work in active imagination on our hatred for someone we should talk to a projection of him or her in our minds, and not directly to the living person.

In *Narcissism* (1993) and *Emotion and Spirit* (1994), Symington develops the ethical and spiritual implications of his views. Parallels with and contrasts between his and Jung's views invite extensive study. Jung was in no doubt about the potential for evil of the objective psyche (see, for example, *CW* 9i, para. 393; *CW* 10, para. 413; *CW* 17, para. 309; *CW* 18, para. 1588).

Implications of Parapsychology Experiments for Understanding the Objective Psyche

The processes involved in parapsychology experiments, healing, prayer, hypnosis and psychotherapy are poorly understood. In so far as we are ignorant of these processes, whether through personal ignorance of the available relevant scientific principles, or because none has been formulated, we work as if by magic. Although ego can exploit these processes to some effect for better and/or worse, they also 'work' on us without ego's involvement, as in the blind PK experiments, and sometimes powerfully in processes of projective identification. In projectively identifying with someone, we put some aspect of ourselves – usually what is difficult to accept – into that person, and take a corresponding attitude to that person. Thus a gay male patient could not accept his own capacities for feeling and love, but saw them as abundantly present in his friend, and also saw his friend's eyes as warm and brown. Days later he was shocked, on noticing that his friend's eyes were actually grey-green, into reflecting that it was his own eyes that were brown. He had put his warm feelings, as well as his eyes, into his friend, where they were safe from his own self-destructive attitude. We may also project our unacceptable destructive attitudes into others, often more powerfully the less consciously we do so (see also Ogden 1992, p. 25; Samuels et al. 1986 under '*participation mystique*' and 'projection'). As receivers of projective identification from others, our counter-transference responses are partly enactments or embodiments of what they put into us (see Field 1991, Grotstein 1986, pp. 200–3). Thus we can get caught by our patients' projections in the counter-transference triumphs and catastrophes described by Giovacchini (1989), as we can when we unknowingly exploit our patients' trance states with comments that act on them as hypnotic suggestions. As psychotherapists we use our science and magic to manage the therapy well enough to allow our patients to discover that they can engage in meaningful dialogues with us and themselves. And we need all the help we can get from science. For example, Schore (1994, pp. 448–52) discusses the neuroscience involved as a therapist manages the 'archaic bond' with the patient, repeating the original 'system of mutual influences' that went on between the patient and his primary caregiver (see also Chapter 8 by Hester Solomon, this volume). This has to do with keeping the patient's arousal somewhere between mindless boredom on the one hand, and mindless terror and rage, on the other.

Warnings

So far, discussion of effects like those of minds on matter and bodies has been of processes studied with conventional scientific and statistical methodology. The harder such effects are to explain in terms of widely known and accepted scientific principles (but cf. Walker's (1987) coherent attempt), the more magic or occult they seem. But phenomena like hypnosis and projective identification, which are almost as inexplicable, are widely referred to by scientifically respectable therapists. Even when a treatment such as the use of a neuroleptic drug for a psychosis can be understood in terms of underlying mechanisms (of neurotransmitter systems), we may not understand all its failures, as when neuroleptic drugs fail to help patients who hear voices linked to prior abuse or trauma (Healy 1997, p. 15).

My warnings are connected with my main thesis about the potentially creative symbolic processes that can occur when science, magic or miracles are not enough. Jesus' abandonment on the cross may become for Christians a meaningful symbol of God's incarnation because he, with his prior miracle-working history, will not and/or cannot un-nail himself (see, for example, Spufford 1989, p. 38). Because a symbolic process – like a dream or an I Ching reading – generates meaning for a particular individual in a particular situation, there is nothing a statistical test can say about that meaning. Thus the following discussion is not about scientific proof. Whether therapies or religious lives which make explicit reference to symbolic processes are more effective by some operational criterion of satisfaction, or whether one can use the I Ching to make money on the stock exchange, are questions in principle accessible to science, if we could in practice apply the appropriate double-blind methodology. How this may be done is not considered here.

Symbolic Approaches

Here, I develop a view of the objective psyche as a source of meaning in stuck situations rather than as something to be exploited to bring about effects in a gears-and-levers way. I suggest how we can take a symbolic approach to discover how to question the objective psyche about the attitude we should take to the particular situations we find ourselves in. After doing that, it is up to us whether and how we go on to act in the light of our resulting attitude.

Meanings beyond Causes

Synchronistic occurrences highlight aspects of the symbolic process. For example, Jung described how the persistent tapping of a rose-chafer beetle against his window coincided meaningfully with his patient telling him her dream about a related scarabeid beetle (*CW* 8, para. 982). Synchronicity denotes the meaningful connection between the minds of patient, Jung and the rose-chafer. It can be a source of meaningful archetypal imagery and symbols from the psychoid unconscious (defined above). In this case it 'punctured the desired hole in her rationalism and broke the ice of her intellectual resistance' (*CW* 8, para. 982). While synchronicity was an empirical concept for Jung (*CW* 8, para. 960), a symbol for him is a metaphysical concept, in so far as it is grounded in the irrepresentable psychoid unconscious. In his definition of a symbol as 'the best possible description or formulation of *a relatively unknown fact*, which is none the less known to exist, *or postulated as existing*' (*CW* 6, para. 814), the phrases italicised by me refer to the contents of the objective psyche alongside the more accessible and knowable facts.

In the closing paragraph of his paper on synchronicity, Jung wrote that synchronicity is 'no more baffling or mysterious than the discontinuities of physics', our difficulties in understanding it being due to the ingrained belief in 'the sovereign power of causality' and the improbability of the idea that coincidences have causes (*CW* 8, para. 967).

Science has the paramount statistical convention that we should discard any hypothesis about how things go together if we cannot discard the alternative 'null' hypothesis that they could have come together by chance. This convention is embodied in the conclusions of successful scientific studies, including those in psi, in phrases like 'produce the "right" outcome for the experimenter significantly more often than would be expected by chance' – or 'statistically significant', in other words.

However, synchronistic occurrences are beyond the conventions and methodology of statistical testing, and thus of science. This is because, in conducting statistical tests, one needs to classify occurrences so as to group them to produce big enough numbers for testing. Meaningful occurrences are so unique that they are one-off events. That such events cannot be tested by the statistical methods of science may make them meaningless to some scientists, but it is bad logic to infer that 'not statistically significant' equals 'meaningless', unless we adhere to a fundamentalist position that nothing, meaningful or not, should exist outside science's purview.

It follows that one cannot, as a scientist, say whether or not synchronistic events have causes, and in that sense they are 'acausal'. There can be no scientific judgement about their meaningfulness; it is up to us what sense we make of them. As with the one-off events of synchronicity, so it could be for the unobservable, separate, so-called random events producing the statistical data of quantum mechanics: a single quantum event may form part of a pattern that is as meaningful in the objective psyche as the fall of a single sparrow may be to God.

I Ching Consultation as a Dialogue with Objective Psyche

In consulting the I Ching, the ancient Chinese book of wisdom and divination, one formulates a question and presides over a process which produces a series of events that science would view as random, but which are seen to provide a meaningful symbol directing one to particular texts in the I Ching, which constitute its answer. The events may be six blind selections out of a bag or bowl of coloured balls, or tossing three coins six times (Karcher 1997, pp. 34–6). Thus the result of a particular sequence of eighteen coin tosses is regarded by the I Ching as a sequence uniquely connecting the user with one out of 4096 possible readings.

Jung's approach to the I Ching (described in his foreword to Wilhelm 1984, and in *CW* 11, paras 964–1018), encourages us to think about how the ego and the objective psyche can interact in the paradoxical and impossible process of divination, to which we may resort in stuck situations where the ego feels it has exhausted all possibilities.

Because the I Ching seeks to plot the processes of transformation or change in the individual and in the collective group, it is particularly helpful when we want to discover where in our attitude and situation we are blocked, and where change might be possible. Each act of divination produces a stack, or hexagram, of six lines, each of which may be yin, symbolised as _ _, or yang, symbolised as ___, and each may be either stable or changing. Each hexagram is a symbol, connecting the reader in his or her situation to a particular reading of the texts, which may also provide more symbols, or put the reader in the way of other symbols connecting him or her to the objective psyche; for example, from dreams, active imagination or synchronistic events. Over the whole of the matrix, sixty-four hexagrams are possible. Special readings go with particular changing lines, and changing lines become their opposites, to produce a second hexagram called a change hexagram.

Because each hexagram can change to sixty-four others (including the case when it stays the same because no lines were changing lines), sixty-four times sixty-four, or 4096, readings are possible. For example, in writing this chapter I asked the I Ching for its comments on my attitude to my difficulty in finding the words and tone for what I felt there was for me to say. Hexagram 13, T'UNG JEN or 'concording people' (Karcher 1997, p. 78), resulted.

The Chinese pictorial ideogram for T'UNG JEN portrays a mouth and the sign for cover, echoing my difficulty with words, and pointing to silent understanding and things that fit together (Karcher 1997, p. 78). I felt it recognised that I was trying to write about things that either could not be said or are difficult to convey.

The change hexagram that followed indicates how the situation may change if the reading provided by the first hexagram is taken to heart. In my case there were three changing lines, resulting in hexagram 31, or HSIEN ('conjoining'; Karcher 1997, p. 114). Its ideogram shows a 'broken piece of pottery, the halves of which join to identify partners' (Ritsema and Karcher 1994, p. 362). Karcher's own translation (1997, p. 114) refers to an influence that connects with you and excites you into action, the attraction between the sexes, and to the attraction between the human and the urging of the spirit. Together, the original hexagram and the resulting change hexagram indicated that my difficulty in finding words was recognised, for I was writing about the partnership between myself and the objective psyche whose contents were beyond formulation in words. The readings also underlined that the urgency of the spirit or objective psyche's desire for connection can be as passionate as the attraction between the sexes, requiring a correspondingly passionate response from me.

The readings can be sharply direct. Thus in a subsequent question I half hid a challenge to the I Ching's unknown sage, the spirit of the book, to tell me how he worked, in the half hope of an impressive answer for me to put into this chapter. The first hexagram (number 43) had a moving line, giving me: 'a bad start' ... 'stop now' (Karcher 1997, p. 139). The change hexagram, 'loosening' (number 40), gave me the ideogram for a pointed ivory instrument for undoing knots (hexagram 40; Karcher 1997, p. 132), connecting me with the role of double-binds in stuck situations. Thus the harder one pulls at a stuck knot, the tighter it gets, until one lets go into a more unravelled frame of mind, and lets the pointed instrument of spirit find its way into the knot's spaces, to let unravelling begin.

Meaning and Pattern in Creation

Jung has described how he believed that the 'psychic non-ego' of the objective psyche (*CW* 18, para. 1720) is encountered by so-called primitive people as they talk with spirits, trees and animals (*CW* 17, para. 315). The physicist David Peat (1995) studied the Blackfoot Indians' 'indigenous science' which is 'firmly rooted in the concrete' and also 'enfolded within the language'. This is a language which 'grows out of the spirit of a place' (Peat 1995, p. 85), like a shaman's song, with its sounds of rivers, ocean waves, and bird and animal calls.

The I Ching is rooted in shamanism (Karcher 1997, p. 3), and the use of symbols in 'indigenous science' as described by Peat (1995, p. 257) parallels the I Ching's use of ideograms, whose images point in a figurative way to show how spirit might find its way through the crannies and past the blockages of a 'stuck' situation. Thus attending to the I Ching symbol HSIEN could allow 'conjoining' to sing through us, in the sense that Blackfoot Indians let song sing the singer (Peat 1995, p. 143), the singing for them being the primary reality, and the primal act of creation being with the word (in the Bible, see

John I: 1–16). Peat (1992, 1995) discusses how the direction and form of healing activity could involve subtle energy, as do the form and coherence of a dance performed by a *corps de ballet*. Such energy is a metaphor for the focus and direction of the meaning and expressive passion of the dance. Of course, the processes of healing, and the movements visible in dancing, *also* need energy supplied by the biochemical action of the Krebs cycle in the mitochondria understood by Western science. Doubly blessed are those who can appreciate both the choreography of classical ballet and this amazing biochemical choreography.

An Impossible Profession: Faith, Scepticism and Double-binds in Analysis

Eigen (1981) has drawn attention to the role of 'faith' in analysis, especially in the work of Bion, Winnicott and Lacan. There is a kind of faith that holds us in stuck and impossible places long enough for the transcendent function to work. It may also be what is needed if we are to resonate to the resultant symbols as if to a passionately alive other. This can be seen in Jung's writing in 'Answer to Job' (*CW* 11, paras 553–758). Also to be seen there and also needed is the equally passionate scepticism of Jung's motto 'all very well, but not entirely' (Jung 1963, p. 209); applicable equally to the answers of science and the objective psyche.

In analysing or performing psychotherapy we half absently let our attention 'evenly hover', and we may follow Bion (1970) to a place without memory or desire, where 'O' can 'become' (like archetypal images) but not 'be known' (like objective psyche) (Bion 1970, p. 26). 'It [O] is darkness and formlessness but it enters the domain K' (Bion 1970, p. 26).[3] The ultimate ability to be at one with 'O' is an act of what Bion called 'faith' (1970, p. 32). Bion went on to suggest that events in analysis are therapeutically greater if they are conducive to transformations in 'O'. He also wrote that, 'Too great a regard for what I have written obstructs the process I represent by the terms "he becomes the 'O' that is common to himself and myself"' (1970, p. 28).

We may notice how neatly Bion demonstrates the double-bind in his approach: he catches us in it. If we go back to re-read what he has written, to make sure that we have understood what he meant, we may interfere with letting ourselves do creative analytic work. But we may also want to go back, because perhaps we feel that we did not understand what he meant, because we gave too little 'regard' on first reading. Or we may feel that we had been reading with too much regard, and try to undo that, by reading with less regard. Milton Erickson has also described double-binds which depotentiate consciousness, facilitating a 'creative interaction between the conscious and unconscious' (Erickson and Rossi 1975, p. 424; and case example in Erickson 1980, pp. 374–82).

Jungians may encounter double-binds in striving to know an unknowable Self, as Winnicott (1964, p. 450) noted in his tender review of Jung's (1963) *Memories, Dreams, Reflections*. Winnicott wrote that Jung 'started off "knowing", but [was] handicapped by his own need to search for a self with which to know. At the end of a long life Jung reached the centre of himself, which turned out to be a blind alley.' But is the blindness in the alley? Perhaps we are blind where our conscious rational thinking reaches its limit. For Jung, 'one's getting stuck in a blind alley or in some impossible situation' is the beginning of the symbolic process whose goal is the means by which the situation is overcome at a higher level. This process may be compressed into a short moment of experience, or it may take a lifetime (*CW* 9i, para. 82). And of course it can occur outside of an ongoing 'Jungian' analysis, as in Spufford's powerful contemporary account (1989) of twenty-two years living in the pain of her own osteoporosis and her daughter's terminal cystinitis.

Conclusion

This chapter is about finding the 'right spirit' with which to work with the objective psyche, in our own lives and in science; especially when we find ourselves stuck beyond the help of any known scientific or magical or psycho-therapeutic technique. Implicit in this chapter is the same question for the science we now do and apply.

After introducing Jung's view of the unconscious as objective psyche, in which we are all 'members one of another', and which is the source of creative inspiration for each of us, I have indicated how recent research on the paranormal and the new physics challenges science as we have known it. Thus it presents 'impossible' paradoxes which make it harder to ignore the currently irrepresentable and magic-seeming processes involving matter and psyche. I trust that the recent scientific analyses of so-called paranormal phenomena will spur on the best kind of science, which sticks with the impossible paradoxes forced on it by hard evidence, until some quite new understanding breaks through. I used the I Ching to illustrate how, when we feel stuck beyond reason, magic or science, the symbolic function can connect us with the objective psyche, suggesting that the very 'impossibility' of the method can engender in us a creative openness to the movement of spirit. I suggested that 'double-bind' situations, inherent in most psychotherapeutic situations, can facilitate creative work.

For want of space, I have not considered the 'systems' views in biology that have been developing since the middle of the twentieth century (see, for example, Capra 1996). This suggests a more subtly feminine way of containing the more masculine one-way, come-too-soon thrust of the science of the last century. A truly fertile union needs the give and take of good love-making, and all the help it can get from Hermes' or Mercurius' genius; a word with its roots in *generere*, 'to generate' (Woodman 1993, p. 82; Woodman and Dickson 1996, pp. 3, 4, 221).

It may be for want of adequate respect for human individuals as spiritual beings as well as systems embedded in wider social systems, that medical science remains baffled by such twentieth-century diseases as cancer and schizophrenia. A less serious but nevertheless sometimes agonising example is chronic fatigue syndrome. The challenges it offers medical science and analytical thinking are discussed both jointly and separately by Simpson, Bennett and Holland (1997). Meanwhile, sufferers have the right to complement the not-altogether-certain magic of medical science with the less understood alternatives that suit them best.

Scientists in touch with systems views, and passionately articulating a more balanced approach, also include Lewontin (1991), Ho (1998), Pert (1998) and Damasio (1994). Lewontin (1991) shows how the 'gear-and-lever' mechanistic 'central dogma' (exemplified by the sequence genes produce RNA which produces enzymes which produce proteins which determine our traits), can make it easy for us to accept doing little for people who do less well than us, because the dogma suggests that at root their feckless 'selfish' genes are to blame. We transfer 'causal power from social relations, for which we are all responsible, to inanimate agents that seem to have a life of their own' (Lewontin 1991, p. 5), ignoring the many intricate systems of feedback loops involving the cytoplasm, other tissues, and the external environment, which complicate the one-way process that the dogma depicts so neatly. Ho (1998) extends the argument and the warning. Thus, to 'engineer' bits of genetic material to help us move 'genes' from one species to another where they do not belong, we have to design them to overcome the feedback systems in the cells in which they are to operate. Thereby we may inadvertently engineer genes that actually are selfish enough to get into organisms for which they were not intended, possibly including those contributing to the fertility of soil communities. Here we enter the field of ethics (see Chapter 12 by Hester Solomon, this volume).

Finally, systems views are helping us to see how intimately our brains are embodied (Damasio 1994, p. 118), in the sense that our brains are indivisibly parts of feedback systems extending to the remotest parts of our bodies. For example, the peptide system with its simple messenger 'molecules of emotion' (Pert 1998) connects events in our brains to the immune systems which extend throughout our bodies.

If mind can influence the integrity of heart muscle, or the walls of blood cells, then it could also affect other tissues, including those of our brains.

Thus changes in the cell membranes, on which receptors to peptide molecules are sited, could affect what is communicated by the peptide molecules. Similarly, changes in the surfaces of the walls, axons and dendrites of the cells in our nervous systems, including our brains, could affect our thinking and behaviour. This is how we, as embodied brains and embrained bodies, could also be 'in mind'. This is where body and mind meet, interact, and produce the self.

Notes

1. Jung referred variously to the objective psyche as numinous (*CW* 8, para. 405), and having the living autonomy (*CW* 7, para. 184; *CW* 12, para. 51) and seemingly absolute authority (*CW* 8, para. 311) of an inspiration (*CW* 17, paras 167, 168), dream (*CW* 7 para. 210; *CW* 10, para. 312), archangel (*CW* 18, para. 1505), spirit (*CW* 17, para. 315), God or devil (*CW* 17, para. 309).
2. Hume (1739–40) pursues his argument in a delightfully open and direct manner; see especially pp. 75–94, 134, 177.
3. For Bion, 'O' denotes ultimate reality, which can 'become but not be known'. Thus the analyst does not know the 'ultimate reality' of a chair, or of anxiety, or of time or space, but he can know the events that are 'evolutions of "O"' (Bion 1970, p. 27). 'K' denotes the activity of knowing (Bion 1962, p. 50), especially in the sense of being conscious enough of emotional experience to be able to abstract a statement that will represent the experience adequately. Hence conflicts of 'K' present particular difficulties, like those involved in the relation between our Love ('L') and (Hate ('H'). In allowing us to understand this relationship, 'K' lets us experience informed passion (Freeden 1999, p. 30).

References

Achterberg, J. (1985) *Imagery in Healing: Shamanism and Modern Medicine*. Boston, MA: Shambala.

Achterberg, J. and Lawlis, G.E. (1987) *Imagery and Disease: Image-CA, Image-SP, Image-DB: A Diagnostic Tool for Behavioral Medicine*. Champaign, IL: Institute for Personality and Ability Testing, Inc.

Bion, W.R. (1962) *Learning from Experience*. London: Heinemann.

Bion, W.R. (1970) *Attention and Interpretation: A Scientific Approach to Insight in Psychoanalysis and Groups*. London: Tavistock.

Bloom, A. (1987) *The Closing of the American Mind: How Higher Education has Failed Democracy and Impoverished the Souls of Today's Students*. New York: Simon and Schuster.

Braud, W.G. (1990) 'Distant mental influence on rate of hemolysis of human red blood cells', *Journal of the American Society for Psychical Research*, 84: 1–24.

Bright, G. (1997) 'Synchronicity as a basis of analytic attitude', *Journal of Analytical Psychology*, 42: 613–35.

Broughton, R. (1991) *Parapsychology: The Controversial Science*. London: Rider.

Capra, F. (1996) *The Web of Life: A New Synthesis of Mind and Matter*. London: HarperCollins.

Collingwood, R.G. (1940) *An Essay on Metaphysics*. Oxford: Clarendon.

Damasio, A.R. (1994) *Descartes' Error: Emotion, Reason and the Human Brain*. New York: Putnam, and London: Picador.

Dossey, L. (1993) *Healing Words: The Power of Prayer and the Practice of Medicine*. San Franscisco, CA: Harper.

Eigen, M. (1981) 'The area of faith in Winnicott, Lacan and Bion', *International Journal of Psychoanalysis*, 26: 413–33.

Erickson, M.H. (1980) 'Impotence: facilitating unconscious reconditioning', in *Innovative Hypnotherapy. The Collected Papers of Milton H. Erickson*, Volumes I–IV, ed. E.L. Rossi New York: Irvington Publishers, Inc., Volume IV.

Erickson, M.H. and Rossi, E.L. (1975) 'Varieties of double bind', *American Journal of Clinical Hypnosis*, 17: 143–57 (and in Erickson 1980), Volume I.

Eysenck, H.J. and Sargent, C. (1993) *Explaining the Unexplained: Mysteries of the Paranormal*. New York: Avery.

Field, N. (1991) 'Projective identification: mechanism or mystery', *Journal of Analytical Psychology*, 36: 93–109.

Freeden, I. (1999) 'The claustrum and the reversal of the alpha-function: a case of a post-autistic adolescent girl', *Journal of the British Association of Psychotherapists*, 36: 29–45.

Giovacchini, P.L. (1989) *Countertransference Triumphs and Catastrophes*. Northvale, NJ, and London: Aronson.

Grimm, J. and Grimm, W. (1983) *The Complete Grimm's Fairy Tales*. Reading: Cox and Wyman Ltd.

Grotstein, J.S. (1986) *Splitting and Projective Identification*. Northvale, NJ, and London: Aronson.

Healy, D. (1997) *Psychiatric Drugs Explained*. London: Times Mirror.

Ho, M.-W. (1998) *Genetic Engineering – Dream or Nightmare? The Brave New World of Bad Science and Big Business*. Bath: Gateway Books.

Hume, D. (1739–40). *A Treatise of Human Nature*, ed. L.A. Selby-Brigg. Oxford: Oxford University Press, 1978.

Humphrey, N.K. (1995) *Soul Searching: Human Nature and Supernatural Belief*. London: Chatto and Windus.

Jung, C.G. (1963) *Memories, Dreams, Reflections*. London: Collins/Routledge and Kegan Paul.

Jung, C.G. and Pauli, W. (1955) *The Interpretation of Nature and the Psyche*. London: Routledge and Kegan Paul (first published in German, 1952).

Karcher, S. (1997) *How to Use the I Ching: A Guide to Working with the Oracle of Change*. Shaftesbury, Dorset: Element.

Lewontin, R.C. (1991) *Biology as Ideology: The Doctrine of DNA*. New York: Harper Perennial.

Lorenz, K. (1977) *Behind the Mirror: A Search for a Natural History of Human Knowledge*. London: Methuen.

Naparstek, B. (1995) *Staying Well with Guided Imagery*. London: Thorsons.

Ogden, T.H. (1992) *The Primitive Edge of Experience*. London: Karnac.

Peat, F.D. (1992) 'Towards a process theory of healing: energy, activity and global form', *Subtle Energies*, 3(2): 1–40.

Peat, F.D. (1995) *Blackfoot Physics: A Journey into the Native American Universe*. London: Fourth Estate.

Pert, C.B. (1998) *Molecules of Emotion: Why you Feel the Way you Feel*. London: Simon and Schuster.

Radin, D.I. (1997) *The Conscious Universe: The Scientific Truth of Psychic Phenomena*. New York: Harper Edge.

Redfearn, J.W.T. (1977) 'The self and individuation', *Journal of Analytical Psychology*, 22: 125–41.

Ritsema, R. and Karcher, S. (1994) *I Ching: The Classic Oracle of Change: The First Complete Translation with Concordance*. Shaftesbury, Dorset: Element.

Samuels, A., Shorter, B. and Plaut, F. (1986) *A Critical Dictionary of Jungian Analysis*. London: Routledge and Kegan Paul.

Schore, A.N. (1994) *Affect Regulation and the Origin of the Self: The Neurobiology of Emotional Development*. Hillsdale, NJ: Lawrence Erlbaum.

Sheehan, E. (1995) *Self-hypnosis: Effective Techniques for Everyday Problems*. Shaftesbury, Dorset: Element.

Simpson, M. (1997) 'A body with chronic fatigue syndrome as the battleground for the fight to separate from the mother', *Journal of Analytical Psychology*, 42: 201–16.

Simpson, M., Bennett, A. and Holland, P. (1997) 'Chronic fatigue syndrome/myalgic encephalomyelitis as a twentieth-century disease: analytic challenges', *Journal of Analytical Psychology*, 42: 191–9.

Spufford, M. (1989) *Celebration: A Story of Suffering and Joy*. London: Mowbray.

Stanford, R.G. (1990) 'An experimentally testable model for spontaneous psi events: a review of related evidence and concepts from parapsychology and other sciences', in S. Krippner (ed.), *Advances in Parapsychological Research*, Vol. 6. Jefferson, NC, and London: McFarland & Co., Inc., pp. 54–167.

Stevens, A. (1982) *Archetype: A Natural History of the Self*. London: Routledge and Kegan Paul.

Stratton, E. (1996) *Touching Spirit: A Journey of Healing and Personal Resurrection*. New York: Simon and Schuster.

Symington, N. (1985) 'Phantasy effects that which it represents', *International Journal of Psychoanalysis*, 66: 349–57.

Symington, N. (1993) *Narcissism: A New Theory*. London: Karnac.

Symington, N. (1994) *Emotion and Spirit: Questioning the Claims of Psychoanalysis and Religion*. London: Cassell.

von Franz, M.-L. (1986) *Shadow and Evil in Fairy Tales*. Dallas, TX: Spring Publications.

Walker, E.H. (1987) 'Measurement in quantum mechanics revisited: a response to Phillips' criticism of the quantum mechanical theory of Psi', *Journal of the American Society for Psychical Research*, 81: 333–69.

Walker, P.M.B. (ed.) (1991) *Chambers Science and Technology Dictionary*, Edinburgh, NY: Chambers.

Whitehead, A.N. (1960) *Science and the Modern World*. New York: Mentor.

Wilhelm, R. (1984) *The I Ching or Book of Changes*. London: Routledge and Kegan Paul.

Williams, M. (1963) 'The indivisibility of the personal and collective unconscious', *Journal of Analytical Psychology*, 8: 45–50.

Winnicott, D.W. (1964) Review of *Memories, Dreams, Reflections* by C.G. Jung, *International Journal of Psychoanalysis*, 45: 450–5.

Woodman, M. (1993) *The Ravaged Bridegroom: Masculinity in Women*. (Studies in Analytical Psychology by Jungian Analysts). Toronto: Intercity Books.

Woodman, M. and Dickson, E. (1996) *Dancing in the Flames: The Dark Goddess in the Transformation of Consciousness*. Dublin: Gill and Macmillan.

Yapko, M.D. (1990) *Trancework: An Introduction to the Practice of Clinical Hypnosis*. New York: Brunner/Mazel.

Suggested Reading

Mansfield, V. (1995) *Synchronicity, Science and Soul Making: Understanding Jungian Synchronicity Through Physics, Buddhism and Philosophy*. Chicago and La Salle, Ill: Open Court.

10
The Environment – Our Mother Earth

Jean Pearson

After his break with Freud in 1913, Jung began what he described as his own personal confrontation with the unconscious in order to deal with a period of deep inner uncertainty. He became engrossed in a study of dreams – his own as well as those of his patients – and was particularly impressed by their common mythological content as distinct from those traces of the dreamer's personal life history which lie buried in the personal unconscious. This led him to speculate about the existence of what he called the collective unconscious – a repository of humanity's psychic heritage – which he believed to be as much a living force within us today as it must have been for our forebears.

During this process Jung became aware of a persistent feeling of oppression within him which he sensed did not spring entirely from his own psyche: there was a strong sense of an external reality to it. Gradually this crystallised into images thrown up in visions and dreams which seemed to Jung to be graphic expressions of a problem of world proportions. He felt a growing sense of urgency to comprehend this problem fully.

The process culminated in December of that year when Jung had the following dream.

> I was with an unknown, brown-skinned man, a savage, in a lonely rocky mountain landscape. It was before dawn: the eastern sky was already bright, and the stars fading. Then I heard Siegfried's horn sounding over the mountains and I knew that we had to kill him. We were armed with rifles and lay in wait for him on a narrow path over the rocks.
>
> Then Siegfried appeared high up on the crest of the mountain, in the first ray of the rising sun. On a chariot made out of the bones of the dead he drove at furious speed down the precipitous slope. When he turned a corner, we shot at him, and he plunged down, struck dead.

159

Filled with disgust and remorse for having destroyed something so great and beautiful, I turned to flee, impelled by the fear that the murder might be discovered. But a tremendous downfall of rain began, and I knew that it would wipe out all traces of the dead. I had escaped the danger of discovery: life could go on, but an unbearable feeling of guilt remained. (Jung 1963, p. 204)

Reflecting on the dream after waking, Jung felt that Siegfried represented the Germans who were about to plunge humanity into total war by their imposition of an idea on the world by sheer force of will. He felt that this portrayed a dangerously one-sided tendency within us to live life according to our conscious attitudes alone, ignoring those values in life which are higher than the ego's will. The image of the brown-skinned savage Jung attributed to the primitive life force within us which our ego consciousness had been trying to subjugate. This life force was now turning against us, personified in Siegfried, in an effort to resolve the conflict between consciousness and the unconscious before utter destruction ensued.

This marked the beginning of Jung's search for reconciliation between those warring opposites within our psyche – to find through insight 'a common *modus vivendi*' between them. As part of this search Jung decided to undertake a series of journeys outside Europe, notably to the continent of Africa – the Dark Continent, as it had been christened by the imperialistic West. He was seeking to gain a clearer picture of the European ego-dominated character from an outside perspective – to see the white races and their environment from the perspective of other cultures (Jung 1963, p. 272).

The outcome of these travels for Jung was his discovery that these other cultures had a very different mode of apprehending and relating to the environment. People were much more grounded in their emotional reaction to the world and more easily affected by their inner impulses. Although they were sufficiently orientated in time and space to function adequately in the outside world, they were not given to reflection about themselves. For them, ego consciousness did not have primacy, so their lives lacked the degree of self-direction and will-power which is evident in the West. But what was so compelling about their lifestyle was the intensity and meaning with which it was endowed. Jung described how he found himself falling under the spell of this so-called 'primitive' way of being which he felt had been forgotten in the Western world.

The fascination of this experience is vividly conveyed in Jung's description of a train journey to Nairobi, when, at the first light of dawn, he glimpsed a brownish-black figure leaning on his spear, standing motionless on a jutting rock above the train. He wrote:

I was enchanted by this sight – it was a picture of something utterly alien and outside my experience, but on the other hand a most intense *sentiment du deja vu*. I had the feeling that I had already experienced this moment and had always known this world which was separated from me only by distance in time. It was as if I knew that dark – skinned man who had been waiting for me for five thousand years. (Jung 1963, p. 283)

Through reflecting on experiences like this, Jung felt that he had gained an insight as to the cosmic significance of the development of human consciousness, for although primitive people had lived in what has been described as a participatory harmony with the world around them, their life had been entirely governed by predetermined, instinctive patterns. Jung developed a mythologem for this early stage which has been beautifully described by Erich Neumann, a student of Jung:

The world is experienced as all-embracing, and in it man experiences himself, as a self, sporadically and momentarily only. Just as the infantile ego, living this phase over again, feebly developed, easily tired, emerges like an island out of the ocean of the unconscious for occasional moments only, and then sinks back again, so early man experiences the world. Small, feeble, and much given to sleep, ie., for the most part unconscious, he swims about in his instincts like an animal. Enfolded and upborne by great Mother Nature, rocked in her arms, he is delivered over to her for good or ill. Nothing is himself, everything is world. The world shelters and nourishes him, while he scarcely wills and acts at all. (Neumann 1954, p. 15)

In actual fact, as Neumann points out, such a paradisal state could only have existed during prenatal existence in the womb, for the harsh rigours of living in the outer world must have compelled our forebears very early on to acknowledge its negative aspects. Presumably it was these rigours which must have stimulated the development of a germ of ego consciousness as people struggled to find ways of adapting to this mixed environment. But this developing consciousness entailed a growing awareness of what had been lost – the protective containment within the mother's body – experienced through projection on to the outer world as an original Garden of Eden. This is the stage which is represented through the universal symbol of the uroborus (a snake eating its own tail), thus forming an enclosure within which life is completely self-supporting.

A further stimulus to the development of ego consciousness was, as Jung pointed out, a growing awareness of a profound meaninglessness about this vegetative existence. Originally, Jung suggested, everything was experienced projectively; not only what was actually external, but also what belonged to the inner world (*CW* 11, para. 375). It was only through projection on to the crude material presented by the outer world that people gradually became aware of their own inner processes. This led them to become more conscious of the distinction between themselves as observing subjects and a world which they were beginning to perceive as having an objective reality, separate to themselves. If this had not occurred, said Jung, the world – and humankind with it – might have gone on whirling around in space in a state of primordial darkness until extinction. In other words, the world needed human beings to give it an objective existence, just as human beings needed the external phenomenon of the world to give them a sense of their own existence.

His travels in those 'primitive' cultures he encountered on the African continent enabled Jung to get a glimpse of those instinctive patterns of collective behaviour which he had earlier posited as *a priori* structures in the human psyche, by means of which the human species had survived in and understood the world. These inherited psychic structures, which Jung called archetypes, gave our forebears a means of apprehending and adapting to the world which ensured that each generation did not have to experience the world totally afresh. There was an instinctive awareness of what was dangerous and what was benign in the environment, and hence how best to relate to it.

Developing on from Jung's mythologem, the archetypal patterning involved in the first two years of life – the most formative period in human development – has been described by Jungian analyst Anthony Stevens:

1. First distinguish your mother from yourself and from everybody else at the same time as forming a secure bond with her: then form bonds with the other people around you who will subsequently reveal themselves to you as father, uncle, aunt, brother, sister, grandmother etc.
2. Having formed a bond with your mother and having started to take your place in the family, begin as a matter of urgency to distinguish people and objects that are familiar to you from those which are strange: then approach and socialize with the familiar and withdraw and escape from those which are strange – they could harm you, attack you, or eat you alive.
3. Having registered and acted on these instructions, proceed to explore and familiarize yourself with your immediate environment and, when possible, play with your peers, never straying very far from mother, frequently checking that she is near, and returning to her directly you encounter anything frightening and strange. (Stevens 1982, p. 85)

In view of the centrality of the mother in early childhood it is not surprising that the earliest archetype from which all others developed was that of the Great Mother. We know from cave paintings, stone carvings and other archaeological evidence that the image of an all-powerful goddess figure was prevalent across the entire populated world from the earliest times and must surely have arisen from that great pool of human experience which Jung had brought to light and came to call the collective unconscious. It is generally believed that through this universal image of the Great Mother, people sought to give expression to their relationship to, not so much their human mother, the vessel who had borne them, but, more importantly, that primordial matrix – Mother Earth – out of whose *materia* they were made, through whose abundance their life was sustained and to whose depths they returned in death.

Jung emphasised the polarity of this central archetype of the Great Mother – she who gives light at sunrise only to take it back again at night, and ultimately she who gives life only to take it back again in death. At first this twin aspect of the Great Mother was conceived of as a unity – a paradoxical simultaneity of good and bad – and thus the image possessed enormous numinous power, hence the divine nature ascribed to the Great Mother. Jung used the term 'numinous' to describe that which 'has a dynamic agency or effect not caused by an arbitrary act of will. On the contrary, it seizes and controls the human subject, who is always rather its victim than its creator' (*CW* 11, para. 6). It was only later, through the growing power of ego consciousness, that people began to ponder on this paradox and, in striving to apprehend it, began to differentiate the archetypal image of the Great Mother into its good and bad aspects. Thus, in order to find ways of reconciling this paradoxical experience, the images of the Good Mother and the Terrible Mother arose.

Jung's mythologem continued: this was a decisive event in the history of our relationship with the world in that an awareness of good and bad had developed, which was then experienced projectively through the outer environment. Before this happened, people had lived in an indiscriminate state of coexistence with the world; in a state of *participation mystique*, as the anthropologist Lévy-Bruhl describes it (Lévy-Bruhl 1926). Once the fruit of the Tree of Knowledge had been tasted, consciousness of both the negative and the positive elements of the Great Mother developed. Thus arose a terrifying awareness of helplessness in the face of Nature.

Erich Neumann gives a graphic description of these dualities:

Thus the womb of the earth becomes the deadly maw of the underworld, and beside the fecundated womb and the protecting cave of the earth and mountain gapes the abyss of hell, the dark hole of the depths, the devouring womb of the grave and of death, of darkness without light, of nothingness. For this woman who generates life and all living things on earth is the same who takes them back into herself, who pursues her victims and captures them with snare and net. Disease, hunger, hardship, war above all, are her helpers, and among all peoples the goddesses of war and the hunt express man's experience of life as a female exacting blood. This Terrible Mother is the hungry earth, which devours its own children and fattens on their corpses: it is the tiger and the vulture, the vulture and the coffin, the flesh-eating sarcophagus voraciously licking up the blood seed of men and beasts and, once fecundated and sated, casting it out again in new birth, hurling it to death, and over and over again to death. (Neumann 1955, p. 149)

The emergence of this terrifying awareness must have been another powerful factor in humankind's struggle to develop its own conscious powers, for a more developed consciousness could enable humans more effectively to understand their place in the world about them and to develop knowledge of its naturally recurring patterns in order to predict how to adapt to them and survive. This led to observations about the lunar and solar cycles which governed their days and nights, and the seasonal fluctuations which governed the life of the vegetation on which they fed. All of these patterns, previously experienced indiscriminately as attributes of the Great Mother who governed all, were now differentiated according to their positive or negative valency, as attributes of either the Good Mother or the Terrible Mother.

Jungian analysts Baring and Cashford, in their seminal work on the evolution of the image of the Great Mother Goddess, describe how, once this differentiation had been consolidated in humanity's thinking, the image of another deity began forming, which eventually led to the degeneration of the original image of an all-powerful Mother Goddess (Baring and Cashford 1993).

Baring and Cashford describe how the inextricable linking of life and death, good and bad, which had all been contained in the central archetype, was eventually challenged by the formation of a male deity. This deity was first represented as the Son of the Great Mother, produced parthogenetically, since in the beginning there was no male principle by whom she could have conceived. Mythology describes how the Great Mother went on to marry her Son and how he, in his later guise as the Great Father, was eventually ascribed equal powers with the Great Mother who bore him. This idea is thought to have arisen at the time when early people had begun to realise the part men played in the impregnation of women and the birth of offspring.

This new god was an image which represented humankind's development of consciousness – the coming of light into the world of preconscious darkness. It was projected on to the sun as an obvious symbol of light, who, in his place in the heavens, could see all that happened on earth and thus give mankind the knowledge of how to control life on earth. This was another decisive stage in humankind's relationship with the environment in that people began to conceive of the idea that the power ascribed to the Great Father – the power of logical thought – was capable not only of understanding but also of controlling the powers of the Great Mother – the earth and the instinctual relatedness which she represented – and the Great Father was hence the more powerful of the two deities.

By the end of the Bronze Age, there is evidence that the worship of the Great Mother had been mostly suppressed by the patriarchal culture which was developing through humankind's increasing knowledge of the world around it and its own powers of creation. However, although the all-powerful Great Mother had now been superseded by the Great Father, people did not want to relinquish her benign aspect as the Good Mother. Thus this positive image has remained constant throughout our evolution as a solace and refuge from the inevitable vicissitudes of life which could still not be controlled, whilst her negative qualities in the guise of the Terrible Mother have been repressed into the unconscious, returning to haunt us in nightmares, the fears of contamination by women's sexuality and the belief in malign forces such as witchcraft. Or conversely, by a process of reaction formation, the dark qualities of the Terrible Mother have resulted in the idealisation of women, leading in actuality to oppressive restrictions on the role of women in society.

The subsequent desacralisation of the earth and the world of nature led to the development of an exploitative and controlling relationship to the world. Humankind no longer perceived itself as the steward of nature's bounty, but saw itself rather as nature's master with a divine right to rape and pillage the resources of the world. The three great monotheistic religions which emerged during the patriarchal era – Judaism, Christianity and Islam – all refer to the earth and our corporeal body as 'feminine' aspects to be subjugated to the 'masculine' world of the spirit. So there arose a decisive splitting between what was feminine and conceived of as inferior, and what was masculine and conceived of as superior.

Thus the change in our attitude to the earth was paralleled by a change in our attitude to the body. It was a logical extension to the idea of the supremacy of mind and spirit over the natural world that there developed a consequent denigration of the body, since it was born of woman and the material world. People began to be dangerously cut off from their instinctual core, in which their life had previously been grounded. Body became subjugated to the world of the spirit.

This belief in the superior powers of the intellect constituted another monumental turning point in our relationship with the environment, culminating in the Renaissance during the fourteenth, fifteenth and sixteenth centuries and followed by the Enlightenment of the seventeenth and eighteenth centuries. It was the thrust which gave birth to the emergence of a value-free science from the previous religious and philosophical ways of apprehending the world.

Although the development of science has undoubtedly improved the quality of our life on earth by reducing the impact of disease, hardship and famine, it has become a double-edged sword. We have become so detached from our instinctual roots that, as Jung pointed out, we have lost access to the vigour and creativity which springs from the collective unconscious. With this we have lost a rightful sense of our own place in the order of things and have aspired to become masters of life and death. As the ancients warned, there is a terrible price to be paid for this hubris.

Greek mythology tells the story of Icarus who failed to heed his father's warning. His father had given him the means – wings of wax and feather – with which he could fly up to the heavens; but he also counselled him to keep a course which was not so low that his wings would become sodden in the sea, nor so high that the sun would melt his wings, causing him to plummet to his death. This is a story that symbolises the gift of ego consciousness – humanity is given the means with which to ascend to the world of the mind – but it also symbolises the necessity of not becoming too far removed from the world of matter and the instinctual life, grounded in the unconscious. If this warning is not heeded a disastrous degree of ego inflation ensues and humankind is destroyed.

Jung described this as the vital question of modern humanity's existence. He asked: 'How long can human beings be successful without falling victim to their own pride or, in mythological terms, to the jealousy of the gods?' (Jung 1964, p. 106).

We now have the power to destroy the world through nuclear war and have brought its natural resources close to extinction through our greedy pursuit of material wealth. We now also have the power to create life in a test tube. As a result, we are tempted to believe we are gods of the universe. In psychological terms, our ego has become identified with the archetype of wholeness which Jung designated as the Self – 'the god in us'. Jungian analyst, Edward Edinger describes Jung's concept of the Self as embodying 'all the attributes traditionally assigned to God. These include immortality, universality or totality, omnipotence, omniscience, divine vengeance or wrath, and supreme central value' (Edinger 1960, p. 6).

But how inevitable is it that in our hubris we will proceed to destroy the planet which sustains us and thus destroy our own existence? Jung's study of alchemy, the forerunner of modern chemistry, has shown us how early scientists had managed to combine their thinking with a deeper, more instinctual wisdom derived from our archetypal roots in the collective unconscious. Science had not yet become an amoral way of dominating the natural world; rather, it was a way of relating to it in the hope of sharing in its wisdom. As Anthony Stevens writes:

Before Alchemy became Chemistry all knowledge had a sacred dimension: unlike modern scientists, alchemists revered matter and expected to be spiritually transformed by their work ... the alchemist's intention extended far beyond mere greed for gold: what he wanted was not so much to enrich his coffers as to transform his soul. (Stevens 1982, p. 281)

How, then, does Jung's view of the split between the intellect and the natural world and the consequent inflation of the ego help us to reorientate ourselves to the world in which we live? Obviously, we cannot close the lid on the Pandora's box we have opened and simply revert to the stage of preconscious harmony with the world. As Jung said, this would be a return to a state of pure barbarism. Rather it is a question of balance – finding a balance between valuing the discoveries that modern science has made but also remaining in touch with the values which we have inherited through the collective unconscious. Jung said:

Science is the tool of the Western mind, and with it one can open more doors than with bare hands. It is part and parcel of our understanding and only obscures our insight when it claims that the understanding it conveys is the only kind there is. (*CW* 13, para. 2)

Jung finds a solution to this question in the concept of individuation. This is an inner process whereby we can find a way of healing the split between the 'masculine' world of ego consciousness and the 'feminine' world of unconscious relatedness. This entails giving up our over-valuation of rationality and its consequent ego inflation (the Siegfried part of ourselves) in favour of using those very powers of consciousness to rediscover our archetypal roots (the brown-skinned savage in us) and, in so doing, to take up a conscious attitude of revaluing this instinctual wisdom. It must be emphasised that this is not to suggest the development of a romanticised return to Nature, but rather a conscious marriage of the warring opposites within us, producing a synthesis which is more than the sum of the two parts.

To describe this reconciliation, Jung adopted the term *coniunctio* which the alchemists had used to describe the symbolic union of unlike substances leading to the birth of a new element. He saw *coniunctio* as an archetype of psychic functioning – an image of the wholeness to which we are eternally striving – and a conscious relatedness between mind and body and the feminine and masculine principles within.

Today, as we look around us, there are several hopeful indications that this process is under way. The ecological movement is educating our awareness of our dependence on the life of our planet and is having some degree of political effectiveness in the world arena in terms of conservation of endangered species, protection of the rain forests and the atmosphere, and the reduction of pollution. It has been said that probably the greatest benefit of the space travel programme has been to give us a glimpse from outer space of the fragile beauty of our planet – a shining blue orb suspended in the blackness of infinity. We have been made conscious of how much this beautiful world now depends on our conscious commitment to its survival and, equally, how dependent we are on the planet for our ultimate survival as a species.

A new branch of science is also emerging, known as the new physics, which is addressing the previous split in scientific thinking between subject and object. Although at first there had been a necessary differentiation between subject and object which had enabled ego consciousness to develop, this differentiation had culminated in a science whereby the scientist, as the observing subject, felt empowered to treat the object – the *materia* which was under observation – as inanimate, without soul. The new physics, however, is showing quite decisively that this split is untenable. The findings of microphysics and astrophysics have superseded the universal application of Newtonian physics, demonstrating that the universe can only be understood fully as an intricate web of relationships between particles rather than as a system of causes and effects. Thus the old split between observer and observed is no longer tenable, for there is a relationship between them which fundamentally affects the outcome of observation. (See this volume, Chapter 7 by Helen Morgan and Chapter 9 by Michael Simpson, for a further elucidation of these ideas.)

At the individual level, there is a growing awareness of our need for psychological well-being, and counselling, psychotherapy and psychoanalysis are becoming more widely accepted as a means to this end. Beginning with Freud and his 'discovery' of the unconscious, we have come to realise the ill-effects of instinctual repression on both psyche and soma, and this has contributed to a more positive attitude towards the individual's body and its instinctual needs. We are now acknowledging our need to take care of and respect our physical well-being and to discover the optimum environment in which it can be nurtured. One could say that a healthy body narcissism is emerging.

Finally, and perhaps most importantly, the feminist movement, with its roots in the emancipation of women earlier in the twentieth century, has obliged us to confront the existence and value of a complementary 'feminine' way of relating to life. It has shown how, through a fruitful coexistence, the masculine and feminine principles within the psyche can be reconciled – a synthesis that Jung foresaw would lead to greater wholeness of life for everyone.

References

Baring, A. and Cashford, J. (1993) *The Myth of the Goddess: Evolution of an Image*. London: Arkana Penguin.

Edinger, E. (1960) 'The ego–self paradox', *Journal of Analytical Psychology*, 5(1): 6.

Jung, C.G. (1963) *Memories, Dreams, Reflections*. London: Fontana.

Jung, C.G. (1964) *Man and His Symbols*. London: Picador.

Lévy-Bruhl, L. (1926) *How Natives Think* (translated from the French by Lilian A. Clare). London: Allen and Unwin.

Neumann, E. (1954) *The Origins and History of Consciousness*. London: Karnac.

Neumann, E. (1955) *The Great Mother*. Princeton, NJ: Princeton University Press.

Stevens, A. (1982) *Archetype: A Natural History of the Self*. London: Routledge and Kegan Paul.

Part IV
Jungian Thought and the Religious, Ethical and Creative Spirit

11

Jung and Christianity – Wrestling with God

Christopher MacKenna

My life-work is essentially an attempt to understand what others apparently can believe.

Jung, *Letters*, Volume I, p. 502

Introduction

Jungian thinking about Christianity has largely been determined by the pattern of Jung's own life and work, which he regarded as indivisible: 'The way I am and the way I write are a unity. All my ideas and all my endeavours are myself' (Jung 1963, p. 14). If we want to understand Jung's approach to Christianity, we will have to see how it arose from the circumstances of his life.

This raises delicate issues. Jung's life began with two major dislocations. First, he was born into a rapidly changing cultural situation in which it seemed, to many thoughtful observers, that Christianity had become obsolete. Jung's father, a Swiss Reform pastor, was a victim of this cultural crisis, and his loss of faith convinced Jung of the inadequacy of traditional Christian formulations. Second, there was domestic dislocation caused by the trauma of Jung's parents' marital problems and his mother's mental illness. These troubles had a profound impact on the way Jung internalised his early Christian teaching.

Stein (1985) has argued that Jung's attitude to Christianity was fundamentally that of a psychotherapist towards a patient. His aim was to help this ailing religion overcome its internal splits, repressions and one-sided developments. I believe that this is an important, but one-sided, view. Western Christianity has indeed suffered from the dualism inherent in Augustinian, Cartesian and Newtonian thought, and Jung was acutely aware of the damage this causes to the psyche. His psychology is a powerful attempt to transcend the gulf between subject and object.[1] However, I believe that Jung was also a victim of his own culture and upbringing. In my view, it was because of the continuing and unreconciled splits in his own inner world that Jung was unable to appreciate the potential of Christian symbols to hold together the opposites (God and humanity, good and evil, spirit and matter, masculine and feminine) which were his lifelong preoccupation. In order to substantiate this claim I will examine Jung's intellectual response to the nineteenth-century crisis of faith, brought about by the impact of scientific materialism. I will look briefly at the way in which Jung reinterpreted Christianity, and then explore three critical moments in his early development. I will attempt to show that the splits which then developed in Jung's inner world, as a defence against intolerable mental pain, had a lifelong effect on his struggles with the God of Jewish and Christian tradition, and that they underlie his most passionate work 'Answer to Job'.[2]

The Nineteenth-century Crisis of Faith

The Protestant Churches were particularly vulnerable to the escalation of scientific knowledge in the nineteenth century. In the heyday of the Reformation, new learning, especially in the field of biblical studies, enabled reformers like Luther and Calvin to rediscover crucial elements of early Christian experience, and to use this as an authority with which to criticise the teachings of the medieval Church. But by the end of the nineteenth century a more rationalistic approach to textual criticism had grown up within the Protestant Churches which was threatening to undermine the authority of the Bible, upon which those Churches were founded. Lacking an adequate religious and intellectual foundation, more stress tended to be laid on the need to believe, as if this could be achieved by an act of will. The result was often harmful. The Swiss theologian Karl Barth (1886–1968) suggests that, having lost touch with the essentials of their faith,

> it is not an accident if the psychology particularly of the theologians and churchmen of the period (and especially about the turn of the 19th century) has for the most part been one of a pronounced lack of humour, of weariness and depression, even of melancholia. Could it have been otherwise when for all the subjective solidity of the effort they were fighting for a kind of lost cause? (Barth 1956, p. 351)

Barth might have been describing the father, of whom Jung wrote:

It was the tragedy of my youth to see my father cracking up before my eyes on the problem of his faith and dying an early death. This was the objective outer event that opened my eyes to the importance of religion. (Jung 1976, p. 257)

Jung's life-work can be seen as an attempt to reclaim the possibility of a genuinely religious vision in face of the forces which caused his father to despair.

In later years, Jung sometimes wrote as if the religious dimension of his psychology was merely the product of his empirical researches:

my whole psychology derives from immediate experience with living people, ... My experience is a medical one in the first place, and only in the course of many years I began to study comparative religion and I also studied primitive psychology, partially in the field. But all that came afterwards and it merely substantiated what I had found with modern individuals. There is not one single thing in my psychology which is not substantiated essentially by actual experiences. (Jung 1973, p. 465)

What this claim to detached empiricism conceals is the fact that, during the years when he was training as a doctor, Jung was also involved in a passionate philosophical search to find some way of describing religious experience so that it could be defended against the assaults of nineteenth-century scientific materialism.

How intensively Jung pursued this quest only became clear in 1983, with the publication of the 'Zofingia Lectures' (Jung 1983) – five talks given by Jung to his student confraternity (1896–99) – which contain the seeds of much of his later thought. Here we find him expounding the philosophy of Kant, for Kant had shown that our sense organs, on which scientific materialism depends for knowledge, can never give a complete account of all that really is (Jung 1983, paras 195f.). Jung claims that, far from having objective knowledge of the external world, all we really have are subjective impressions in the psyche. As he later put it: 'there is, in a certain sense, nothing that is directly experienced except the mind itself' (*CW* 8, para. 623). At the same time, coupled with this neo-Kantian ontology, derived through Schopenhauer and Hartmann (Jung 1983, para. 199), Jung professed a mystical form of Christianity:

We should and must interpret Christ as he himself taught us to interpret him ... as a prophet, a man sent by God ... The mystery of a metaphysical world, a metaphysical order, of the kind Christ taught and embodied in his own person, must be placed centre stage of the Christian religion ... (Jung 1983, para. 287f.)

To the end of his life Jung stoutly maintained his Christian identity, once calling his position 'a sort of left-wing Protestantism' (Jung 1976, p. 334). Such a statement conceals the complexity of his relationship with Christianity. According to his autobiography, by 1912 he realised that he no longer lived by the 'Christian myth' (Jung 1963, p. 195). Then, during the years of the First World War, as he struggled to contain the eruption of the primitive contents of his inner world triggered by the loss of his relationship with Freud and his intensive study of mythology, he survived through discovering the value of simply accepting the contents of his dreams and fantasies, *as if they were direct communications from God.*[3]

Unburdened now by any doctrinal allegiance to the Christian Church, Jung's unconscious feelings about life gradually took shape, not without resistance, until, in 1916, they spontaneously burst forth in the form of *The Seven Sermons to the Dead* (*VII Sermones ad Mortuos*) (Jung 1916) (see Chapter 13 by Dale Mathers, this volume). Now Jung had a 'myth' which gave a sense of meaning to *his* life: Man, the creature, is the one in and through whom all the infinite and unreconciled possibilities of life – everything that exists in the 'absolute realm' (he called it the 'Pleroma') – are destined to find expression. This was a 'religious' position to which he could give whole-hearted allegiance. It endowed his life with a sense of meaning which he had never found in the dogmatic teaching of the Christian church.[4]

Jung is always punctilious in maintaining that the symbols which arise from the unconscious – as he saw them, the raw material of our religious experience – are not to be confused with the God of metaphysical belief:

> I have no religious or other convictions about my symbols. They can change tomorrow. They are mere allusions, they hint at something, they stammer and often they lose their way. They try only to point in a certain direction, viz. to those dim horizons beyond which lies the secret of existence. (Jung 1976, p. 290)

But this did not prevent Jung from having his own thoughts about the nature of the reality which lies at the heart of existence.

Writing to his close friend and colleague Erich Neumann in March 1959, Jung wrestled with the question as to whether the creator is conscious of himself (an article of faith in orthodox Judaism and Christianity). Relying on his theory of archetypes, Jung was able to posit 'an all-pervading, latent meaning' in the universe, 'which can be recognised by consciousness'.[5] But he could not subscribe to the idea of a conscious creator giving birth to creation.

> Why should the Creator stage-manage this whole phenomenal world since he already knows what he can reflect himself in, and why should he reflect

himself at all since he is already conscious of himself? Why should he create alongside his own omniscience a second, inferior consciousness – millions of dreary little mirrors when he knows in advance just what the image they reflect will look like? ... [God] is just as unconscious as man or even more unconscious. (Jung 1976, p. 495f.)

What is remarkable about this passage is the extreme narcissism of the picture which Jung projects of God. Jung might have imagined a creator moved by love and generosity; a God who possesses being longing to bring others into being with whom to share God's life and joy. Instead, there is something terribly solitary about this vision of a creator, for whom creation could mean nothing more than the creation of 'millions of dreary little mirrors' in which to reflect himself (I am reminded of Jung's reported comment, handed down in Jungian oral tradition: 'Thank God I am Jung, and not a Jungian!'). This projection is in stark contrast to the Christian vision of God as a Trinity of persons-in-relationship; of God creating because it is of the nature of love to be creative. What we are encountering here, I believe, is a painful glimpse of Jung's narcissistic isolation – the long-term effect of childhood trauma on his inner world.

Reinterpreting Christianity

According to Jung, Christianity no longer reflects the unconscious life of modern men and women. He believed that the Christian image of God must die before a more adequate image can be born, which he thought would differ from the old Christian image in three crucial ways. First, the distinction between natural and supernatural will disappear: it no longer makes sense in the new scientific age. Second, the masculine traits of the Christian God will be transformed by the inclusion of the feminine principle. Third, the picture of a God of light and goodness will be transcended, so that darkness and evil can find their place in God. In Jung's terms, the Trinity must become a Quaternity through the inclusion of three disowned elements – matter, the feminine, and evil – which he believed Christianity had relegated to its shadow (*CW* 11, paras 243–85). Jung reached these conclusions through the study of Gnosticism and alchemy, esoteric traditions which, he thought, expressed the repressed areas of the Christian mind.

The importance to Jung of his ideas about religion can be gauged by the fact that, whereas psychoanalysis offers a theory of individual psychological development, Jung offers a developmental theory of the Western (Christian) mind. As a psychiatrist he was fully aware of the importance of individual psychopathology; but his prime concern was with healing our collective cultural dislocations. In his view we are sick (indeed, his father was the first important example for him of this sickness), not just because of our early environment, but because we are out of touch with the instinctive wellsprings of unconscious life. The great religions once regulated our intercourse with these unconscious depths; but religions breed dogmas which ossify. As a consequence, change must come. Analytical psychology, as Jung called his school of thought, is 'religious' in that it helps us carefully to attend to the symbols which emerge from the unconscious, receiving them as believers have traditionally received the voice of God. As Iris Murdoch has written, 'Jung is not just offering a therapeutic tool, he is offering what he feels to be a relevant and necessary metaphysic' (Murdoch 1993, p. 135).

Jung's conviction that Christianity must change to comprehend the insights of Gnosticism would have startled the early Christian fathers. At a theological level Gnosticism and Christianity are poles apart, but it is instructive to review their conflict from the perspective of developmental psychology. A comparison of their creation stories will serve as an example. The biblical story begins with hope, and alienation only occurs after Adam and Eve have become fully conscious of their existence. In the Gnostic myths, the world itself 'is the product of a divine tragedy, a disharmony in the realm of God, a baleful destiny in which man is entangled and from which he must be set free' (Rudolph 1983, p. 66). These stories reflect different orders of early mental experience, before and after the self has been securely differentiated. The Gnostic view – with its endless emanations, in place of the one creator God – corresponds to primitive states in which there is little perceived difference between self and other; and in which the other (the parent) is already deeply disturbed. The biblical story suggests a scenario in which the self has achieved unit status in relation to a good object before the principal trauma occurs.

I believe that Jung's difficulty in appreciating the developmental differences underlying Gnosticism and Christianity stemmed from unresolved disturbances in his own psychological development, which crucially affected the way in which he internalised his earliest Christian teaching. These disturbances are clearly illustrated in three episodes which Jung describes in his autobiography, *Memories, Dreams, Reflections* (Jung 1963), to which I will now turn.

Fractured Vision

(a) Lord Jesus

When Jung was three, his mother returned from several months in hospital and taught him an evening prayer. It began, 'Spread out thy wings, Lord Jesus mild, and take to thee thy chick, thy child.' Jung said it gladly: it eased his fear of the night. He then describes an internal process by which 'comforting Lord Jesus' became associated with the undertaker's men whom he had seen at work in his father's churchyard. In this way, being 'taken' by 'Lord Jesus mild' acquired the terrible undertones of being buried (Jung 1963, p. 24f.).

By his own account, Jung was an inquisitive child who had evinced a lively curiosity in death. At the age of three he found the sight of blood and water, coming from the corpse of a drowned boy, 'extraordinarily interesting'. Slightly later he was 'fascinated' by the sight of a dead man, and by watching a pig being slaughtered – which his mother thought 'terrible' (Jung 1963, p. 30f.). Yet now he feared for his life. Where did these disturbed and disturbing thoughts come from? Jung presents his changed feelings about Lord Jesus as if they were the outcome of his own thoughts. This seems improbable, given his age and otherwise robust attitude to death. Much more likely, I believe, is that Jung picked up his mother's feelings along with the words of the prayer.

We know too little about Emilie Jung. One of the many important details which Jung omits from his autobiography is the fact that he had an elder brother, Paul, born in August 1873,[6] who lived only a few days (Ellenberger 1994, p. 662). What effect did little Paul's death have on his parents? Jung tells us that the months his mother spent, apparently in a mental hospital in Basle, 'presumably ... had something to do with the difficulty in the marriage' (Jung 1963, p. 23). We might imagine – if Jung's silence about Paul reflects his parents' inability to speak of him – that the effects of unresolved grief became an obstacle between his mother and father, filling his mother with fearful and ambivalent feelings about the well-being of her second child. Had not Paul already been 'taken' by Lord Jesus, and buried? I believe Jung's complicated and frightening feelings about Lord Jesus were created as his mother unconsciously transferred to him her own inexpressible, and perhaps unthinkable, distress about Paul's death, coupled with her consequent hostility to God.

A darker thought is that the words of the prayer, '*take* to thee ...' may have expressed a death wish towards her child. In his autobiography, the first case Jung describes under Psychiatric Activities is that of a young mother, admitted to the Burgholzli suffering from melancholia. Using the Word Association Test, Jung discovered that she had murdered her two children (1963, p. 135f.). As a child he was deeply disturbed by his mother's divided personality. She could be 'most companionable and pleasant', but also 'archaic and ruthless' (Jung 1963, pp. 65, 67). Sadly, not least for Jung's later attitude towards Christianity, there was no therapist present to analyse the parental anxieties through the dreams or fantasies of the child. Instead, a deep split between the fear and love of God began to form in Jung's mind, with no safe container in which his ambivalence could be contained.

(b) The Underground Phallus

Jung had his first remembered dream between the ages of three and four. Beneath a meadow near his home he found a stone-lined chamber, entered through a green curtain. Before him, on a low platform, was a gold throne on which something like a tree trunk was standing. The 'tree' was made of flesh. It did not move, 'yet I had the feeling that it might at any moment crawl off the throne like a worm and creep towards me. I was paralysed with terror.' At that moment, Jung heard his mother calling, 'Yes, just look at him. That is the man-eater.' He woke scared to death and unable to sleep for many nights (Jung 1963, p. 26f.). The dream haunted Jung for years. Only much later did he realise that he had seen a phallus, and it was decades before he connected this 'man-eating' phallus with the rituals of cannibalism.

Jung used this example from his autobiography to introduce his concept of the archetype: an inherited, universal predisposition to experience and conceptualise life in certain almost stereotypical ways. He is overwhelmed with amazement by the fact that, as a child of three or four, he dreamed of a phallus almost as he might have seen it in an Indian temple. He instinctively sets this 'underground God' alongside, and in secret opposition to, 'Lord Jesus' (Jung 1963, p. 28). What Jung does not provide is any commentary on why *this* archetypal image should have appeared in his dream just then, or why it should so obviously exist in opposition to Lord Jesus.

Jung's own theory suggests that archetypal images appear in dreams in order to compensate a one-sidedness in our conscious attitude to life. What meaning could this dream have for a three-year-old? In another place, Jung wrote: 'The dreams of small children often refer more to the parents than to the child itself' (*CW* 17, para. 106). The phallus is a symbol of masculinity. But 'Father', to Jung, meant 'reliability and powerlessness' (Jung 1963, p. 23). From what Jung tells us, we know his parents were sleeping apart during his early school years (Jung 1963, p. 33). This, and the fact that his only younger sibling was not born until he was nine,[7] suggests that sex was a difficult subject for them, and perhaps for the whole family. For example, at the age of six, Jung remembered being berated, by an aunt who had taken him to Basle Museum, just for looking, in wonder, at some classical statues. Only when she cried out: 'Disgusting boy, shut your eyes!', did Jung see that the figures were naked (Jung 1963, p. 31). If – in Jung's Christian family – sexuality was wrapped in a powerful taboo, 'not to be named', then Lord Jesus could certainly have nothing to do with *that*. Sadly, the rich, earthy, erotic symbolism of the Bible, where Yahweh is pictured as the husband of his people, and Jesus comes as the bridegroom to claim his bride 'made ready for her husband' (Revelation 21: 2), seems to have found no expression in Jung's parents' marriage, nor in their religion. Not surprising then if, in accordance with Jung's idea of psychic compensation, the repressed instinctual ingredient erupted in his dream.

A three-year-old cannot act as a container for his parents' sexuality. But Jung's dilemma was even greater. The phallus dream also reflects his own nascent sexuality. In his discussion of the dream, Jung explained the green meadow and green curtain as symbols of 'the mystery of Earth, with her covering of green vegetation' (Jung 1963, p. 28). In personal terms, the dream is about his mother and Jung's instinctive longing to penetrate her 'underground'. He is terrified when he thinks the phallus may move towards him, fearing it will devour him. He cannot bear the excitement caused by the thought of uniting with the phallus, of becoming sexual. Very likely, he was also terrified of being 'eaten' by his mother's feelings.

This interpretation is confirmed by one of Jung's earliest memories of his mother, the only memory he retained of her when she was still 'a slender young woman', before she became 'older and corpulent' (Jung 1963, p. 32). He was out walking with her and she was wearing a dress 'of some black stuff printed all over with little green crescents'. They came to a Catholic church. Moved by curiosity, which was mingled with fear, Jung slipped away from his mother and peered through the open door into the interior.

> I just had time to glimpse the big candles on a richly adorned altar ... when I suddenly stumbled on a step and struck my chin on a piece of iron. I remember that I had a gash that was bleeding badly when my parents picked me up. My state of mind was curious ... I felt I had done something forbidden. 'Jesuits – green curtain – secret of the man eater ... So that is the Catholic Church which has to do with Jesuits. It is their fault that I stumbled and screamed.' ... For years afterwards I was unable to set foot inside a Catholic Church without a secret fear of blood and falling and Jesuits ... Not until I was in my thirties was I able to confront Mater Ecclesia [Mother Church] without this sense of oppression. (Jung 1963, p. 32)

Linked together, these impressions and associations are what Jung later called a 'feeling toned complex' (*CW* 8, para. 18). Here is a collection of incredibly powerful memories, glimpses, half-thoughts and wishes: green curtain/dress, mother, peering/stealing a glimpse, big (phallic) candles, blood, curiosity, excitement, fear – all abruptly brought to an end by an 'accidental' fall, which executes immediate punishment. What we are dealing with here, I imagine, are either actual memories or unconscious fantasies of sexual intercourse, of seeing mother (or another woman) naked, of blood, of desire for her, and terror of being 'eaten' by her, all clustered round an archetypal 'crystallisation point', and charged with paranoid anxiety: it was the Jesuits' fault he stumbled and fell.

The fact that Jung resorts to the Latin *Mater Ecclesia* (Mother Church) suggests the continuing force of this complex in his memory.[8] In his own discussion of the dream Jung becomes bombastic and argumentative, inveighing against those 'good, efficient, healthy minded people', who would like 'to banish something terribly inconvenient that might sully the familiar picture of childhood innocence' (Jung, 1963, p. 29). Who are those people? His parents? Clearly expecting his 'revelation' to be greeted with cries of horror, Jung – sounding almost like Job – perseveres in his most grandiose and Nietzschean tones:

> Who spoke to me then? Who talked of problems far beyond my knowledge? Who brought the Above and Below together, and laid the foundation for everything that was to fill the second half of my life with stormiest passion? Who but the alien guest who came from both above and below? (Jung 1963, p. 30)

It would be difficult to overestimate the importance of this passage for understanding Jung's later struggles with Christian theologians about the nature of God, and his contempt for the scholastic belief that the essence of evil is a privation of good. For Jung, evil is a force in its own right, and Christianity is deficient to the extent that it denies evil a place in God. However, a Christian might suggest that the strength of Jung's feelings about his vision appears to be interfering with his capacity to think. Sexuality cannot be evil, in the Christian sense, although it might appear so to a child brought up in a prudish and repressive home. The 'good' and 'bad' to which Jung seems to be referring, here, are judgements reflecting his parents' conscious attitude of mind towards the raw material of our physical and emotional endowment. For them, presumably, Lord Jesus was 'good', and sexuality 'bad'. This is quite different from the Christian notion of evil as a privation of good which, in psychological terms, as we will see below, is an important insight into the nature of envy.

The phallus dream enabled Jung to say he had experienced God in split form: as Lord Jesus, and as his underground counterpart the 'subterranean God "not to be named"' (Jung 1963, p. 28). Over the course of time, despite Jung's frequent repudiation of metaphysics, these two poles seem to have acquired substance, so it becomes an article of 'Jungian faith' that God is light *and* dark, good *and* evil. Much of Jung's later work, the alchemical studies and his passionate explosion in 'Answer to Job' (*CW* 11), were driven by his consuming need to reconcile these opposites. Jung represented God's motive in the Incarnation as the need to have his irreconcilable opposites reconciled in man (*CW* 11, paras 659, 739–44). It is equally possible to interpret this, as Winnicott suggests (1989, p. 484), as a desperate search for self-cure by a man whose inner world had early been shattered by his parents' tragedy, and who was then saturated with their uncontained projections. I think this latter explanation is the more likely, and I suspect from his bluster that Jung thought so too.

What Jung could not do was to extricate himself from his psychology once it had been formed. The three-year-old child whose months of separation from a probably deeply depressed mother expressed themselves in a general eczema, for whom 'woman' for a long time meant 'innate unreliability', who first experienced sexual longing in relation to a black-haired, olive-skinned maid, 'quite different from my mother' (Jung 1963, p. 23), was never able, in childhood or adult life, to find a container safe and accepting enough to hold him through the terrible trauma which would have been involved in allowing his deeply split feelings and experiences to come together. Had this been possible, I think Jung would have achieved a picture of God in which love and hate could have been allowed to wrestle together, with love proving ultimately the stronger. Because this did not happen, Jung advanced into later life passionately convinced that God is split: 'that whatever we call "good" is balanced by an equally substantial "bad" or "evil"' (*CW* 11, para. 357).

(c) The Cathedral Vision

When he was about eleven, Jung came out of school and went to the cathedral square:

> I was overwhelmed by the beauty of the sight, and thought: 'The world is beautiful and the church is beautiful, and God made all this and sits above it far away in the blue sky on a golden throne and ...' Here came a great hole in my thoughts, and a choking sensation. I felt numbed, and knew only: 'Don't go on thinking now! Something terrible is coming ...' (Jung 1963, p. 52)

Jung was in agony, unable to sleep for three nights, convinced that to think the thought would be to commit the unforgivable sin, and so cause his damnation and bring unbearable pain on his parents.

He then described the reasoning process which finally released him. God had created every human being, back to Adam and Eve, exactly as we are. We can only sin because God has made us capable of sinning. Therefore it is God's intention we should sin.[9] Fortified by these considerations Jung allowed the thought to come, and saw an enormous turd fall from under God's throne and shatter the cathedral: 'So that was it! I felt an enormous, an indescribable relief.' The experience was 'an illumination', a 'miracle of grace' which, tragically, his father had never known, because 'he had taken the Bible's commandments for his guide' (Jung 1963, p. 56f.).

In his memoirs, Jung tells the story (Jung 1963, pp. 49–58) of this vision immediately after recalling a humiliating incident in which the father of a school friend gave him a first-class dressing down for disobeying orders in a rowing boat. Jung was furious, but rendered speechless by his recognition of the absolute difference in importance between himself, a schoolboy, and this 'rich, powerful man'. The incident was so painful that it induced a split in Jung's mind. He suddenly felt he was really two people: an ignorant schoolboy, and 'a high authority, a man not to be trifled with, as powerful and as influential as the manufacturer'. He then adds the 'annoying tradition' that his grandfather was a natural son of Goethe.[10]

Jung experienced this reprimand as an intolerable wound to his fragile self-esteem. God's turd is the expression of his immense, split-off rage, not just against his friend's father, but much more against his own parents who seemed so pathetically inadequate by comparison (hence the need to identify himself with Goethe). How sad it would be for his parents 'if their *only* son, ... should be doomed to eternal damnation!' In his rage, Jung had annihilated his brother, thinking of himself as his parents' only son. Unable to accept his desire to banish his parents to hell, Jung unconsciously reversed the wish and made himself, not only their protector, but also the possessor of a new revelation about God which would, in due course, reveal even God as morally inferior to the righteous Job (with whom Jung identified himself).

This interpretation is confirmed by the comments Jung adds to the cathedral vision. At one level, it filled him with certainty and wonder: he was amazed God's grace should have been revealed to a 'corrupt, inferior person' like him (Jung 1963, p. 58). At a deeper level, the vision increased his sense of inferiority, leaving him feeling he had fallen into something bad, evil and sinister (Jung 1963, p. 57). What Jung had fallen into, I believe, was an indirect awareness of the enormous amount of 'shit' – repressed pain and anger – he was carrying. Sadly, once again, there was no therapeutic container available to him in which he might have begun to integrate his shadow side and re-experience his feelings, gradually linking them up, through the experience of the transference, with experiences which had originally occasioned them.

Instead, as Winnicott observed, Jung embarked on his journey of self-cure. The repressed contents of his inner world were projected into God, the only safe container for them. Jung's God thus became a vehicle to hold unlived, unknown, unprocessed primitive thoughts and feelings, which constantly press towards consciousness. God carried Jung's shadow.

It is noticeable that Jung resisted any tendency to analyse these experiences.[11] Lacking a therapeutic relationship within which the trauma of re-membering could be contained, and his memories reconstituted in consciousness, he was forced to deal with his inner world in what he called an 'objective' manner. He wrote, 'I am a bundle of opposites and can only endure myself when I observe myself as an objective phenomenon' (Jung 1976, p. 78). Because Christianity, as Jung was introduced to it, was too rationalistic and too full of unrealistic sweetness to allow any expression of primitive feeling, he was forced to look in other directions for help. He found much of his inner experience reflected in Gnostic texts, especially those which spoke of gathering the scattered fragments of light.[12] He also devoted himself to the study of alchemy, which 'has performed for me the great and invaluable service of providing material in which my experience could find sufficient room' (*CW* 14, para. 792). Even so, he was left with deep, disturbing and unresolved intimations from his early days.

Throughout his long working life he pursued his researches on the 'objective' level, trying to understand religious symbols by a process of comparison.[13] But the childhood questions kept returning until, in the spring of 1951, at the age of seventy-five, when confined to bed with a spell of liver trouble (Jung 1976, p. 21), he finally erupted in his most personal work, a '*tour de force* of the unconscious' (Jung 1976, p. 17f.): 'Answer to Job'. This was Jung's own great turd directed at an unreceptive church, or, as he described it, 'a straightforward application of my psychological principles to certain central problems of our religion' (Jung 1976, p. 241).

'Answer to Job'[14]

Taking the Book of Job as his starting point, Jung turns on God hoping to express 'the shattering emotion which the unvarnished spectacle of divine savagery and ruthlessness produces' in many people (*CW* 11, para. 561). Jung identifies with Job. He feels he has been the victim of God's violent, unjust, thoughtless and cruel behaviour. Job/Jung is innocent. Yahweh must be put on trial and forced to acknowledged the unconsciousness which led him to forget his wisdom and allow his wily son, Satan, to cause the human race to sin. Psychological thought and theological language are conflated as the conscious part of Jung confronts the terrible splits in his inner world.

In the white heat of his fury we suddenly find mention of

> a prototype of the early-departed Abel who was dearer to God than Cain, the go-ahead huntsman (who was no doubt instructed in these arts by one of Satan's angels). Perhaps this prototype was another son of God of a more conservative nature than Satan, no rolling stone with a fondness for new and black-hearted thoughts, but one who was bound to the Father in childlike love, who harboured no other thoughts except those that enjoyed paternal approval, and who dwelt in the inner circle of the heavenly economy. That would explain why his earthly counterpart Abel could so soon 'hasten away from the evil world,' in the words of the Book of Wisdom, and return to the Father, while Cain in his earthly existence had to taste to the full the curse of his progressiveness on the one hand and of his moral inferiority on the other. (*CW* 11, para. 618)

I find it difficult to read these lines without thinking of Jung as a little boy. Like Cain he must have felt that he could never be loved like his early-deceased brother. Instead, he was made to feel that his fondness for new thoughts made him wicked, black-hearted, and inferior.

Characteristic of Jung is the suggestion that Satan and his angels are a progressive influence. A Gnostic idea which, when presented in apparently theological language, is guaranteed to evoke an apoplectic response from Christian theologians. What Jung is meaning to say, psychologically, is that the opposites which emerge into consciousness from the self, especially those which appear antagonistic to our conscious attitude, are of great significance for our future individuation. (Jung knew this from his own early experience, where a prudish conception of Lord Jesus needed to be complemented by the daemonic underground phallus.) Christianity can, all too easily, be perverted by a one-sided conscious attitude into becoming a force of repression, preventing conscious engagement with these apparently negative aspects of our potential selves. This important insight into the value of apparently 'evil' contents emerging from the unconscious led Jung – for example, in his letters to Father Victor White (Jung 1973, 1976) – passionately to reject the Christian notion of evil as a privation of good. Unfortunately, Jung was aiming at the wrong target. The concept of evil as a privation of good is the theological expression of a different, but equally important, psychological mechanism: the psychology of envy. Satan, in Milton's *Paradise Lost*, is a wonderful illustration of this destructive force which can only destroy, and not create. An envious attitude of mind which is memorably expressed in Nietzsche's defiant cry, '*if* there were gods, how could I endure not to be a god! *Therefore* there are no gods' (1961, p. 110). This is a different psychological process to the one intended by Jung, when he speaks of Satan as a progressive influence, but the confusion between these different understandings of Satan and evil has endlessly bedevilled (!) discussions between analytical psychologists and Christian theologians. Jung recognised the psychology of envy (*CW* 11, para. 980), but appears not to have related it to the theological understanding of evil.

More disturbing, in 'Answer to Job', is Jung's sudden suggestion – a thought which has no parallel in Jewish or Christian sources – that some human beings, the chosen ones, are descended from Adam and Eve, while the rest are descended from the animals (*CW* 11, para. 576). This splitting of the human race, characteristic of Gnosticism (Rudolph 1983, p. 91f.), is a catastrophic undoing of the symbol for the unity of humankind which Jews and Christians find in Adam; but it powerfully expresses Jung's heartfelt identification with Job as 'a half-crushed human worm, grovelling in the dust' (*CW* 11, para. 565).[15]

What did Jung achieve through 'Answer to Job'? First, he experienced enormous relief from having, finally, put Yahweh in the dock. Unlike his father, he had dared to quarrel 'with God, the dark author of all created things, who alone was responsible for the sufferings of the world' (Jung 1963, p. 112f.) Second, in the face of Christian insistence on a God of love, he found courage to proclaim his conviction that God is less righteous than humankind, and it is only in and through humankind that the contradictions in God will finally be resolved. To all who would hear, Jung proclaimed his revision of the Christian message: the gospel of love must be balanced by a gospel of fear (*CW* 11, para. 732). But relief from inner tension was bought at some cost. As Jung wrote concerning the effects of having produced 'Answer to Job', 'I have attained ... a certain state of peace within, paid for by a rather uncomfortable state of war without' (Jung 1976, p. 242).

Jung insisted that he did not have to *believe* in God because he *knew* God (McGuire and Hull 1980, p. 383). As he wrote, 'I don't *believe* [in a personal God], but I do *know* of a power of a very personal nature and an irresistible influence. I call it "God"' (Jung 1993, p. 274). Understandably, given all the circumstances of his life, Jung could not worship. In an evocative dream he was led by his father 'into the highest presence'. His father knelt and touched his forehead to the floor. Jung tried to do the same, but could not quite touch the ground (Jung 1963, p. 245f.). If God is terrible and to be feared, we are wise not to entrust ourselves completely to him: watchfulness and control will remain the order of the day. Consciousness becomes all important. From the time of his mother's hospitalisation, Jung could say, 'I have always felt mistrustful when the word "love" was spoken' (Jung 1963, p. 23).

Conclusion

Jung's greatest gift to us is the integrity with which he lived his life, and his readiness to share the deeply personal experiences which formed him. I have argued that Jung carried the scars of those experiences to his dying day, and that they seriously impaired his ability to comprehend important dimensions of the Christian symbols which were his lifetime study. It was a tragedy that, in a time of rapid cultural and intellectual change, when so many landmarks were being swept away, the Protestant Church – split between pietism and rationalism – was unable to provide the safe container within which Jung might have been able to wrestle with the extremes of his experience. Yet Jung has enriched the Christian Church. Particularly, he has reminded us that there is no direct route to knowledge of God, but that all our talk of God is symbolic: the symbols we are bound to use are drawn from the common symbol-stock of humankind. He has also made us aware that the knowledge of God is not just to be found in overtly religious places, but that the religious journey demands that we face up to the reality of our inner worlds, with all their darkness and confusion and with all their fullness of creative potential.

From the Christian point of view, it is as we wrestle with the full truth about ourselves that we begin to find the symbols and the metaphors which give substance to the experience – which Jung called the transcendent function – of being in real communion with One who is truly Other (Ulanov 1996), in whom all the opposites are already reconciled and enfolded, in whose image (as a Trinity of persons-in-relationship) we have somehow already been made. The perception of this wholeness – glimpsed in moments of worship, prayer and reflection, as well as inner struggle – is itself a healing and uniting factor in the process of individuation.

Notes

1. It is instructive to compare Jung's work with that of his great Swiss contemporary, the theologian Karl Barth (1886–1968). Barth's work, although still largely ignored or misunderstood in Christian circles, is also an attempt to break out of the dualism inherent in Western thought. Jung and Barth were intensely sensitive to the paradigm shift in our self-understanding which is most easily seen in the move from Newtonian to Einsteinian thought. For an introduction to Barth, see Torrance (1990), especially the chapter 'Karl Barth and the Latin Heresy'.
2. In addition to Stein (1985), readers should consult Dourley (1981, 1984), Edinger (1973) and Jaffé (1984, 1989) for discussions of Jung's psychology of religion which are more accepting of Jung's basic presuppositions about Christianity than I am. See, also, the valuable collection of papers in Ryce-Menuhin (1994).
3. For example, Jung wrote to Father Victor White: 'My personal view in this matter is that man's vital energy or libido is the divine pneuma all right and it was this conviction which it was my secret purpose to bring into the vicinity of my colleagues' understanding' (Jung 1973, p. 384). Compare this with: 'Suddenly I understood that God was, for me at least, one of the most certain and immediate experiences' (Jung 1963, p. 80).
4. Note Jung's poignant words about his teenage situation: 'For God's sake I now found myself cut off from the Church and from my father's and everybody else's faith. In so far as they all represented the Christian religion, I was an outsider. This knowledge filled me with sadness and was to overshadow all the years until the time I entered the university' (Jung 1963, p. 74).
5. For an admirable discussion of Jung's psychology of religion in relation to this 'implicate order', see Aziz (1990).
6. C.G. Jung was born on 26 July 1875.
7. Johanna Gertrud,' born 17 July 1884 (Ellenberger 1994, p. 662).
8. As he explains in his 'Studies in word association':

   > Perhaps in order to be less obvious, perhaps because it takes less effort, the complex expresses intimate feelings by cliches such as quotations, words of songs, titles of stories, and such like. Quotations are frequently masks. We use them in everyday life, too, in this sense. One sings certain songs in certain moods, often because one does not want to express the thoughts that underlie the moods; so they become masked. (*CW* 2, para. 273)

   Unlike Freud, Jung never did overcome his '*Mater Ecclesia* complex' sufficiently to visit Rome (Jung 1963, p. 319; Gay 1995, pp. 32–6).
9. 'God in His omniscience had arranged everything so that the first parents [Adam and Eve] would have to sin. *Therefore it was God's intention that they should sin*' (Jung 1963, p. 55; original emphasis).
10. Aniela Jaffé adds a footnote saying that no proof of this item of family tradition has been found, and it is not supported by circumstantial evidence (Jung 1963, p. 52).

11. Jung was evidently not unaware of what he was doing. When commenting, in archetypal terms, on a dream from the time of his mother's death, he said: 'Undoubtedly, I could have found out a good deal more by looking at its subjective meaning' (Jung 1963, p. 347). Perhaps he most clearly explained his antipathy to looking at the subjective side of his material in his final letter to Father Victor White, where he rather bitterly imagined what effect a personal interpretation of Job's struggles might have had on Job (Jung 1976, pp. 544–6). Smith's comment is right: 'Jung's highly creative use of religious images was for him a largely unconscious mode of intuitive psychotherapy' (Smith 1996, p. 139).

12. See Jung (1976, p. 564):

> We must bear in mind that we do not *make* projections, rather they *happen* to us. This fact permits the conclusion that we originally read our first physical, and especially psychological, insights in the stars. In other words, what is farthest is nearest. Somehow, as the Gnostics surmised, we have 'collected' ourselves from out of the cosmos. That is why the idea of 'gathering the seeds of light' played such an important role in their systems and in Manichaeism.

'Collecting ourselves' from the cosmos is part of every individuation process, but it takes on a special urgency and difficulty for those who, like Jung, are deeply dissociated through their borderline condition (cf. *CW* 11, paras 399–401).

13. Jung distinguishes 'interpretation by faith' from his own method of 'interpretation by comparison':

> Interpretation by faith seeks to represent the experienced content of a vision ... as the visible manifestation of a transcendental Being, and it invariably does so in terms of a traditional system and then asserts that this representation is the absolute truth.* Opposed to this is my view, which also interprets, in a sense. It interprets by comparing *all* traditional assumptions and does not assert that Transcendence itself has been perceived; it insists only on the reality of the fact that an experience has taken place, and that this is exactly the form it took. I compare this experience with all other experiences of the kind and conclude that a process is going on in the unconscious which expresses itself in various forms. I am aware that this process is actually going on, but I do not know what its nature is, whether it is psychic, whether it comes from an angel or from God himself. We must leave these questions open, and no belief will help us over the hurdle, for we do not know and can never know. (Jung 1976, p. 379)

* Jung is too sweeping. Such dogmatic fundamentalism represents the *failure* to achieve symbolic thinking. This is as dangerous, theologically, as it is psychologically.

14. Of the enormous literature on 'Answer to Job', see especially Newton (1993) and Weisstub (1993). On the Book of Job as an account of a creative illness, see Kahn and Solomon (1975).

15. It is probably significant that Jung makes no mention of this wild, personal idea when writing more objectively and dispassionately. See, for example, his discussion of the symbolism of Adam in *CW* 14, paras 552–8.

References

Aziz, Robert (1990) *C.G. Jung's Psychology of Religion and Synchronicity*. Albany: State University of New York Press.

Barth, Karl (1956) *Church Dogmatics I.2: The Doctrine of the Word of God*. Edinburgh: T and T Clark.

Dourley, John P. (1981) *The Psyche as Sacrament*. Toronto: Inner City Books.

Dourley, John P. (1988) *The Illness That We Are*. Toronto: Inner City Books.

Edinger, Edward F. (1973) *Ego and Archetype*. Baltimore, MD: Penguin.

Ellenberger, H.F. (1994) *The Discovery of the Unconscious*. London: Fontana.

Gay, P. (1995) *Freud, A Life for our Time*. London: Papermac.

Jaffé, Aniela (1984) *The Myth of Meaning*. Zurich: Daimon Verlag.

Jaffé, Aniela (1989) *Was C.G. Jung a Mystic?* Zurich: Daimon Verlag.

Jung, C.G. (1916) *The Seven Sermons to the Dead (VII Sermones ad Mortuos)*. London: Watkins, 1967.

Jung, C.G. (1963) *Memories, Dreams, Reflections*. London: Fontana, 1995.

Jung, C.G. (1973) *Letters of C.G. Jung*, Volume I, 1906–1950. London: Routledge and Kegan Paul.

Jung, C.G. (1976) Letters *of C.G. Jung*, Volume II, 1951–1961. London: Routledge and Kegan Paul.

Jung, C.G. (1983) *The Zofingia Lectures*. London: Routledge and Kegan Paul.

Kahn, J. and Solomon, H. (1975) *Job's Illness: Loss, Grief and Integration*. Oxford: Pergamon.

McGuire, William, and Hull, R.F.C. (eds) (1980) *C.G. Jung Speaking*. London: Pan Books.

Murdoch, Iris. (1993) *Metaphysics as a Guide to Morals*. London: Penguin .

Newton, K. (1993) 'The weapon and the wound: the archetypal and personal dimensions in "Answer to Job"', *Journal of Analytical Psychology*, 38(4): 373–95.

Nietzsche, Friedrich (1961) *Thus Spoke Zarathustra*. London: Penguin.

Rudolph, Kurt (1983) *Gnosis*. Edinburgh: T and T Clark.

Ryce-Menuhin, Joel (ed.) (1994) *Jung and the Monotheisms*. London: Routledge.

Smith, Robert C. (1996) *The Wounded Jung*. Evanston, IL: Northwestern University Press.

Stein, Murray. (1985) *Jung's Treatment of Christianity*. Wilmette, IL: Chiron Publications.

Torrance, Thomas F. (1990) *Karl Barth, Biblical and Evangelical Theologian*. Edinburgh: T and T Clark.

Ulanov, A. B. (1996) *The Functioning Transcendent*. Wilmette, IL: Chiron Publications.

Weisstub, E. (1993) 'Questions to Jung on "Answer to Job"', *Journal of Analytical Psychology*, 38(4): 397–418.

Winnicott, D.W. (1989) *Psycho-Analytic Explorations*. London: Karnac.

12
The Ethical Self

Hester McFarland Solomon

The peculiarity of 'conscience' is that it is a knowledge of, or certainty about, the emotional value of the ideas we have concerning the motives of our actions.

Jung, *CW* 10, para. 825.

[F]or Jung ... ethics [is] the action of the whole person, the self.

Stein, *Jung on Evil* (1995b), p. 10.

Preamble

Common usage often conflates ethics and morals. In this chapter a distinction is implied throughout between morality and ethics. Morality is indicated by the adherence to a set of stated principles or rules which govern behaviour (for example, the Ten Commandments, or a professional Code of Ethics), whereas ethics implies an attitude achieved through judgement, discernment and conscious struggle, often between conflicting rights or duties (for example, the duty of confidentiality versus the duty of protecting a person from potential harm). In this I follow Jung who made the following useful distinction:

[I]n the great majority of cases conscience signifies primarily the reaction to a real or supposed deviation from the moral code, and is for the most part identical with the primitive fear of anything unusual, not customary, and hence 'immoral.' As this behaviour is instinctive and, at best, only partly the result of reflection, it may be 'moral' but it can raise no claim to being *ethical*. It deserves this qualification only when it is reflective, when it is subjected to conscious scrutiny. And this happens only when a fundamental doubt arises as between two possible modes of moral behaviour, that is to say in a conflict of duty. (*CW* 10, para. 855)

Introduction

This chapter seeks to address the question of whether Jung's model concerning the structure and processes of the psyche can offer us a specific and helpful approach to understanding the ethical attitude, and, in particular, the ethical attitude underpinning psychotherapeutic practice. Inevitably, any discussion of Jung's model of the psyche brings us to the core concept of the self, including its defences and dynamics, both in personal as well as in archetypal terms. The question of the nature of the self has a direct bearing on the question of Jungian thought and the ethical attitude. Are we born with a capacity for ethical thinking and behaviour, or do we learn it through the socialisation processes of identification, internalisation and introjection?

Depth psychologists approach issues about the self according to two main theoretical frameworks, roughly corresponding to the nature/nurture debate. It is tempting – indeed, in classical scientific conceptualisation it has been habitual – to keep the terms of the nature/nurture debate regarding the ontology of the self as separate lines of enquiry. When it comes to identifying the sources of the capacity to understand complex situations in ethical terms, and to behave in ethical ways, the nature/nurture debate is of central importance in assessing whether, or the extent to which, the ethical attitude is innate or learned. Both have implications for our understanding of the ethical bases of our behaviour as human beings and as psychotherapists and analysts.

The first framework, corresponding to the nature side of the debate, centres on the idea of a primary self with innate, universal deep structural features that are instinctual but which have archetypal imaginal correlates connected to and often arising at the time of the individual's passage through the major life stages. This is the self that the individual is born with, containing the potential for his or her future development. It includes the very hardwiring of the brain that underpins such functions as the instinctual drives, emotional responses and intellectual capacities. (See Chapter 8 in this volume.)

It is not immediately evident that an enquiry into the sources and origins of the ethical attitude might be found on the nature side of the debate, where the focus is more often on understanding the hardwiring components of the self. However, recent scientific evidence gives some support to the view that there is an innate, genetically based ethical capacity. From the field of evolutionary genetics, Sober and Wilson (1998) have argued that altruism has evolved for purposes of survival and reproduction (the so-called 'altruistic gene').

Intuitively, it might at first seem plausible that the sources of the ethical attitude are located in environmental caretaking, partly because the self's relationship and conduct towards another is the foundation of the ethical attitude, and partly because, in reflecting on the instinctual life of animals, who, as far as we know, are sentient but not conscious, we do not usually attribute to them a capacity for ethical judgement and behaviour.

Thus, on the nurture side of the debate, there is abundant evidence of the impact of the environment on developmental processes. In Winnicott's (1964, p. 88) famous phrase: '"there is no such thing as a baby" – meaning that if you set out to describe a baby, you will find you are describing a *baby and someone*. A baby cannot exist alone, but is essentially part of a relationship.' This succinctly expresses the depth of the impact of those external sources on the self's ontology by articulating the view that the self can never, from its very beginnings, be considered apart from another self: this is clear from the fact that the neonate is totally dependent on others for its protection and sustenance. The methods and modes of relating that contribute to and are the vehicle for the development of an individual's identity have been elaborated variously by object relations theory (see Kohon (1986) for an overview), attachment theory (Bowlby 1969), and intersubjectivity (Stein 1995a, Aron 1996, Kumin 1996).

An interactive model of the impact of innate and environmental influences on the origins of the self would seem the most credible, and recent scientific evidence supports this view. For example, the new field of psychoneurobiology has shown that the development *post partum* of the neural circuitry and structures of the infant's brain which regulate the development of the higher human capacities are dependent on the existence and quality of the earliest interactions between infant and mother or caregiver (see my discussion of the implications of these findings in Chapter 8 in this volume, and in particular, Schore 1994, 1996). Daniel Stern (1985) has made a powerful contribution to this area from the field of developmental psychology, where he has analysed the different modes of fit and attunement between the infant and its mother that create the basic patterns of being and becoming that characterise individuals as their unique selves. The emphasis here is on mutuality, with both infant and mother actively generating exchanges, with direct impact on the development of the neural circuitry of the infant.

Thus, since the infant instinctively seeks to participate in activating the type, number and timing of these mutual exchanges, we can infer that the infant, a proactive partner, is thereby participating directly in the development of its own neural circuitry, in its own neural growth. Moreover, it is this particular circuitry that determines the cognitive and socioaffective responses which must eventually have bearing on and underpin the achievement of the ethical capacity. This suggests that there are grounds for considering that the ethical capacity is, at least in part, innate, derived from the earliest, instinctually driven exchanges with its primary caregiver, and, at least in part, influenced by environmental factors, by the impact of that very caregiver's capacity to be responsive to and to initiate appropriate and meaningful inter-actions with the self.

It is for these reasons that the ethical capacity should be located firmly in the overall study of the self, and, in particular, that it has a claim for a central place in analytic thinking. It is therefore surprising that, with some notable exceptions, there is a dearth of theoretical work or published clinical material within the broad psychoanalytic and Jungian analytic *opus* that seeks directly to address an understanding of the origins of the ethical attitude, to integrate it within a view of the self in developmental and archetypal terms, and to locate it as an intrinsic, *a priori*, component of the analytic attitude, in which the exchanges between patient and analyst are so intimately connected to these earliest levels of the self's experience.

Whereas the major focus of this chapter will be within the discourse of analytical psychology (Jungian theory and practice), the relevance of the psychoanalytic enquiry is enormous, and will be integrated where appropriate. The underlying assumption is that, as the ethical attitude is an inherent human capacity, whatever we might venture to propose from the study of ethics within a depth psychological framework will pertain to both the Jungian and Freudian theoretical and clinical traditions. There is no doubt that an ethical or moral dimension is deeply involved in the sense of self and plays a major role in the development of the self over time as it unfolds both through its genetic endowment as well as within its environment.

The Contemporary Jungian Position Concerning the Self

Jung pursued his studies concerning the structure and dynamics of the self throughout the decades of his working life until his death, and a number of contemporary Jungian theorists and clinicians have carried on the enquiry that Jung began. The Jungian enquiry into the nature, structure and processes of the self does not claim to offer a definitive or unified theory. Nevertheless, it has provided the means for a discourse that avoids the pitfalls of envision-ing the self as a unified whole, while at the same time affording the possibility of thinking about the self as a psychic totality, encompassing many disparate, often conflicting aspects. I consider that this can be most satisfactorally accom-plished by adopting a theoretical position that encompasses the nature/nurture polarities.

In this chapter I will follow Fordham's view (for example, Fordham 1985), as offering a useful and persuasive theory concerning the archetypal and developmental roots of the self, and how the concomitant processes continue throughout life. Starting with the concept of a primary self, Fordham suggests that the basic identity of the individual, known as the primary integrate, is the fundamental given from which the self unfolds through the processes of deintegration and reintegration. The self develops when a part of the self reaches out to the environment and has an experience there (deintegration). For example, a toddler plays a game with its mother, and then rests contentedly for a time in the playpen. The toddler has taken the experience of playing with the mother and has reintegrated it back within the self. The shape and quality of this experience becomes part of the self's ongoing growth, development, and identity, attaching itself to the ego or to other aspects of the psyche. A relaxed and happy experience with the mother will make a very different impact on and contribution to the internal world of the self than will, say, an anxiety-ridden experience.

Through the processes of deintegration and reintegration, the quality of experiences with the external world inevitably influences the quality of experiences in the internal world, and vice versa. Fordham offers a guiding theory concerning the self that allows us to place it theoretically and clinically within a developmental and an archetypal, nature/nurture framework. Here we have a view of the self both as a primary integrate endowed with a capacity to reach out and gather experience with its environment which it can then internalise and use to grow, allowing for a view of a multiplicity of selves, or part selves, arising partly through childhood complexes, partly through identifications with internal and external archetypal figures that form the foundation of each person's self experience. At the same time, it is possible to understand the conditions under which an habitual attitude might develop in a very young self to turn away from experiences with another, particularly when the other is the source of trauma and pain to it.

The dynamic growth of the self can thus be thought of as the result of a constant interaction between the impact of nature and of nurture. These influences, both internal and external, will vary in both type and in quality, because of the ordinary variation of differences between individuals as well as because of variations in the environment in which growth occurs. Thus, how the self as an ethical agent may arise, and also how the ethical capacity may be thwarted, can be considered according to two intersecting dimensions: on the one hand, the deep structural aspects of the self, its innate capacities; and on the other hand, the environmental influences impacting on the self and interacting with the deep structural components of the self.

Along with these underlying concepts regarding the foundations of a primary self and its development over time, there remain further possible dimensions that contribute to a view of the complexity and richness of the internal world of the self. These have to do with understanding the self not as an entity that achieves a state of wholeness and integration through a unifying process of integration and combination of all elements, but rather a self that is whole or a totality in the sense that it is composed of a multiplicity of internally and externally generated components, subsystems, complexes, divisions, splits, structures, internal objects and unconscious phantasies (to name only a few concepts found in analytic theory). This self is in turn dependent on important others in its external environment for a sense of its identity and continuity, others who themselves are equally subject to such complexity and multiplicity of internal and external influences on their self-identity and behaviour.

Jung stressed the self's capacity for integration and wholeness. For example, he documents in his autobiography (Jung 1963) that he turned to drawing mandalas in 1916, having just written *VII Sermones ad Mortuos* (*Seven Sermons to the Dead*) (Jung 1916). Drawing mandalas was a way of self-healing, representing the state of the self at any given moment, and thereby creating a container for 'the self, the wholeness of the personality, which if all goes well is harmonious' (Jung 1963, p. 221). The *VII Sermones* was a powerful and immediate record of how Jung was overtaken by numerous, intense and disturbing fantasies, numerous figures, complexes, sub-personalities and oppositions that erupted into his conscious mind from his unconscious. So rich and multiple were these fantasies that Jung considered that:

> All my works, all my creative activity, has come from those initial fantasies and dreams which began in 1912 ... Everything that I accomplished in later life was already contained in them, although at first only in the form of emotions and images. (Jung 1963, p. 216)

Thus, Jung was clearly fully aware of the self as 'an extremely composite thing, a "conglomerate soul"' (*CW* 9i, para. 634).

On the other hand, there is the view propounded eloquently by Jungian analyst Polly Young-Eisendrath in which 'selves are created and sustained in relationship, from birth to death' (Young-Eisendrath 1995, p. 22). She emphasises that the sense of the self's continuity in time and space, in face of its own plurality, is dependent on the context of human relationships.

Thinking about the complexity of the self that we are evoking here, divided as it is in a number of ways, with a panoply of internal archetypal imageries, identifications, projections, and warring opposites, hence a self that is both primary and plural, brings us back to the topic at hand, to ethics. What are the implications of this view of a complex, multiplex self for our depth psychological understanding of the self's ethical capacity, where the self is nevertheless expected to have to struggle within this complexity and still achieve an authentic ethical attitude, to arrive at an authentic ethical decision, or to perform an authentic ethical behaviour? Which part of this multiplex self is ethical? How are ethical doubts and uncertainties to be understood? And what would it mean if two individuals, struggling with ethical concerns, do not agree?

The Ethical Self

Unlike developmental psychology,[1] neither psychoanalysis nor analytical psychology has offered a unified view of the growth of an ethical attitude within their general theories of the overall development of the self. However, both have formulated theories, at least implicitly and in some respects explicitly, that seek to understand those psychic states and mechanisms that can effect the attainment of the ethical attitude and the conditions that underpin it, and, at the same time, of what may happen within the personality that can pervert or block its attainment. Freud and Jung each made considerable contributions to this understanding. They shared a starting position that regarded the psyche as suffused with the ubiquitous presence of unconscious conflict, of psychological processes and behaviour that are multi-determined and multi-motivated, of unconscious and subversive impulses and desires that can undermine conscious intent,[2] and of the counterbalancing possibility in the psyche of conscious ego choice, moral energy and ethical struggle. To this shared view Jung added a deep conviction regarding the overriding teleological nature of the self's continued search to become itself, even in the face of dire internal resistance or malign external forces. All these elements are components of a profound view of the psyche that have a direct bearing on our understanding of the attainment of an internal ethical position.

Freud's Contribution

Through his metapsychology and his clinical writings, Freud formulated a rich and complex view of the workings of the mind that have direct relevance to considerations regarding the origins of the ethical attitude. In brief terms, classic psychoanalytical metapsychology delineates two regulating systems relevant to moral behaviour: (i) the superego, which first emerges at around eighteen months of age and is related to the internalisation of figures representing power and authority (hence the role of shame and humiliation, and their opposite, triumph, in regulating human behaviour); and (ii) the notion of the ego ideal, which generally develops around the time of the child's working through of the Oedipus complex and is based on empathic guilt and the wish to preserve and identify with the internalised good parents.[3] It is the quality of the caregiving that the child receives at both these stages, and the child's responsiveness to it, that will determine his or her capacity to develop a moral or ethical sense, whether this is experienced as the imposition of a set of commandments or constraints, or whether it is integral to and congruent with the sense of self. Since they were first elaborated by Freud, there has been much further discussion concerning the nature and development of these two capacities, but they point to two roughly distinct modes of mental functioning that remain salient to our understanding of the achievement of an ethical attitude.

Freud's notion that all behaviour is motivated, including unconscious behaviour, meant that the psychoanalytic task was to bring to the light of consciousness the motives that are embedded in the unconscious, as in his famous phrase, 'Where id was, there ego shall be' (Freud 1933, p. 80). The implication, although not stated as such, is that thus all behaviour has an ethical dimension, at least in the sense that the impulse to fulfill instinctual desires (the id) must be met by conscious judgment and control in order to protect both the self and others (through the ego or superego). Whether this is accomplished through the agency of a harsh superego, or the more flexible and discriminating agency of the ego ideal, depends upon the developmental stage and the quality of the internal world. Through the mechanism of subli- mation and the ego's eventual capacity to take responsibility for the actions of the self, choices can be made that will ensure that the social nature of the self is active in moral ways. As he stated, '[t]he patient's capacity for subli- mating his instincts plays a large part [in the cure] and so does his capacity for rising above the crude life of the instincts' (Freud 1940, cited in Wallwork 1991, p. 243, note 43).

The later psychoanalytic contribution of Melanie Klein (for example, Klein 1957) and her followers is relevant to our discussion. Klein described the impulses belonging to the more primitive internal world as functioning through part-object representations that operate according to the talionic principle, a ruthless, aggressive, and vengeful reaction to the past, present or possible future pain of relating felt by the self. This way of relating is charac- teristic of the paranoid-schizoid position. The dynamics of whole object relating, called the depressive position, however, are characterised by a capacity for concern and impulses of reparation towards the other. These are akin to agapaic responses, whereby the other is perceived in a more realistic way, as a subjective other, a real person occupying a real position in the world external to the self.[4] Britton (1998) has described how the ongoing cyclical oscillation between the paranoid-schizoid and the depressive positions can account for the possibility of a continued psychic growth and development – how well established psychic systems can 'unfreeze' in order for new levels of integration to be achieved. The Kleinian and post-Kleinian view has clear implications for the development of an ethical capacity through the develop- ment of a capacity for concern and the wish to make reparation.

Jung's Contribution

Although taking account of the importance of the classic psychosexual stages, a Jungian approach to understanding how the self may achieve an ethical attitude can be located within the context of the unfolding of the self over the stages of an entire life. Thus, an ethical capacity would be considered in the context of a teleological view of the self, imparting meaning and value at each stage. This suggests a universal ethical capacity that is innate (as might be understood by archetypal theory) but which, to unfold, depends on the quality of caregiving that the child receives during its early development.

If human beings have an innate capacity to behave both individually and in groups in recognisably ethical ways, such that unethical or immoral behaviour is also recognisable and demonstrable, then we can say that embedded in the human psyche are templates or deep structures that correspond to this moral intent, shaping thoughts, feelings and our ethical behaviour accordingly. Any such archetypally based theory which considers there is an innate capacity that seeks to identify, struggle with and eschew unethical or immoral behaviour is bound up with the ubiquity of what Jung called the shadow. The outcome of this struggle brings us right to the heart of the struggle to find and maintain an ethical attitude, for it is a matter of whether the self retires into a self-protective, defensive, or autistic state where no other is admitted, or whether the self allows itself to recognise and engage with another, the not-self, acknowledging the other as having a place in the self's universe, with all the consequences and risks to the self that this entails.

The Struggle between the Shadow and the Self

The concept of the shadow is central to Jung's understanding of the self as an ethical entity, and its recognition and integration is crucial to the self's capacity to develop and grow. For Jung, the shadow is that portion of the self that the ego designates as bad and unwanted. The shadow carries what is treacherous and subversive – what is unethical – in the self, and hides it, relegating its contents to unconscious areas in the psyche where it can then be lived out in projection, using the other as a vehicle to hold the bad aspects of the self. When the ethical capacity is still undeveloped and in a compensatory relationship to the shadow, then the shadow assumes archetypal, unmitigated proportions. In order for the self's nascent ethical capacity to achieve human dimensions, the archetypal shadow must be brought to consciousness, or somehow to be tolerated in the dynamics between unconscious and conscious, thereby to be mitigated. Jung was in no doubt about the tremendous struggle that this process requires. It is tantamount to acknowledging and integrating to the fullest extent possible at any given moment the most comprehensive knowledge of oneself to date, whether positive or negative, including the full, horrific nature of the shadow. Thus, we could say that a certain primitive moral discrimination operates as a function of and in relation to the shadow. The shadow is the inferior part of the personality, and as such is incompatible with the conscious attitude.

In the face of the pain of shame and humiliation in acknowledging hateful and undesirable aspects of the self, the shadow is usually first dealt with by projecting its attributes outside the self. The bad aspects of the self are thus located elsewhere, in a friend, a parent, a lover, a spouse or a child. In the meantime, the shadow has gone underground, deep into the personality, thus avoiding the light of consciousness, seeking to remain hidden and incognito, and taking with it the self's knowledge of its participation in what is deplorable in and to the self. In the depths of the unconscious, the shadow struts about, in a parody of rectitude and decked out in all its moral finery, crying 'Shame!' at its neighbour, oblivious to the fact that what it finds reprehensible in the other is located within. While this state of affairs pertains within the psyche, there are enormous psychic blindspots about oneself and about the reality of others. When the shadow is in command, there can be no knowledge of the reality of the other. A state of narcissism prevails.

Jung's notion of the shadow belongs to an understanding of the primitive splitting mechanism of projection that seeks to protect the self against the pain of traumatisation that has already happened to the self when the self had reached out to another and was injured. The effect of such retreats from relating is to

> isolate the subject from his environment, since instead of a real relation to it there is now only an illusory one. Projections change the world into the replica of one's unknown face. In the last analysis, therefore, they lead to an autoerotic or autistic condition. (*CW* 9ii, para. 17)

Jung points time and again to the difficulty of the moral task of acknowledging one's shadow, since to do so requires that the self face the painful recognition that the shadow projections belong within.

> The shadow is a moral problem that challenges the whole ego-personality, for no one can become conscious of the shadow without considerable moral effort. To become conscious of it involves recognizing the dark aspects of the personality as present and real. This act is the essential condition for any kind of self-knowledge, and it therefore, as a rule, meets with considerable resistance. Indeed, self-knowledge as a psychotherapeutic measure frequently requires much painstaking work extending over a long period. (*CW* 9ii, para. 14)

The idea that shadow projections can and must be withdrawn and reintegrated within the personality is often stated by clinicians, but it may be difficult to reckon on the degree of struggle and suffering that the task requires. And yet, this is the very grounds for the eventual transformation of the self, the aim of analysis. Jung was very clear about the struggle involved.

Although, with insight and good will, the shadow can to some extent be assimilated into the conscious personality, experience shows that there are certain features which offer the most obstinate resistance to moral control and prove almost impossible to influence. These resistances are usually bound up with *projections*, which are not recognized as such, and their recognition is a moral achievement beyond the ordinary. (*CW* 9ii, para. 16)

A battle of titanic proportions ensues, whereby the self struggles to risk letting go of its habitual protective barriers erected via defensive splitting and projecting of the shadow which guard it against acknowledging the existence of another who may cause the self pain. The shadow aspects of the psyche pit themselves against the forward movement of the self, forcing psychic splits to come to the fore. The splitting of internal experience into pairs of opposites is often the method by which the self seeks to defend itself against unbearable and overwhelming pain that accompanies being open to another human being, thereby maintaining the reign of the shadow. The effort to manage and tolerate the reintegration and metabolisation of such states can be gruelling. In this situation, the self is liable to evoke its narcissistic self-care defences (Kalsched 1996, Solomon 1997b).

Archetypal, instinct-based experiences occur initially in very early or primitive states of mind as pairs of opposites, thus providing a way of ordering experience according to either/or categories, making it possible for the self to gain some sense of safety and primitive understanding. Defensive patterns of splitting in order to organise experience and protect the self can become hardened, habitual and difficult to shift, even if the circumstances that first called forth the defence no longer pertain. Jung understood this situation in the psyche in dialectical terms (see Solomon 1994). In order to overcome the conflict of opposites, he evoked the concept of the transcendent function (*CW* 8, paras 131–93), the symbolic function of the psyche which is essential to it if it is to change and grow. The transcendent function, characterised by its teleological function to bring the psyche forward out of polarised, oppositional defensive states, thus enabling the individuation process, operates through symbol creation. In the self's agony as it labours within the split and stuck inner situation, the unconscious may, perhaps through a dream image, offer a symbol or image to conscious awareness which is meaningful and can be used by the self to move forward. This process inevitably brings pain, suffering and resistance, as the old order breaks down and before new habits and more adaptive ways are securely established. Nathan Field's (1996) notion of 'breakdown and breakthrough' is relevant in this respect, as is Britton's (1998) notation ($Ps(n) \rightarrow D(n) \rightarrow Ps\ (n + 1)$) regarding the cyclical oscillation between the paranoid-schizoid and depression positions.

Although it is contentious to speak of change occurring at the neurobiological level as a result of psychological shifts, the degree of suffering that is often involved cannot be discounted, and at times may be tantamount to giving up an addiction, with its attendant neurobiological and neurochemical correlates. This has a parallel with the earlier discussion in this chapter concerning the infant's participation in its own self-regulatory processes, including the energy and effort involved in initiating interactions with another. The quality of the humanity of the patient is thereby attested to, through their recognition of the pain, waste, and destruction that the old ways of living life have exacted of the self, and indeed how others in the person's life have suffered as a result by the ongoing struggle – and failure – to integrate the shadow. It is through engaging in this struggle that the ethical capacity has been activated, and meaning and value thereby generated.

The Struggle to Find the Other

The self is not called upon to be ethical in a vacuum. The ethical attitude implies recognition and value of the substantive reality and subjectivity of the other. It requires the withdrawal of shadow projections so that the reality of the other can be known about, acknowledged internally and responded to. This idea is reminiscent of Buber's (1937) concept of the 'I–Thou' relationship as a dialogistic encounter between two subjectivities. The teleological project of the self to achieve wholeness requires in the first instance the withdrawal of projections, since the self cannot be whole if parts of it are unknown and projected outside itself. In particular, what is often projected is exactly that which the self experiences as an immoral, unethical, bad part of itself.

A clear theme that emerges both in this chapter and throughout this volume is that the self becomes itself gradually over time as it unfolds in relation to another. My subjectivity impacts on the subjectivity of the other, and vice versa. Helen Morgan (Chapter 7, this volume) has discussed the perspective of the new physics which demonstrates that the observer changes what he or she observes by the very act of observing. Similarly, the observer will be changed by being observed. Just as the self may treat itself as either subject or object in healthy or unhealthy ways, so it may treat the other. Thus we can say that the primary self is embued with a primary instinct for relatedness, if for no other reason than that the infant must seek out interactions with its caregiver in order to ensure nourishment, care and protection, so that the optimal development of its own neural networks, particularly those that regulate cognitive and socioaffective behaviour, can occur. (See Solomon, Chapter 8, this volume, and also Solomon 1997a for a fuller description of this situation.) This is an expression of a general self-protective and self-generative purposefulness which also includes acts on the part of the self to rid itself of unwanted, bad aspects, a self-protective, self-immunisation. Thus we have an archetypal and developmental relational set-up in which the other is both needed and desired but may also be deprecated and eschewed by the self as a receptable of unwanted, bad internal aspects projected by the self outside itself.

The self is at once separate and related, divided against itself and instinctively seeking integration. How is the self to properly find the other in these circumstances, in order to find the fullest expression of its self as an ethical being? The contemporary British moral philosopher Bauman (1993) has pointed out that it would be incorrect to consider as equivalent subjectivities the two persons interacting in an ethically laden situation. Contrary to Buber's supposition, in ethical discourse 'I' and 'Thou' are not equals in a reciprocal relationship:

> The 'we' ... is not, therefore, a plural of 'I' ... In a moral relationship, I and the Other are not exchangeable, and thus cannot be 'added up' to form a plural 'we'. In a moral relationship, all the 'duties' and 'rules' that may be conceived are addressed solely to me, bind only me, constitute me and me alone as an 'I' ... The moral person and the object of that person's moral concern cannot be measured by the same yardstick – and this realization is precisely what makes the moral person moral ... Being a moral person means that I *am* my brother's keeper ... whether or not my brother sees his own brotherly duties in the same way I do ... It is this uniqueness ... and this non-reversibility of my responsibility, which puts me in the moral relationship. (Bauman 1993, pp. 50–1)

Bauman points out the ontological separateness of each one from the other, as exemplied by God's question to Cain, 'Where is your brother?', and Cain's reply, 'Am I my brother's keeper?' This emphasises that the ethical attitude is predicated on the reality of the separateness of the self from the other. Following the French moral philosopher Levinas (Levinas 1985), Bauman argues that ethics comes *before* ontology (Bauman 1993, p. 71). Morality is a transcendence of being, a face-to-face experience, an authority which I give to you that you then have over me. Thereby, he states, 'I am fully and truly for the Other ... I give myself to the Other as hostage ... My responsibility ... is unconditional' (Bauman 1993, p. 74). The ethical capacity cannot be derived from shared ontological reality, the facts of existence; rather, it is derived from value and meaning, which are different, 'higher' and unconditional.

Bauman and Levinas seem to be pointing to a fundamental human mode of relatedness that has as its first expression the 'ordinarily devoted mother' (Winnicott 1964), a deeply ethical mode in its instinctual and unconditional devotedness to another, her infant. This must include the mother's capacity to struggle with her own internal shadow impulses to rid herself of the ethical and nurturing burden that she has accepted in attending to her infant. The first ethical experience of the infant, no doubt at a deeply unconscious level, is as a 'me' at the breast of another who is devoted to me, despite whatever struggle she may have with her shadow impulses towards me. So the infant is free to use the breast ruthlessly (Winnicott 1971), without fear of retaliation. In so doing it becomes possible for the infant to experience itself as an authentic being, without undue regard for its survival on placating another, which would have the effect of skewing the development of the infant's self.

I am proposing here that this is the condition that lays the foundation for the infant's potential to eventually develop an ethical capacity. The infant takes in the experience of non-talionic relating at the primordial, pre-verbal level of being, at the breast. Through the experience of the unconditional availability of the mother, who has had to manage internally, through her own capacity for containment (as in Jung's idea (*CW* 12, para. 187) of the *vas bene clausum*), her inevitable negative, shadow responses towards her infant, the infant is thereby nourished physically, mentally and emotionally. This may be the *a priori* condition through which the ethical capacity is catalysed. Equally, this may be the *a priori* condition through which the infant falls in love with the beauty of the breast (Meltzer and Williams 1998). The link between the ethical and aesthetic capacity has also been signalled by Bauman (1993). These events trigger the next stages in the development of the primitive mind, those primordial acts of discriminating, splitting and projecting, that organise the subjective experiences of the early world of the infant.[5] The discriminating, splitting and projecting activities are in turn the very preconditions of the creation of the shadow.

So the situation of the self which struggles to find the other reconfirms elements of the situation of the self we have been examining when we posited the self as a primary integrate – I am alone as a moral being – while at the same time I find my moral nature in relation to another. In order to find its inherent moral condition, the self must struggle to find another, whether or not the other is moral in relation to the self. It represents a transcendence of narcissistic ways of relating, in which the other is appropriated by the self for 'use' in the self's internal world, such that the object's subjective reality, their freedom to be other, is attacked or denied, through to a capacity to encounter the truth of the other, a genuine capacity to relate to another, a move in the furtherance of, or development beyond, the depressive position. This situation has direct implications for what happens in the consulting room between the analytic couple. The ethical attitude develops, personally and professionally, through the self progressing from a narcissistic mode of relating. Just as the basis for the eventual development of the infant's own capacity through its earliest experience of unconditional devotedness of the caregiver, notwith-standing the infant's attacks and the caregiver's own inevitable (but hopefully not too overwhelming) failures, such that the infant is allowed to develop mentally and emotionally, as well as physically (as does the caregiver in a way appropriate to his or her self); so in the consulting room the patient experiences an ongoing capacity in the analyst to maintain an unconditional analytic and ethical attitude that survives, despite the patient's attacks on or denial of what is available, and despite the inevitable (but hopefully not too overwhelming) failures of the analyst, such that the patient may develop and grow (as does the analyst in a way appropriate to his or her self).

The Struggle to Find the Other in the Consulting Room

Jung provided in the concept of the *coniunctio* a way of conceiving the self's archetypal capacity to enter into relation with another in all its various aspects and vicissitudes, while at the same time remaining the unique individual self as it was born and has become. Much of the work between patient and analyst in the consulting room concerns the variations in the modes of and capacity for *coniunctio*. A major difficulty that is often addressed in the analytic work is that of finding and sustaining a relationship with another. In the patient's unconscious search for what he or she needs from the analysis and from the analyst, two opposing scenarios often present themselves: either the self may hide itself from the possibility of intercourse with the other, locking itself away in an internal asylum; or else the self may attack or otherwise seek to invade, damage or undermine the other, thus avoiding the possibility of true relating. Both scenarios pre-empt the freedom of authentic interaction with another, in this instance, with the analyst.

Of the many possible vicissitudes of the *coniunctio*, there is an archiac and typical one that is often encountered in analytic work, or during some phase of it, whereby the *coniunctio* itself is negated, with the consequence that the experience of the difference between self and other, as well as the potential to relate to each other, is annulled. The reality of the other as a separate self is denied, exchanges between self and other occur in projective and identificatory ways such that it is difficult to decipher the two separate entities in the consulting room. The person may never have experienced a safe-enough *coniunctio* with an important other in order for the self to allow its defensive self-care system to fall away (Solomon 1997b); or else he or she may never have experienced another who was available mentally or emotionally and so instead survived by using up his or her own vital resources in an empty void where no one is allowed entry (Solomon 1998b); or else the person may have experienced an early loving relationship, but with another who was crazy or unable to relate in a way which was enduring (Solomon 1998a).

Jung emphasised the importance of the mutuality of the relationship that patient and doctor enter into in undertaking analysis, and at the same time he was very aware of the psychological dangers inherent in the situation and the ethical considerations that arise from this.

[I]n therapy, ethical values must not be injured on either side if the treatment is to be successful. Yet what happens in the therapeutic process is only a special instance of human relationships in general. As soon as the dialogue between two people touches on something fundamental, essential, and numinous, and a certain rapport is felt, it gives rise to a phenomenon which Lévy-Bruhl fittingly called *participation mystique*. It is an unconscious identity in which two individual psychic spheres interpenetrate to such a degree that it is impossible to say what belongs to whom. If the problem is one of conscience, the guilt of the one partner is the guilt of the other, and at first there is no possibility of breaking this emotional identity. (*CW* 10, para. 852)

In the notion of *participation mystique*, Jung clearly identified the strengths and dangers of these primitive levels of communication, as they were liable to lead to a state where there was little distinction or difference between two individuals within the relating pair. The positive aspect of this is that an immediate and intimate communication between them is possible; but there is a negative aspect in that, because self and other can become mixed up, there is a very real danger that the discriminating function essential to the capacity to behave according to the unconditionality of the ethical attitude may be perverted. To counter this danger, Jung warned that

[f]or this a special act of reflection is required ... Although the first step in the cognitive process is to discriminate and divide, at the second step it will unite what has been divided, and an explanation will be satisfactory only when it achieves a synthesis. (*CW* 10, para. 852)

Differentiation: The Notion of Boundaried Space

The notion of boundaried space has a long analytic tradition. For Jung, the idea of the *vas bene clausum* (*CW* 12, para. 187), and for later psychoanalysts that of the analytic frame (Langs 1974; see also Gabbard and Lester 1995 for a fuller discussion), referred to the boundaried and protected space of the analytic vessel within which analytic work can take place safely and therefore to its fullest extent. This chapter has emphasised that analytic work brings together the two fundamental conditions of being human: the unique individuality of the self, which implies the unique individuality of the other, and, at the same time, the possibility of the intermingling of psychic states of mind between the self and the other such that the boundaries between them can become blurred. In the analytic situation, this happens in a context of an avowedly unequal relationship between the two participants, patient and analyst. In this situation, the analytic frame provides the possibility of experiencing the fundamental conditions of the self in relation to another within the safety of a boundaried space. Within the secure and protected analytic frame, the analytic work proceeds through exploring the patient's conscious and unconscious inner world, as well as through the unfolding relationship between the patient and the analyst. As Gabbard and Lester point out:

> One of the central paradoxes of the analytic situation is that the professional boundaries must be maintained so that both participants have the freedom to cross them psychologically. In other words, processes such as empathy and projective identification oscillate back and forth across the semipermeable membrane constructed by the analytic dyad. The analyst expects a therapeutic regression to occur in both participants so that more primitive states of fusion and exchange are possible. (Gabbard and Lester 1995, pp. 42–3)

Earlier, I suggested that the emergence of a capacity for an ethical attitude in the young mind was predicated on the mother's secure attachment to her own capacity to offer an unconditional devotedness to her infant at the breast, whatever inevitable failures might occur and whatever subsequent interactions unfold through the developmental process. I am arguing here that it is by the very nature of the analyst's secure attachment to their own inner ethical attitude, within the safety of the boundaried analytic space, that the patient may him- or herself safely divert from his or her usual moral or ethical attitudes at the adult level, including the socially accepted norms of behaviour to which the social self usually adheres. Instead, the patient can allow him- or herself the psychological freedom to seek to test, assault, damage or destroy, as well as to love, cherish, protect and nurture, the contents of his or her own inner world, the inner world of the analyst, and the world of the analytic relationship. Only thus can the patient achieve whatever unconscious need he or she had of the analytic process when analysis was entered. This is what Jungians understand as steps towards wholeness and psychic integration, which will inevitably include regressions to disturbing states of mind. Without the analyst's capacity to maintain the ethical attitude in the face of the dramatic, often life-and-death struggle that can occur during the course of an analysis, if talionic rather than agapaic responses prevail within the analyst, then the assault on the ethical attitude within the analyst and between the analyst–patient pair will have prevailed. The primitive defences of the patient or the analyst, or both, will have triumphed over the search for greater health and integration within each. This does not mean that knowledge is to be eschewed of the talionic, aggressive, sadistic, masochistic or destructive responses, as well as of the loving and nurturing responses, evoked within the analyst through working with the patient. On the contrary, the fullest knowledge that the analyst can achieve of those experiences in his or her own inner world, including the shadow side, along with the interaction of his or her inner world with that of the patient, is exactly the 'special act of reflection' which the analyst is called upon to perform (*CW* 10, para. 852).

The unbalanced nature of the analytic dyad resembles the situation described earlier by Bauman (1993) in which one person takes on unconditional ethical responsibility towards another who is not obliged to reciprocate in an equal way. Essential to this is the recognition of the differences between the pair in the analytic dyad, and the special responsibilities of the analyst in maintaining an agapaic attitude towards the patient while allowing for the more primitive, talion responses of each to be known about. Within the urgency of the situation, which can at times reach dramatic, archetypal proportions, both patient and analyst may feel that no solution is evident or forthcoming. It is then, Jung stated, that 'the transcendent function manifests itself as a quality of conjoined opposites' (*CW* 8, para. 189). This is tantamount to finding how the self in its separateness and uniqueness can with safety be open enough to the reality of the existence of another such that authentic relating is possible. This requires evidence that neither the self nor the other will in fact revert to talionic acts of defence and aggression. If the analyst maintains his or her ethical attitude, it should be possible to meet such a challenge, even if with a struggle, particularly as the analyst will already have faced through his or her own analysis a similar struggle to the one that faces the patient. For the patient, within the special conditions of the analytic frame, this will be won only through a struggle of enormous proportions. It means going from a two-dimensional existence in which the other may be ignored with impunity, to a three-dimensional existence in which the other is acknowledged and related to. However, the enormity of the struggle may lead to a creative solution and to further integration of the personality, through the work of the transcendent function.

> Only the creative power of the ethos that expresses the whole man can pronounce the final judgment. Like all the creative faculties in man, his ethos flows empirically from two sources: from rational consciousness and from the irrational unconscious. It is a special instance of what I have called the transcendent function, which is the discursive co-operation of conscious and unconscious factors or, in theological language, of reason and grace. (*CW* 10, para. 855)

Maintaining Relatedness in Boundaried Space

In the situation we are imagining, provided that the safety of the boundaried space is maintained, the patient is not required to heed the usual ethical or moral imperatives in relation to the analyst. Scope is created thereby for the analytic exploration of exactly the internal position of the patient where there is no experience of another with whom to relate. Here, the self may be sequestered into a closed, internal space, uninhabited by others, the claustrum (Meltzer 1992). This is the area patrolled by the defences of the self which seek to control the traffic between the self and the other in order to protect the self from the conditions that made possible the original trauma and required such defences to be erected (Kalsched 1996). Where these conditions prevail, admitting another into this space would be tantamount to the most enormous achievement, a revolution in the internal world of the patient, an achievement with deep moral implications since the other would be discovered, acknowledged and related to.

We know that in such circumstances there can be a life-and-death struggle in the consulting room between what Kalsched (1996) has called the diabolical shadow and the forces of health and life in the patient. This includes the analyst's relationship to his or her ethical attitude, since inevitably the analyst will be tested in one way or another at this level by the patient. The opposites have now been constellated, and there appears within the analytic situation no solution available to the conscious mind. In Rosenfeld's (1987) terms, a psychic impasse has been reached, which requires a creative breakthrough, but which may end up in a defensive splitting or psychic retreat (Fairbairn 1951, Steiner 1993).

It is here where the analyst can feel most fully engaged in a struggle which has ethical dimensions. The analyst adheres to the knowledge that the patient eschews knowing about the reality of the existence of another, usually the analyst, for profound reasons that have to do with the survival of the self. There may be a defence against relating to an object that must inevitably be shared, as amongst siblings or with the other parent. But usually the trauma has come from narcissistic damage caused when the self had been seeking contact with another who was then catastrophically traumatising to the self. Perhaps there was an inability to respond, or a sudden absence, or an inappropriate mode of relating that was intrusive or abusive. Whatever the circumstances, the self had learned to create a place of safety for itself by ensuring that the other was excluded and thereby rendered impotent and incapable of going on harming the self. Inevitably, of course, maintaining such isolation requires that the self use up its own resources for self-nurturing. A real life-and-death situation may then arise when there are fears for the patient's physical or psychological safety. This situation has already been alluded to and described clinically (Solomon 1997b, 1998a, 1998b).

In this situation, the analyst is required to be empathically with the patient in their internal solitary confinement, while at the same time maintaining a knowledge of and relationship to the possibility for proper *coniunctio* in which self and other may live in separateness and mutuality. This is an achievement which is equivalent to a position beyond the terms usually understood as the depressive position.

Beyond the Depressive Position

Much of the argument of this chapter has suggested that the attainment of the ethical attitude is a developmental achievement, such that it is possible to venture a view that the ethical attitude is a developmental position. Here, 'developmental position' is meant in much the same way as Klein (1957) or Bion (1957) when they referred to the paranoid-schizoid or the depressive positions as stages in the developmental process. Hinshelwood defines the term 'position' as 'the characteristic posture that the ego takes up with respect to its objects', adding that Klein adopted the term 'to convey ... a much more flexible to-and-fro process between one and the other than is normally meant by regression to fixation points in the developmental phases. She wanted also to convey an emphasis on relationships' (Hinshelwood 1989, p. 382).

In the Kleinian framework,[6] there evolves a gradual demarcation between self and other, as the self achieves a fuller experience of its own subjectivity in relation to the subjectivity of another. Involved in this view is the infantile equivalent of the withdrawal of the projections of those negative aspects of the self that in adults we might call shadow projections, through to a gradual capacity to view the self along with the other as separate but interrelated subjectivities. It must be emphasised that the view offered here is of a continuous oscillation, an ongoing dynamic, between these states or positions.

As Jung stressed at the level of adult functioning, so Klein stressed the importance of internal integration and synthesis of the self in relation to the other at the earliest level of infantile mental functioning, although she did not bring out the teleological implications of this.

> [F]rom the beginning of life the ego tends towards integrating itself and towards synthesizing the different aspects of the object. There appear to be transitory states of integration even in very young infants – becoming more frequent and lasting as development goes on. (Klein 1948, p. 34)

However, without recourse to a teleological explanation for this ongoing process of integration, the Kleinian formulation can only be predicated on the mother's capacity to maintain and support the infant at those earliest times when the young mind is liable to be overwhelmed by the force of its own experiences without adequate means to achieve integration on its own. And yet, Klein's explanations were centred on the *internal* dynamics of the self. Although she acknowledged the importance for the infant's development of the quality of the mothering provided, she did not particularly elaborate on how this interaction would impact on the infant's self.

None would deny the crucial role of early nurturing and the provision of a 'good enough environment' for the self to develop and grow (Winnicott 1965). Jung stressed the teleological implications of a view of the self in which the innate capacity for the self to become itself through the process of individuation was a fundamental aspect. It seems to me that this represents a crucial difference between the Jungian and Kleinian view of the self, with implications for the understanding of the development of an ethical attitude, as discussed above. In that view, the ethical attitude is not predicated on the ethical behaviour of the other towards the self, but rather is triggered by the earliest experience of the unconditional devotedness of another in relation to the self, regardless of the self's relation to the other. In Klein's view, on the other hand, the capacity for guilt, concern and the wish for reparation seen in the infant results from the self's capacity to imagine the damage it has caused the object, and thus how the object's wish or capacity to go on loving the self will be diminished. Here is an internal accounting system at work which remains related to the talion law.

In the teleological perspective in which the self is always becoming more itself, there is a further dimension in which the self is supported in its development through the symbolic capacity of the transcendent function and the creative resources of the unconscious. In speaking about the self's struggle with an ethical conflict which can leave the self feeling locked in a dilemma from which there seems to be no development or recourse, Jung states:

> The deciding factor appears to be something else [than an accepted rule or custom]: it proceeds not from the traditional moral code but from the unconscious foundation of the personality. The decision is drawn from dark and deep waters. ... If one is sufficiently conscientious the conflict is endured to the end ... The nature of the solution is in accord with the deepest foundations of the personality as well as with its wholeness; it embraces conscious and unconscious and therefore transcends the ego ... a conflict of duty [finds] its solution through the creation of a third standpoint. (*CW* 10, paras 856–7)

We have seen that it is not always possible to achieve a positive outcome to the struggle to find another in such a way as to relate in an ethical manner. This is as true in the consulting room as outside it, and involves an ethical struggle on the part of patient as well as analyst. It may be that the achievement of an ethical attitude will depend on the apprehension of being related to ethically prior to the development in the self of an ethical capacity. Freedom from appropriation for use in another's intimate, internal world, may preceed the ability to relate ethically to an intimate other. In conditions where such freedom was not available, the self may have had to devise ways of protecting itself from such incursions, and a loss of ethical capacity may have ensued. Much analytic work is then devoted to reinstating such freedom.

Conclusion

The struggle for psychological wholeness and the integration of the projected shadow brings pain and requires sacrifice. But it is also a satisfying achievement to the self to attain ever increasing states of truth, moral freedom, meaning and value. The achievement of an accommodation between the conflicting needs for closeness and the need for differentiation require the self to be in constant struggle with itself and with the close other, the pitfalls of which are seen in the varieties of narcissistic object relating that occur outside and inside the consulting room. This struggle is at the source of the ethical capacity. It is when the fit between states of closeness and states of differentiation are wrong, skewed or intolerably uncomfortable, that we can find ourselves cast out of the ethical domain and into a part-object, perverse way of relating.

In this chapter I have explored the ways in which the self finds, defines, creates and struggles with ethical value. An ethical attitude is a crucial part of the analytical and psychotherapeutic relationship, and not just an addendum to the practitioner's work. It may take some time in working analytically for a practitioner to appreciate how integral the ethical attitude is to analytic practice. It is just as difficult a task for the patient. If it is experienced as the patient's problem, then analytic work becomes essentially no more than an intellectual exercise, and the Code of Ethics a mere checklist that may be forgotten as long as it is not transgressed. Analytic practice and the ethical attitude are intimately bound together; each permeates the other and defines and gives value to the other. This reflects the analytic relationship itself in which both partners make themselves available to, and are liable to be changed by, the encounter with the other. This is the essence of the analytic work and of the ethical attitude.

Notes

1. See, for example, Kohlberg (1963, 1984) and Kohlberg and Lickona (1986), who have made a particular study of moral development of children.
2. All of these can be included under the rubric of philosopher Paul Ricoeur's idea that the practice of psychoanalysis is tantamount to a 'hermeneutics of suspicion' (Ricoeur 1970). The implication is that embedded in the psyche are latent meanings

that cannot immediately be made sense of, or be made conscious, for a variety of motivated reasons (for example, to avoid the experience of psychic pain). Things are not what they appear, but although concealment is motivated, there is enough revelation of concealed meaning for interpretations to be more or less safely made.

3. Wallwork has provided a close study of the ethical implications in Freud's writing. For example, he states that,

> Freud sometimes seems to equate the superego or conscience, with the whole of moral functioning ... In *The Ego and the Id*, Freud states that the 'injunctions and prohibitions' of parents and other authority figures that are introjected into the ego at the close of the oedipal complex 'remain powerful in the ego ideal and continue, in the form of conscience, to exercise the moral censorship' ... 'In this way,' Freud writes a year later: 'the Oedipus complex proves to be ... the source of our individual ethical sense, our morality'. (Wallwork 1991, pp. 221–2, note 2)

4. Jungian analyst Kenneth Lambert (1981) made the useful distinction, relevant to our ethical enquiry, regarding the activation of the talion law versus the agapaic response in the context of the relations between analyst and patient. In particular, he warned the analyst against expressing the natural talionic instinct to reward or punish like by like; for example, to retaliate against a patient's negative transference by making punishing interpretations designed to hurt, humiliate or create distance from the patient. By contrast, he encouraged the analyst to adopt an agapaic attitude towards the patient, characterised by a respectful, reliable approach that is without exploitation or retaliation.

5. James Fisher provides a lucid account of this situation arising from work as a psychoanalytic marital psychotherapist and as an individual psychotherapist (Fisher 1999). He proposes a two-stage developmental model. In the first stage, the infant achieves a capacity to face the reality and truth of its own experience as a result of the mother's capacity to respond meaningfully to her infant's spontaneous gesture. In the second stage, the self achieves the capacity to face its own truth as well as that of the other in all their subjectivity, a situation in which both struggle to maintain their internal truths while at the same time come to terms with their experience of a shared external world. This creates triangular space that allows for the possibility of genuine intercourse, such that a new creative solution, an unpredicted outcome, or a real child, can emerge. Most importantly for our discussion here, Fisher considers that 'the achievement of the first stage may be dependent on an intimate relationship with someone who has achieved the second stage' (Fisher 1999, p. 8). This is a profile of exactly the situation that is being considered here, and can be linked to that situation described by Schore (1994, 1996) at the neurobiological level.

6. It might be useful briefly to review at this point Klein's formulations concerning the development of the young mind. At the most primitive level, Klein considered that, because of the massive onslaught of internal and external stimuli on its limited mental capacities, the infant was suffused with psychotic states of mind causing profound anxieties that were primarily managed defensively through splitting and projection, where communicating, relating and using the other psychologically take place via projective identification (Klein 1946). Hence self and other are mixed up, and parts of each are allocated to different and separate psychic locations, either internally or externally in the self or in the other. Klein called this the paranoid-schizoid position, where the bad and good parts of the self and the other are not found together, and where relating was at the level of part objects. In a later development, called the depressive position (Klein 1935), the infant is more able to experience the other as a whole object, containing both good and bad aspects. Thus

the infant's feelings of love and hatred for the object, which had previously been experienced as separate, are now capable to being held together in the infant's mind, giving rise to feelings of ambivalence towards the object, as well as feelings of guilt and the wish to repair the damage that the self might have wrecked on the object in the previous, part-object mode of relating. Ogden (1989) made a further contribution to the Kleinian view of the primitive mind of the infant when he offered the concept of the autistic-contiguous position, the earliest of the three positions, in which the sense of the boundary between the self and the other was derived from the rhythmicity, periodicity, and 'skin-to-skin "molding" ... that are the ingredients out of which the beginnings of rudimentary self-experience arise' (Ogden 1989, p. 32).

References

Aron, L. (1996) *A Meeting of Minds: Mutuality in Psychoanalysis*. Hillsdale, NJ: The Analytic Press.

Bauman, Z. (1993) *Postmodern Ethics*. Oxford: Blackwell.

Bion, W. (1957) 'Differentiation of the psychotic from the non-psychotic personalities', *International Journal of Psycho-Analysis*, 38: 266–75.

Bowlby, J. (1969) *Attachment and Loss, Volume 1: Attachment*. London: Hogarth Institute of Psycho-Analysis.

Britton, R. (1998) *Belief and Imagination: Explorations in Psychoanalysis*. London: Routledge.

Buber, M. (1937) *I and Thou*, 2nd edition, trans. R.G. Smith. Edinburgh: Clark, 1958.

Fairbairn, R. (1951) 'A synopsis of the development of the author's views regarding the structure of the personality', in *Psycho-Analytic Studies of the Personality*. London: Routledge/Tavistock.

Field, N. (1996) *Breakdown and Breakthrough*. London: Routledge.

Fisher, J. (1999) *The Uninvited Guest: Emerging from Narcissism towards Marriage in Psychoanalytic Therapy with Couples*. London: Karnac.

Fordham, M. (1985) *Explorations into the Self*. Library of Analytical Psychology, vol. 7. London: Academic Press.

Freud, S. (1933) 'The dissection of the psychical personality', Lecture 31, *New Introductory Lectures*, in James Strachey (ed.), *The Standard Edition of the Complete Psychological Works of Sigmund Freud [S.E.]*, 24 vols. London: Hogarth, 1953–73, vol. 22, pp. 57–80.

Gabbard, G. and Lester, E. (1995) *Boundaries and Boundary Violations in Psychoanalysis*. New York: Basic Books.

Hinshelwood, R.D. (1989) *A Dictionary of Kleinian Thought*. London: Free Association Books.

Jung, C.G. (1916) *VII Sermones ad Mortuos*. London: Watkins, 1967.

Jung, C.G. (1963) *Memories, Dreams, Reflections*. London: Routledge and Kegan Paul.

Kalsched, D. (1996) *The Inner World of Trauma*. London: Routledge.

Klein, M. (1935) 'A contribution to the psychogenesis of manic-depressive states', *International Journal of Psycho-Analysis*, 16: 145–74.

Klein, M. (1946) 'Notes on some schizoid mechanisms', *International Journal of Psycho-Analysis*, 27: 99–110.

Klein, M. (1948) 'A contribution to the theory of anxiety and guilt', *International Journal of Psycho-Analysis*, 29.

Klein, M. (1957) *Envy and Gratitude*. London: Tavistock.

Kohlberg, L. (1963) 'The development of children's orientation toward a moral order, I: Sequence in the development of moral thought', *Vita Humana*, 6: 11–33.

Kohlberg, L. (1984) *The Nature and Validity of Moral Stages*. San Francisco, CA: Harper and Row.

Kohlberg, L. and Lickona, T. (1986) *The Stages of Ethical Development from Childhood through Old Age*. New York: Harper and Row.

Kohon, G. (ed.) (1986) *The British School of Psychoanalysis: The Independent Tradition*. London: Free Association Books.

Kumin, I. (1996) *Pre-Object Relatedness*. New York: Guilford Press.

Lambert, K. (1981) *Analysis, Repair and Individuation*. London: Academic Press.

Langs, R. (1974) *The Technique of Psychoanalytic Psychotherapy*. Volume II. New York: Jason Aronson.

Levinas, E. (1985) *Ethics and Infinity: Conversations with Philippe Nemo*, trans. R.A. Cohen. Pittsburgh: Duquesne University Press.

Meltzer, D. (1992) *The Claustrum*. Scotland: The Clunie Press.

Meltzer, D. and Williams, M.H. (1998) *The Apprehension of Beauty*. Scotland: The Clunie Press.

Ogden, T. (1989) *The Primitive Edge of Experience*. London: Jason Aronson.

Ricoeur, P. (1970) *The Symbolism of Evil*. New York: Harper and Row.

Rosenfeld, H. (1987) *Impasse and Interpretation*. London: Tavistock.

Schore, A. (1994) *Affect Regulation and the Origin of the Self*. Hillsdale, NJ: Lawrence Erlbaum.

Schore, A. (1996) 'The experience-dependent maturation of a regulatory system in the orbital prefrontal cortex and the origin of developmental psychopathology', *Development and Pathology*, 8: 59–87.

Sober, E. and Wilson, D.S. (1998) *Unto Others: The Evolution and Psychology of Unselfish Behaviour*. Cambridge, MA: Harvard University Press.

Solomon, H. (1994) 'The transcendent function and Hegel's dialectical vision', *Journal of Analytical Psychology*, 39: 1.

Solomon, H. (1997a) 'The developmental school', in P. Young-Eisendrath and T. Dawson (eds), *The Cambridge Companion to Jung*. Cambridge: Cambridge University Press.

Solomon, H. M. (1997b) 'The not-so-silent couple in the individual', *Journal of Analytical Psychology*, 42: 3.

Solomon, H. (1998a) 'Love: paradox of self and other' *British Journal of Psychotherapy*, 14: 3.

Solomon, H. (1998b) 'The self in transformation: the passage from a two to a three dimensional internal world', *Journal of Analytical Psychology*, 43: 2.

Stein, M. (ed.) (1995a) *The Interactive Field in Analysis*. Wilmette, IL: Chiron Publications.

Stein, M. (1995b) *Jung on Evil*. London: Routledge.

Steiner, J. (1993) *Psychic Retreats. Pathological Organisations in Psychotic, Neurotic, and Borderline Patients*. London: Routledge.

Stern, D. (1985) *The Interpersonal World of the Infant*. New York: Basic Books.

Wallwork, E. (1991) *Psychoanalysis and Ethics*. New Haven, CT: Yale University Press.

Winnicott, D.W. (1964) 'Further thoughts on babies as persons', in *The Child, the Family and the Outside World*. London: Penguin.

Winnicott, D.W. (1965) *The Maturational Processes and the Facilitating Environment*. London: Hogarth.

Winnicott, D.W. (1971) *Playing and Reality*. New York: Basic.

Young-Eisendrath, P. (1995) 'Gender and individuation: relating to self and other', in D.E. Brien (ed.), *Mirrors of Transformation: The Self in Relationships*. Pennsylvania: The Round Table Press.

Suggested Reading

Bauman, Z. (1993) *Postmodern Ethics*. Oxford: Blackwell.
Gabbard, G. and Lester, E. (1995) *Boundaries and Boundary Violations in Psychoanalysis*. New York: Basic.
Jung, C.G. (1958) 'A psychological view of conscience', *CW* 10, paras 825–7.
Solomon, H.M. (1997) 'The developmental school', in P. Young-Eisendrath and T. Dawson (eds), *The Cambridge Companion to Jung*. Cambridge: Cambridge University Press.

13

Spirits and Spirituality

Dale Mathers

Introduction

Analytical psychology understands religious experience as an expression of a natural human instinct, of archetypal patterns related to survival, appearing in our social interactions during a lifetime (Stevens 1982). Archetypes unfold from the beginning of life; at birth, in early relationships of dyads, triads and peer groups; during sexual differentiation, initiation, courtship and parenting; through ageing and gaining wisdom, to death with its attendant rituals. All *rites de passage* have archetypal components (Hillman 1983), cultural myths which underpin arts, sciences and religions.

'The archetype of religion' expresses in acts giving spiritual meaning to an object; 'reverencing', 'worshipping' or 'religioning' it. It operates in two relational fields – one between ego and Self, another between Self and collective. I capitalise 'Self', as I do not mean self (me, rather than you) but Self ('the eternal in us'). These bridging relationships express the transcendent function, which leads a part from itself to a larger whole. For ego, religion points beyond its daily role as a time-bound reality tester towards the time-free eternal Self: for Self, from personal uniqueness back to the collective, by sharing in collective myths and rituals (Henderson 1990).

> [F]or in the cosmos there is God, the deus otiosus, a being beyond man's capacity to comprehend him, and there are the bridging functions – the minor gods, sons or messengers – through whom communication between God and man is made possible. A parallel system exists in the psyche. There is the big Self that cannot be expressed directly, and there is the Ego, the area of consciousness. (Gordon 1995 p. 85)

Religion, a mental attitude, shapes perceptions, bringing meaning and purpose to experience. Its structures are describable, as those of any other psychological process. Unfortunately, 'believers' frequently see psychological descriptions as a threat, a point Jung made in his Terry Lectures at Yale in 1937: 'The psychologist, if he takes up a scientific attitude, has to disregard the claim of every creed to be the unique and eternal truth' (*CW* 11, para. 10). The 'creed' could be religious, political or analytic. Claims for 'unique, eternal truth' are characteristic of closed systems – cults and the fundamentalisms.

Born in a 'fundamentalist' Swiss Reform household, Jung recognised that his approach to religion began with the Christian myth system. He studied extensively in the emerging field of comparative religion, taking anthropological trips to East Africa and North America to gain first-hand knowledge of other traditions. His last twenty-five years were spent using his insights to 'treat' Christianity. His narrative treatment reasserted religion's function as a link between individuals and the collective, a natural 'cure' for individual and cultural anomie, alienation and social disintegration (Stein 1987).

As a medical student in Basle, Jung debated in the Zofingia Club – in medieval times, a student duelling society; at his time, an interfaculty intellectual 'duelling ground'. Theological students welcomed a natural philosopher as a supporter of the existence of 'the unknowable' but thought his questioning of their basic assumptions and belief systems, their fundamentalisms, to be disturbed and bizarre.

Analytical psychology is part of depth psychology: a way of looking at how we know; an epistemology as much as a science; a semiotics rather than a new religion. It examines how meaning and purpose attach to experience, including religious experience. It treats ideological concepts as 'Glass Bead Games' (Hesse 1946), differentiating between religion's perceptions of existence (ontology), and describing systemic commonalities between religious systems. It has no 'eternal truths'; privileges no belief system over another. It concerns itself with answerable questions: Is this belief system internally consistent? What is its ability to conduct reality testing successfully for its believers? Is the system open or closed? Can it accommodate change? Analytical psychology speaks to the human condition, saying pluralism, the capacity to hold and contain opposites, measures humanity.

There is also concern for aesthetics, for beauty in the patterns of meaning making. As Oscar Wilde put it (referring to interior design): 'have nothing in your home which is neither beautiful nor useful' – for 'home', read 'heart'. For example, belief systems may make certain foods or acts taboo; they may be internally consistent, perhaps beautiful, but fail on counts of reality testing and utility. Fundamentalism in any system represents premature closure; whether the system be religious or political, it is no longer beautiful nor useful. The word comes from *fundus*, the Latin for 'bottom'. Driven by perverse and primitive states of mind, as well as dropping turds on others, fundamentalists too often become fanatics. Murdering for the sake of mere belief is a premature closure: privileging 'belief' over reality testing, tyranny over freedom.

As Anthony Giddens, the present director of the London School of Economics, has responded when asked what he considered the greatest threat at present to individual freedom and liberty:

> The rise of fundamentalism of all kinds. Contrary to the received wisdom of the moment, I believe we should oppose all forms of moral absolutism. The simplest way to define fundamentalism is as a refusal of dialogue – the assertion that only one way of life is authentic or valid. Dialogue is the very condition of a successful pluralistic order. (Giddens 1997 p. 82)

In a similar vein, the philosopher of religion William Lafleur (1998) stated that,

> Much of what we recognise as 'fundamentalism' in any religious tradition is, at least in its hermeneutic posture, a wholesale rejection of all modern critical approaches and a professed return to a given scripture as authoritative in this sense. It tries to be premodern. (Lafleur 1998 pp. 75–89)

The argument I develop in this chapter is that contemporary analytical psychology, developing from the life and work of Jung, applies a postmodern critique to religion, a position opposite to fundamentalism or a cultish, closed religious system. Such a critique takes religion as narrative myth, a signifying system of symbols and signs which gives meaning and purpose to human life.

Jung's Background

Religious experiences shaped Jung's psyche and his ideas about the mind. How his story is told, like any narrative, depends on who tells it, to whom and why. Like a fugue, with themes and variations, 'Jung' exists in authorised versions: *Jung and the Story of Our Time*, by Laurens van der Post (1976); hagiographies: *Jung*, by Barbara Hannah (1991); in an 'autobiography': *Memories, Dreams, Reflections*, written in part by his loyal secretary Aniela Jaffé (1963); in apologetics: *The Wounded Jung*, by Richard Smith (1996); and in postmodernist critique: *Tabooed Jung*, by Christine Gallant (1996).

Against these stand an 'unauthorised version' – *The Jung Cult* (1994) and its sequel, *The Arian Christ* (1997), both by Richard Noll. He suggests that Jung, at one point, believed himself to be a messianic founder of a pre New Age German *Volkisch* cult, and that analytical psychology is no more than a cult religion masquerading as a profession. Both Noll's scholarship and conclusions have been seriously questioned (Shamdasani 1998). Perhaps enough time has passed since Jung died (1961) for there to be distance between the man, his beliefs and the ideas of analytical psychology? To separate the man from the work, we need to know more about the man.

Carl Jung was born in 1875, the second child of Paul Jung, a Swiss Reform pastor. A brother, Paul, died in infancy, three and a half years before Carl's birth. The ghost lived on (see Chapter 11 by Chris MacKenna, this volume). When Carl was four the family moved to Klein Hunigen, a small village outside Basle, where he attended school. He may well have been known as 'the Pastor's son', a difficult position for any boy in a small village. Jung says he was a dreamy, lonely, haunted child with many doubts about his father and his father's spirituality. For father, 'spirit' meant 'Holy Spirit' – and religion.

His mother, Emilie, suffered from depression. She was treated in a sanatorium when Carl was three and half. He saw her as having two person-alities, one for the day and one for the night. She may have been psychic, like her niece Helene – about whom Carl wrote his doctoral thesis (*CW* 1, paras 1–150). Both had a capacity for dissociation. This goes with being a good hypnotic subject, another of his early medical interests. From his mother, he learnt that 'spiritual' meant 'seances', 'mediums' – and the paranormal.

His father died in 1896, when Carl was twenty-one. He was dependent on relatives to help pay his way through medical school. He also read philosophy – Plato, Kant and the post-Kantians. He was particularly interested in the work of Schopenhauer – an atheist whose major work *The World as Will and Idea* was popular amongst literati – rather than philosophers. His transcendental idealism emphasises 'will' (volition), suggesting that 'divine purposes' (primordial images or archetypes) lie behind observable phenomena. There is a universal will, or life force, of which each object and individual is but a part (Russell 1961). Jung later used these ideas in his analysis of Christianity.

He excelled as a psychiatrist. While Junior Resident at the Burgholzli, Zurich – the University Psychiatric Hospital, an important research centre in Europe (like the Salpêtrière in Paris and the Maudsley in London) – with his Professor, Eugene Bleuler, he defined the basic differences between the functional psychoses, schizophrenia and manic depressive psychosis. This work assures his eminent status in psychiatry, as pioneering research on the Word Association test does in experimental psychology. Yet, with all these achievements, something was felt to be missing. Perhaps his capacity to empathise with severely psychotic patients confronted him with disturbed parts of his own psyche?

Jung became drawn to Freud after reading *The Interpretation of Dreams* in 1906. Freud, in need of experimental validation for his theories, welcomed the already famous Jung whose researches on the Word Association test provided scientific proof for the existence of the unconscious, the proof Freud needed (Solomon 1994). Jung had shown, reliably and repeatably, the existence of psychological mechanisms which push disturbing affects out of consciousness, which he called complexes.

Spirit and the Split with Freud

From strongly contrasting social backgrounds, a generation apart, it was not so much the differences between Judaism and Protestant Christianity that finally split the two apart (Samuels 1996). Perhaps galled at being outshone by someone younger, a gentile and *haute bourgeois* (if only by marriage) with intellectual prestige greater than his own, Freud provided Jung with an excuse for separation by posing a challenge that Jung was unable to ignore within the psychoanalytic enquiry on the freedom to explore 'spiritual' phenomena.

At the start of the twentieth century few boundaries existed between psychology and parapsychology. Freud had difficulties with how the latter was to be understood. He wished to treat both religion and the paranormal as forms of the sexual instinct. Here, Jung (not Freud) belongs in the mainstream: the tradition of William James, Pierre Janet and Anglo-Swiss-Franco-American thinking (Taylor 1996) who kept open minds about the study of spirit, which Freud, given his temperament and extremely difficult political position – a Jew in anti-Semitic Vienna, found hard to do. Jung had wrestled with his parents' 'spirituality' and probably projected unresolved feelings about them on to Freud; first as Idealised Father, then as 'Terrible Mother'. Nor could he bear Freud's 'fundamentalist' reductionism. Their split is symbolised by a pivotal incident: 'the bang in the bookcase'.

In 1909, Jung visited Freud in Vienna. Freud told Jung he was the 'Crown Prince' in his nascent psychoanalytic movement. Jung felt his diaphragm get hot, maybe physically sensing rage at being appropriated by Freud's paternalistic ambition. Immediately, there was a loud bang in Freud's bookcase. Freud was upset. Jung said there would be another bang: it followed (Jung 1963, p. 155). Freud felt his authority challenged. At one level it seems he really did believe that Jung 'used occult powers' to make the noises; at another, he could not let himself believe.

Freud's supporters make much of a three-month study period with Charcot in 1885, Jung's supporters make less of his time with Janet in the winter of 1902–3 (Ellenberger 1970, p. 436). These 'pilgrimages to Mecca' (the Salpêtrière Hospital in Paris) connect both to a parenting tradition, the cultural myth of 'mental science'. These French connections matter to my argument here as Charcot and Janet investigated just such liminal phenomena – those psychic happenings bordering conscious and unconscious – as well as hysterical dissociation, multiple personality, hypnosis and suggestibility. Thus, at the core of the first psychoanalytic enquiries is the Charcot–Janet interest in the borderlands of the mind.

The Anglo-Swiss-French-American psychologists hoped to find scientific evidence for, amongst other things, the basis of religious experience. The problem is described by a leading member, Jung's friend William James (1960, pp. 25–46), in his first Gifford Lecture, given in Edinburgh in 1902. Their work mirrored the work of psychical researchers, such as F.W.H. Myers at the Society for Psychical Research in London, whose concept of subliminal consciousness influenced Jung (Taylor 1996).

Whether the 'bang in the bookcase' is understood primarily as a paranormal phenomena, or as a phenomena critical to the split between Freud and Jung, certainly it was a synchronicity – a coincidence carrying meaning. A 'container of knowledge' split in the outer world, and between them, in the inner world. The history of religion (like analysis) is bedevilled by splitting. Painful feelings go in one place and good feelings in another. Getting rid of the bad and keeping the good is a universal psychological defence mechanism. Jung grew up in a culture which split Protestant and Catholic into light and dark, good and bad. Early attempts at dealing with bad feelings by dissociative splitting are seen in an incident showing his fearful preoccupation with death and his connecting it to Jesuits, the original 'Men in Black' (Jung 1963, pp. 25–30).

He saw a coffin being carried to a grave and a Jesuit in a black coat. He felt frightened. He carved a toy 'man in black', hiding the manikin in his pencil case in the attic. He talked to the manikin in this secret place and felt power over the 'Shadow man'. The little man was comforting and made him feel potent. Retelling the incident in his autobiography, Jung owned the sexual symbolism and linked it to his earliest remembered dream in which he descended into the earth and saw a giant phallus enthroned in a cathedral-like room. He heard his mother saying, 'That is the man eater' (Jung 1963, p. 27).

The manikin, like the phallus, begins as a *sign* – a concrete object, representing things of which he was afraid. As he used the object habitually in anxiety management rituals – taking it out and putting it away, writing private thoughts on scrolls and leaving them with it – it became a *symbol* invested with numinosity (spiritual and sacred significance). This capacity to transform *sign* into *symbol*, to let his manikin become a protective inner companion, is not simply magical, primary process thinking: it is an unfolding of 'the archetype of religion', an exercise of the transcendent function, giving numinous meaning to an object. The ability to do this is vital to individuation (Lambert 1981, pp. 188–92), a word the adult Jung coined for a soul's journey through inner and outer worlds.

Encounters with his inner world often took dramatic forms. As a small boy day-dreaming on a stone, he wondered if it was the stone or he which thought, like the story of Confucius and the butterfly (Jung 1963, p. 35). Doubts about Protestant orthodoxy contrast with experiential certainty about the reality of 'spirit'. Adolescent religious doubts crystallised in a vision of Basle Cathedral being shattered by God's turd. Steeped in religious processes, his life's work was to differentiate himself from family, social and cultural religious matrices. There is no denial of 'religion', nor founding of a new one; rather, Jung developed by repeated *reculer pour mieux sauter* (steps back to leap forward) as traced by Jacoby (1990, pp. 47–9) through his writing.

Religious Themes in Jung's Work

As so much of Jung's work is suffused with spirit, I am going to concentrate on texts which bring together, hold and reconcile opposites – a cultural task of religion and a personal task in analysis. Jung's first major work, 'Symbols of transformation', written in 1911 (*CW* 5), attempted to demonstrate his separation from Freud over the libido theory as applied to spirit. He used poetic fantasies written by Mrs Frank Miller, collected by his colleague Theodore Flournoy. He amplified differences between the *signs* in her text and the *symbols* in her psyche, hoping to show the turbulent psychic life of this 'highly suggestive woman' was not 'all to do with sex'.

The style is sometimes turgid, the tone often tendentious, and the amplifications at times appear as massive digressions rather than clarifications. Yet the work is important. It is Jung's first demonstration of a religious instinct, common across cultures and not reducible to sexual drives. It is a signpost at the start of a difficult journey through previously unmapped territory, the collective unconscious. For, after breaking from Freud, the collective threatened to overwhelm Jung. *The Seven Sermons to the Dead* (*VII Sermons ad Mortuos*), written in 1916 in less than a week by automatic writing, at a time of intense psychic turmoil, inspired much that came after. An extract from the start of the first sermon catches the mood:

> The dead came back from Jerusalem where they did not find what they were seeking. They asked admittance to me and demanded to be taught by me, and thus I taught them: Hear Ye! I begin with nothing. Nothing is the same as fullness. In the endless state fullness is the same as emptiness. The Nothing is both empty and full. One may just as well state some other thing about the Nothing, namely that it is white or that it is black, or that it exists or that it exists not. That which is endless and eternal has no qualities, because it has all qualities. The nothing, or fullness, is called by us the Pleroma. In it thinking and being cease, because the eternal is without qualities. (Jung 1916, in Hoeller 1982, pp. 44–5)

Again, the language is impersonal, grandiose and inflated, perhaps because 'archetypal psychology recognises that psychic reality is inextricably involved with rhetoric. The perspective of soul is inseparable from the manner of speaking of soul' (Hillman 1983, p. 19), or perhaps mythopoeic bombast resulted from 'effort after meaning' – a common symptom in minds in a religious frenzy or on the edge of a psychotic breakdown (WHO 1978).[1]

Key concepts in analytical psychology appear in embryo amongst the *Seven Sermons*. There is the interplay of opposites through paradox, as the unconscious makes good the deficits experienced by consciousness. There is a difference between ego-time ('here and now', outer world, serial, clock or *chronos* time) where moments appear in succession, and Self-time ('eternity', inner world, parallel, non-linear *kairos* time) where moments appear coexistent (Wiener 1996). This distinction appears in the *Seven Sermons* as between Noumena and Pleroma, and underpins the concept of synchronicity (Aziz 1990, pp. 64–6, 75–84).

The *Seven Sermons* contains a huge amount of data in a tiny volume, like a 'Zipfile' in cyberspace. Jung's life-work was to 'unzip' them. Rather than taking his automatic writing as a text for a new religion, he treated it as a series of symbols. That he is sometimes hard to understand is less due to his poor exegesis of this primary text, than as a consequence of difficulties in translating the language of archetypes into 'ordinary human speech' – tuning down the 'language of gods' to the 'language of men'. Significantly, at around the same time as the *Seven Sermons* he wrote his seminal essay on 'The transcendent function' (*CW* 8, paras 131–93), the link between the real and the imaginal through metaphor and symbol formation.

Jung's interpretation of his deep religious and near-psychotic experience required new words. After 1913, he invented the terms 'introvert' and 'extrovert', 'collective unconscious', 'animus' and 'anima', 'persona' and 'shadow', and 'individuation' – signs on his map of the inner world. Intense inner turmoil gradually stabilised through his discovery and exploration of mandalas, through which he arrived at an idea of Self. Again, this is capitalised, meaning the transcendent rather than the personal.

Self is neither a unity nor a deity: it is a process, not a thing – a 'becoming' rather than an 'is'. Self is not a 'higher consciousness' or 'an organising centre', yet it is a whole greater than the sum of its parts (*CW* 6, paras 789–91). Imagine Self as a party of people dancing – a metaphor from a popular Christian hymn 'Lord of the Dance' (Carton 1969). Sometimes many parts of the psyche are on the dance floor, sometimes not; first one has the spotlight, then another. Jung took his idea that such a Self has 'divine purpose' from Schopenhauer (Nagy 1991, pp. 72–4). Over-identification with Self (the Lord of the Dance, Christ) is dangerous, narcissistic psychic inflation (Ledermann 1989, pp. 101–26) –

and common in psychotic states, which can be thought of as a flooding of the ego by the Self.

Jung deepened his concept of Self through work on alchemical texts, building from them sets of metaphors for psychological transformation; the 'purification' of the gold of the Self from the *massa confusa*, the muck in the alchemical vessel (von Franz 1980, pp. 13–14, 207–8). Instead of being projected on to others, this is held and transformed.

In 1933, he wrote 'The spiritual problem of modern man' (*CW* 10, paras 148–96). Separately published as *Modern Man in Search of a Soul*, this deconstructed the then fashionable modernism, showing that the Westerner's obsession with *now (chronos)* alienates him or her from *forever (kairos)*, just as obsessions with 'outside' alienate him or her from 'inside'. This radical idea, placing Self at the centre of life rather than 'selfish ego', is a commonplace sixty years on, particularly amongst the 'New Age' community, those who see in Gaia 'the world as will and idea'.

In 1937, Jung gave the Terry Lectures on psychology and religion at Yale (*CW* 11, paras 1–168). Exploring links between Christianity and alchemy, he defined Self thus:

> I have chosen the term Self to designate the totality of man, the sum total of his conscious and unconscious contents. I have chosen this term in accordance with Eastern Philosophy which for centuries has occupied itself with the problems that arise when even the gods cease to incarnate. (*CW* 11, para. 140)

The union of opposites, a metaphor Jung took from the alchemist's *coniunctio*, is central to the healing task of analysts, both for individuals and with the culture (Samuels 1993, pp. 19–23). Unification in the collective, not fusion, is the task of religion.

> Concern with the psychology of primitives, with folklore, mythology and the comparative history of religions opens the eyes to the wide horizons of the human psyche and in addition it gives that indispensable aid we so urgently need for the understanding of unconscious processes. (*CW* 6, para. 313)

Jung unfolds the alchemical theme in his essays on Paracelsus (*CW* 13, paras 145–238). He identified strongly with this fifteenth-century physician. Both struggled with the same problem – how to bridge the split between an orthodox Christian's dogmatic idea of 'God the Creator' and our experience as 'free spirits' living in that creation.

In 'Answer to Job' (*CW* 11, paras 553–758) Jung gave his polemical view on the split at the heart of Judaeo-Christian-Islamic monotheistic belief, the problem of evil. The duality intrinsic in myths about good and evil dividing the world is shown in the wrestling for Job. Job represents ego. The struggle for his soul represents a split in the Self and in the world, which religion tries to heal. Jung suggests that God needs humankind for God's redemption and individuation, as humankind needs God. He believed that the Christian religion contains its own analysis and could give itself its own treatment. Jung's complaint against God when confronted by Job's cries, is that he did not then look at himself and ask why he had done what he had. It took the birth of Christ to permit this introspective opening, for God to experience human suffering in his own person.

This provoked great controversy. Theologians criticised the religious implications; psychologists the psychological. Jung was playing ideas against each other to clarify the *form* of a discourse, rather than the *content*. The *content* is a Hebrew myth. The *form* is 'as ego equals Job, so Self equals God'. Therefore, as Job becomes healed by reconciliation with God, so ego becomes healed by reconciliation with Self. And, likewise, as Self needs ego to be in the world, so God needs humankind to know itself and become 'healed' through reconciliation with his creation, as fulfilled in the death and resurrection of Christ.

The theme of *'splitting and reconciliation'* (opening and closing) is fully developed in his *magnum opus* 'Mysterium coniunctionis' (*CW* 14). The union of opposites *(coniunctio)* is examined in a series of paradoxes. First, God has both unity and duality, a central tenet of Gnosticism. Second, in alchemical metaphors, the dance of the elements is both the intercourse of spirit, in masculine *sol* and feminine *luna,* and also real sexual intercourse.

By returning to sexual metaphors in the *coniunctio,* Jung completed a task begun in 'Symbols of transformation' (*CW* 5). There, he had used the Miller fantasies to show that dissociative hysteria is not 'just about sex', it is also about problems with symbol formation. This involves ego and Self working together to make meaning, an intrapsychic function of the religious archetype. Interpsychically, this expresses through activities in which the Self and the collective make meaning together. 'Mysterium coniunctionis' seems a long way from his 'dream of the man eater', in which the little boy Carl met the sacred phallus. However, both the initial dream and the two texts show that in the *form* of religion there is the *content* of sexuality. When Jung explains that the penis is just a phallic symbol (*CW* 18, para. 572; *CW* 6, para. 406), he is emphasising that collective meanings come *before* personal.

Herbert Read (1974, pp. 230–47), the art historian, anarchist and editor of the *Collected Works* says, for Jung, 'religion and politics inextricably link as forms of social discourse', as 'without freedom there can be no morality'.[2] 'The undiscovered self' (*CW* 10, paras 488–588) amplifies this, asking what it means to live in an age full of apocalyptic images of universal destruction, in a world where splitting is acted out by hanging an 'Iron Curtain' across Europe. Jung asserts it is our own internal splitting of Self into light and dark, good and bad, that lies at the core of these projected conflicts. Resolution comes about through individuation: for 'resistance to the organised masses can be effected only by the man who is as well organised in his individuality as the mass itself' (*CW* 10, para. 540).

Religion as Archetype

Let us suppose that Jung's work arose from, amongst other things, subconscious wishes to repair damaged parents, exorcise family ghosts, heal his inner splits, and 'explain everything'; like a child wanting to know what life, death and beyond mean. Religious themes were sought, found and explored in medicine, psychology, metaphysics and theology, then applied to human behaviour.

He used an alchemical formula 'as above, so below' – as inside, so outside – to deconstruct splitting. The function of the religious archetype is to make sacred, reverent; to give meaning, to make what has been split whole. This involves seeing the whole repeated in the part (like a hologram), finding the Creator in the creation. It reclaims the projected from the projector, by placing Self (as a venerated object) in place of 'me', as seen in 'the manikin' myth and the myth of the stone on which the boy sat wondering. Maybe our own healing comes through finding sermons in stones? This does not require analysis, though it does require attention.

Jung's central idea is that religion is an archetypal capacity, the function of which is to make meaning. Religion is not a 'belief in …' a concept – or *content* – but a 'capacity to believe …', to have particular *forms* of thought. If we imagine that archetypes function as verbs, 'doing words' in the psyche, then, just as 'mothering' is the name for expressions of the mother archetype, so the verbal noun 'religioning' (making objects symbolic and sacred) names the action of the religious archetype – like 'reverencing', or 'worshipping'. Samuels (1997, pp. 287–316) describes this process as 'resacralising', putting a spiritual dimension back into the political process, but 'religioning' may be an easier word to remember, especially in reference to the individual experience of religion.

Jung's aim was to replace 'religion' as a specific, limited belief system (the fundamentalism of his ancestors) by 'religioning' – the ability, as the Society of Friends states, 'to answer that of God in Everyman' (Quakers 1995, s. 19:32). 'Religioning' is a universal human capacity to find meaning in one's own life or the lives of others. It helps us to recognise, accept and reconcile opposites.

It is an instinct, like sexuality, which expresses deep human needs for unity, wholeness and meaning.

Interplay between sexual and religious archetypes is crucial in the practical work of analytical psychology. In our work with patients we keep a 'bifocal vision', validating perceptions from the ego and the Self of both persons in the room. Using the dance metaphor again, analytical psychologists see individuals *both* as 'individual dancer' *and* 'part of the dance troupe'. Problems in living are *both* related to ego struggling with Self (perhaps expressed in sexual and relational difficulties), *and* Self struggling with the collective (perhaps expressed in religious doubts). Healing comes through replacing *'either–or'*, as operator in our inner logic, with *'both–and'*, creating open systems. The sudden realisation by any individual of being *both* an individual participant *and* the spirit of the dance is numinous. It breaks down anomie. As Jung put it:

> By becoming conscious, the individual is threatened more and more with isolation which is nevertheless the sine qua non of conscious differentiation. The greater this threat, the more it is compensated by the production of collective and archetypal symbols which are common to all men. This fact is expressed in a general way by the religions, where the relation of the individual to God or the gods ensures that the vital link with the regulating images and instinctual powers of the unconscious is not broken. Naturally this is true only so long as the religious ideas have not lost their numinosity, i.e. their thrilling power (*CW* 13, paras 395–6).

The thrilling power of religious behaviour is analysable, but not reducible to repressed sexuality. Analysis validates the way beliefs express, the *form of a belief* (since belief is both possible and necessary) rather than its specific *content*. This is an extremely important point. For, to those *inside* a belief system, validation of their perceptions, feelings and experiences comes through that system. The more fundamentalist (closed) the system, the less that system itself can be questioned, and the less it can cope with change. Analysis, a belief system for observing belief systems, includes its own bias. It acknowledges, with modern physics, the inevitability of observer effects and intersubjectivity. Jung's idea of *coniunctio*, the holding of opposites, encourages us to work with this intersubjective perspective (Hall and Young-Eisendrath 1991, pp. 37–8).

Questioning Religion

Analysts ask certain kinds of question: 'Is the life this person leads consistent with their belief system?', 'Is their belief system consistent with human experience?', or, 'Would the results of their belief system further the growth of any human from any culture at any time in history?'

We have seen that Jung's spiritual project was not to found a cult, but to examine religious systems. Did his project have a selective bias? Yes. To Christianity, to the paranormal, to the interface between Western and Eastern religion, to the problem of evil. Jung never left his ancestor's religion, but in his 'Introduction to the Tibetan Book of the Dead' (*CW* 11, paras 475–526) he states his belief that East and West cannot resolve into each other, but can and must learn from each other in order to counter the materialist inflation of the West and the emotional inertia of the East. He emphasised and contributed extensively to the dialogue between Christianity and other world religions.

Jung emphasised the 'invariants of self: agency, coherence, continuity and emotional arousal' (Hall and Young-Eisendrath 1991, p. 60), as vital links between an individual's belief systems and the regulating images and instinctual powers of the collective unconscious. Taking a concept from systems theory, we can ask: *Is this religious system open or closed?* To caricature, amongst Christians: Quaker (open) and 'Wee Free' Presbyterian (closed); in Judaism: Liberal progressive (open) and Lubovitch (closed); in Islam: Sufi (open) and Taliban (closed).

Religioning (reverencing), our capacity to make experience sacred, makes meaning and connects individuals to the collective. Jung felt it empirically evident that religion, a collective expression of humanity's capacity to form and use symbols, links internal and external reality. What we believe shapes our perceptions, and what we perceive can shape our beliefs. Open systems are not morally better than closed, fundamentalist, ones. However, open belief systems are better able to deal with change. Closed systems tend to be better able to contain anxiety.

The value of using the whole human culture (the collective, both conscious and unconscious) to validate belief systems – the religioning of percepts – cannot be overemphasised. It promotes tolerance. The Cross, a symbol for those raised in Christian cultures, is an example. Its associations are reached out for, and seem to reach out to Christians. Certain perceptions of the image are validated: 'the Cross signifies God's love', might be one. Raised in a Roman Catholic myth system, we may find nothing odd in the image of a naked man scourged and crucified, hanging behind a gilded altar, representing God's love. However, to those from another myth system; for example, a Buddhist, this is a strange sanctification of sado-masochism. Perhaps Christians find gold images of Buddha sitting in the Lotus position a disturbing glorification of passive withdrawal?

Cultural mental attitudes can turn anything into an object of worship. Like all expressions of archetypes (archetype ... ing), religioning relies on the existence of consciousness (*CW* 6, para. 700). Consciousness is perception (having sense experiences) and reflection. It allows negotiation with our instincts, permitting adaptation to the environment, which makes us feel good. A concept of good requires a concept of bad. Paraphrasing Jung in 'Mysterium coniunctionis' (*CW* 14), acts of separation basic to our survival (between open and closed, percept and perceiver, inner and outer, Self and ego, individual and collective), arise from a natural tendency to perceive in pairs of opposites. Splitting is inherent to the psychic experience.

This dichotomising creates the problem of Good and Evil. As separation between Self and ego is essential for individuation, so, having choice (free will) contributes to the problem of evil (*CW* 11, paras 658, 1958). The dichotomy is as natural as that between opening and closing systems. We cannot avoid closing round a set of religious myths, or beliefs. Doing so provides existential security, clarifies boundaries and simplifies reality. Yet it has the inevitable consequence of making 'us' seem good and 'them' seem evil. This further closes down perceptual systems, destroying the possibility of tolerating difference.

The Self has the function of verifying meaning. This depends upon being able to separate Self from object, as explained by Michael Fordham:

> Jung identified ... religious experiences ... with archetypal symbolism: it is often thought that infantile experiences comprise states of mind with which a truly adult person has nothing to do: I contend, on the contrary, that they persist and are progressively integrated into later and more mature living. So in showing that the grandeur, the mystery and the numinosity of religious experience are rooted in infancy and enrich its mature equivalent, I shall make an opportunity to illustrate a thesis about the relation between infancy childhood and maturity.
>
> Unless the links with the helplessness, the dependence and the spontaneity of childhood are maintained, religious experience can lose its true meaning and may become either an empty and formal ritual or merely a rational exercise. (Fordham 1976, p. 25)

Fordham describes what happens if the joyful dance of life becomes empty ritual, when the good goes out of the Gospel, 'for Unless ye are as little children you cannot enter the kingdom of heaven' (St Mark 10: 15). As children, we live more in eternal time and our ego is less rigid. Our drive towards symbol formation, our capacity for magic, awe and wonder, arise from the spiritualising, religious function.

As a child's Self unfolds and perceives (opens, *deintegrates*), it is in a two-way dialogue with the surrounding culture. Ego's response to Self, and Self's response to the culture, question our belief system's internal consistency and reality testing. Religious (meaning-making) negotiations decide when *deinte-*

gration turns to *reintegration;* closure, Self infolding and digesting. Free movement between opening and closing is central to 'religioning'. It gives us choice about moving from oppression and madness towards freedom, as explored by Foucault in *Madness and Civilisation* (1965, pp. 117–59). Jung engaged with the same problem. His insight into religion was to see its function as holding together and transcending opposites. By his struggle to free his own spirit from dogma, he created methods to allow us to do likewise.

Notes

1. For a description of the phenomena from a psychiatric viewpoint, see World Health Organization (1978) p. 27, schizophrenic psychoses (295 group). Jung knew this danger, describing it in 'Paracelsus': '[O]ne employs a special bombastic style full of neologisms which might be described as power words. This symptom is observable not only in the psychiatric clinic but also amongst certain modern philosophers, and above all, whenever anything unworthy of belief has to be insisted on in the teeth of inner resistance: the language swells up, over reaches itself, sprouts grotesque words distinguished only by their needless complexity' (*CW* 13, para. 155).
2. Read refers particularly to 'Two essays on analytical psychology' (*CW* 7, para. 240), 'The assimilation of the unconscious'.

References

Aziz, R., (1990) *C.G. Jung's Psychology of Religion and Synchronicity*. Albany: State University of New York Press.
Carton, Sidney (1969) 'Lord of the dance', in *The Songs of Sidney Carter: In the Present Tense, Book Two*. London: Galliard Ltd.
Ellenberger, Henri (1970) *The Discovery of the Unconscious*. New York: Basic Books.
Fordham, Michael (1976) *The Self and Autism*. Library of Analytical Psychology, Volume 3. London: Heinemann.
Foucault, Michael (1965) *Madness and Civilisation*. Cambridge: Cambridge University Press.
Gallant, Christine (1996) *Tabooed Jung*. London: Macmillan.
Giddens, Anthony (1997) in 'Influences', interview with S. Brasher, *New Statesman* 31 January.
Gordon, Rosemary (1995) *Bridges*. London: Karnac.
Hall, James and Young-Eisendrath, Polly (1991) *Jung's Self Psychology*. New York: Guilford Press.
Hannah, Barbara (1991) *Jung: His Life and Work*. Boston, MA: Shambala.
Henderson, Joseph (1990) *Shadow and Self*. Wilmette, IL: Chiron Publications.
Hesse, Hermann (1946) *The Glass Bead Game*. London: Penguin.
Hillman, James (1983) *Archetypal Psychology*. Dallas, TX: Spring Publications.
Hoeller, Stephan (1982) *The Gnostic Jung and the Seven Sermons to the Dead*. Wheaton, IL: Quest Books/The Theosophical Publishing House.
Jacoby, Mario (1990) *Individuation and Narcissism*. London: Routledge.
James, William (1960) *The Varieties of Religious Experience*. London: Fontana.
Jung, C.G. (1963) *Memories, Dreams, Reflections*, recorded and edited by Aniela Jaffé. London: Collins/Routledge and Kegan Paul.
Lafleur, William (1998) 'Interpretation as interlocution', in Donald Mitchell (ed.), *Masao Abe: A Zen Life of Dialogue*. Boston, MA: Tuttle Publishing.

Lambert, Kenneth (1981) *Analysis, Repair and Individuation*. London: Academic Press.
Ledermann, Rushi (1989) 'Narcissistic disorder and its treatment', in Andrew Samuels (ed.), *Psychopathology: Contemporary Jungian Perspectives*. London: Routledge.
Nagy, Marilyn (1991) *Philosophical Issues in the Psychology of C.G. Jung*. Albany: State University of New York Press.
Noll, Richard (1994) *The Jung Cult*. London: Fontana.
Noll, Richard (1997) *The Arian Christ*. London: Fontana.
The Quakers (1995) *Quaker Faith and Practice: The Book of Christian Discipline of the Yearly Meeting of the Religious Society of Friends in Britain*. London: The Yearly Meeting of the Religious Society of Friends.
Read, Sir Herbert (1974) *Anarchy and Order*. London: Condor.
Russell, Bertrand (1961) *The History of Western Philosophy*. London: Unwin University Books.
Samuels, Andrew (1996) 'Jung's return from banishment', *Psychoanalytic Review*, 83(4): 469–90.
Samuels, Andrew (1993) *The Political Psyche*. London: Routledge.
Shamdasani, Sonu (1998) *Cult Fictions: C.G. Jung and the Founding of Analytical Psychology*. London: Routledge.
Smith, Robert (1996) *The Wounded Jung*. Evanston, IL: Northwestern University Press.
Solomon, Hester (1994) 'The transcendent function and Hegel's dialectical vision', *Journal of Analytical Psychology*, 39(1): 77–100.
Stein, Murray (1987) *Jung's Challenge to Contemporary Religion*. Wilmette, IL: Chiron Publications.
Stevens, Anthony (1982) *Archetype*. London: Routledge.
Taylor, Eugene (1996) 'The new Jung scholarship', *Psychoanalytic Review*, 83(4): 547–69.
van der Post, Laurens (1976) *Jung and the Story of Our Time*. London: Penguin.
von Franz, Marie-Louise (1980) *Alchemy*. Toronto: Inner City Books.
Wiener, Yvette (1996) 'Chronos and kairos: two dimensions of time in the psychotherapeutic process', *Journal of the British Association of Psychotherapists*, 30(1): 65–85.
World Health Organization (WHO) (1978) *Mental Disorders: A Guide to their Classification in Accordance with the Ninth Revision of the International Classification of Diseases*. Geneva: World Health Organization.

Suggested Reading

Clarke, Margaret (1998) 'God could be something terrible', in Ian Alister and Christopher Hauke (eds), *Contemporary Jungian Analysis*. London: Routledge.
Jones, Peggy (1998) 'Process of transformation', in Ian Alister and Christopher Hauke (eds), *Contemporary Jungian Analysis*. London: Routledge.
Meckel, Daniel J. and Moore, Robert L. (1992) *Self and Liberation: The Jung/Buddhism Dialogue*. New York: The Paulist Press.
Stein, Murray and Moore, Robert L. (1997) *Jung's Challenge to Contemporary Religion*. Wilmette, IL: Chiron Pubications.

14

Jung's Influence in Literature and the Arts

John Clay

The arts represent an especially Jungian field. This view has partly grown up through the association of Jung with the arts and the spiritual side of life in general, and with his emphasis on the second half of life – the second half being seen as the opportunity and time for artistic endeavour as a counterbalance against the active and acquisitive first half. I think it is important in this context to mention that artistic endeavour, or creativity to give it its wider name, can refer to all sorts of undertakings, not just the recognised fields of the arts. People can live in a creative way, or exercise thought and judgement and discretion in all sorts of creative and therefore artistic ways. Lateral thinking is one example of this or a more reflective cast of mind. Recent developments in chaos and complexity theory attest, too, to the need to re-view things from different and perhaps more creative perspectives.

Jung wrote widely on the arts. One volume of the *Collected Works* is devoted to this: Volume 15, 'The spirit in man, art and literature', where he emphasises art as reflecting the *Zeitgeist*, the spirit of the age. In another paper written in 1937, 'Psychological factors determining human behaviour' (*CW* 8), Jung considered that the need to create was one of five basic instinctive forces, the others being hunger, sexuality, activity and reflection. Thus, the creative urge was in all of us. Erich Fromm (1947) echoed this: 'To be creative means to consider the whole process of life as a process of birth, and not to take any stage of life as a final stage.' In this context there is a story that Bion took the playwright Samuel Beckett, his analysand, to Jung's Tavistock Lectures in 1934, and that Beckett was particularly struck by hearing Jung talk about people not being properly born. Beckett seems to have incorporated this in his later work – 'giving birth astride the grave', a memorable phrase in one of his plays (Beckett 1954).

In Jung's own case, his first significant experience of artistic creation came after his break from Freud. In 1913, as he describes in his autobiographical *Memories, Dreams, Reflections* (1963), he embarked on a lengthy 'confrontation with the contents of his unconscious'. For Jung it was an extremely long drawn-out affair that took years before he reached 'some degree of understanding' of his unconscious. He shut himself away in his tower by the lake shore at Bollingen. Here was a safe retreat, backed by the security of his family life, where he could pursue the promptings of his unconscious. Having isolated himself, he started to sculpt in stone and draw mandalas, drawing inspiration both from his personal unconscious and from the wellspring of archetypal images that gradually emerged.

He described this process in *Memories, Dreams, Reflections*:

My mandalas were cryptograms concerning the state of the self which were presented to me anew each day. In them I saw the self – that is, my whole being – actively at work. I had the distinct feeling that they were something central, and in time I acquired through them a living conception of the self ... I had to let myself be carried along by the current, without a notion of where it would lead me. When I began drawing the mandalas, however, I saw that everything, all the paths I had been following, all the steps I had taken, were leading back to a single point – namely, to the mid-point. It became increasingly plain to me that the mandala is the centre. It is the exponent of all paths. It is the path to the centre, to individuation. During those years, between 1918 and 1920, I began to understand that the goal of psychic development is the self. There is no linear evolution; there is only a circumambulation of the self. Uniform development exists, at most, only at the beginning; later, everything points towards the centre. This insight gave me stability, and gradually my inner peace returned. (Jung, 1963, p. 187)

This is a central text regarding Jung's view of artistic activity. Everything points to the centre, to individuation : the 'truth' is already there, it needs only to be found. Artistic purpose is to uncover it, to know one's face for the first time, to paraphrase T.S. Eliot. In Picasso's apposite phrase regarding his own artistic undertaking, *'je ne cherche pas, je trouve'* (I do not seek, I find).

Jung's encounter with alchemy at the same time was decisive in this respect, as it linked him with the 'primal world of the unconscious' and emphasised the importance of spirit. The study of alchemy became his mentor, his teacher. He found that the alchemical process replicated the process of creation – from *massa confusa* to *nigredo* to refining process and to whitening, to purification and to the *coniunctio*, to the *lapis*, the philosopher's stone, and finally to gold. His study of alchemy was preceded by a series of dreams. In one he found himself in an adjoining house and discovered an incredible library within, dating from the sixteenth and seventeenth centuries, with large folio volumes along the walls. Among them were a number of books with copper engravings, containing curious symbols such as he had never seen before. At the time he did not know what they referred to; only later did he recognise them as alchemical symbols. He was fascinated by this series of dreams, interpreting the unknown wing of the house as a part of his personality of which he was not yet conscious. Interestingly, some fifteen years later he had assembled a library very like the one in the dream.

Having commissioned a Munich bookseller to send him alchemical texts, he acquired the sixteenth-century text *Rosarium Philosophorum*. This became his main text, which, with its illustrations, Jung elaborated on at great length in Volume 12 of his *Collected Works*, 'Psychology and alchemy'. He commented: 'the experiences of the alchemists were, in a sense, my experiences, and their world was my world' (Jung 1963, p. 196). This was for him a momentous discovery: he had stumbled upon the historical counterpart of his psychology of the unconscious.

> When I pored over these old texts, everything fell into place: the fantasy-images, the empirical material I had gathered in my practice, and the conclusions I had drawn from it. I now began to understand what these psychic contents meant when seen in historical perspective. (Jung 1963, p. 196)

History was important to him, for 'without history there can be no psychology and certainly no psychology of the unconscious' (Jung 1963, p. 197). He was on the path of individuation, and this was the path of creativity.

The unconscious then for Jung, and for Jungians, is seen as a repository of valuable and age-old material. Individual artistic creation draws upon this collective wealth. This was a matter over which Freud and Jung differed. Freud saw the unconscious as the place for suppressed personal material, certainly conflictual, and often pathological by nature. Unconscious drives were to be interpreted in sexual terms. Jung, on the other hand, saw the unconscious as a storehouse for valuable psychic material, both relating to the individual and to a wider context, arising from the collective unconscious. In particular, dreams were not so much seen as emanating from psychological disorders, but were expressions of psychic activity where the process of symbolic transformation could occur. Thus, dreams were often purposive. In his 1930 paper 'Psychology and literature', Jung wrote:

> A great work of art is like a dream; for all its apparent obviousness it does not explain itself and is always ambiguous. A dream never says 'you ought' or

'this is the truth'. It presents an image in much the same way as nature allows a plant to grow, and it is up to us to draw conclusions. (*CW* 15, para. 161)

Jung described two levels of the unconscious, the personal and the collective. The personal had to do with personal acquisitions, dispositions, forgotten or repressed contents. It was where a person's potential resided. The collective unconscious was closer to biology than biography; its contents were ingrained, not the accidents of personal experience, and linked with the common experience of the human race. This distinction led Jung on to develop his theory of the archetypes, with their eternal motifs. It is worth remembering that in the era when Jung was writing, other works of literature were developing similar archetypal ideas – T.S. Eliot's *The Waste Land* in 1921, Spengler's *Decline of the West* in 1923, and Thomas Mann's *The Magic Mountain* in 1924. The need to delve into the past, to re-acquire age-old collective wisdom, was then very much part of the *Zeitgeist*.

Concurrent with this, the emphasis on unconscious mental processes, on interior dialogue, or stream of consciousness, found its way into the novels of Virginia Woolf, and more particularly in James Joyce's *Ulysses* which appeared in 1922. Joyce and Jung had some dealings with each other in Zurich at this time. Joyce's daughter, Lucia, an incipient schizophrenic, had approached Jung for treatment. Lucia had remained mute with her previous other doctors, but with Jung she spoke freely, and for a while she gained weight and seemed happier. But Jung was uncertain about continuing her treatment without her father's support. Jung feared it might lead to her breakdown. Jung commented, in a memorable phrase, 'Both [father and daughter] are swimming in the same water – one is diving, the other drowning', thus expressing the narrow dividing line between artistic creation and madness. Joyce resisted further treatment for Lucia who was, in Jungian terms, Joyce's anima. He did not want her changed. Jung struggled to read *Ulysses* at the time. At first it seemed to him 'like a pitiless stream that rolls on without a break' (*CW* 15, para. 164) and he called it a 'hellish monster-birth' (*CW* 15, para. 164) but he persevered – indeed, he must be one of the few people ever to have read the book right through – and began to see its pattern of creativity and destruction. He commented that 'Joyce's inexpressibly rich and myriad-faceted language unfurls itself in passages that ... attain an epic grandeur that makes the book a Mahabharata of the world's futility and squalor' (*CW* 15, para. 194). He saw similarities to the alchemical process, the book's dark passages leading to a transformation – 'amid acid, poisonous fumes and fire and ice, the homunculus of a new universal consciousness is distilled' (*CW* 15, para. 201). Mostly he liked its emphasis on the inner world as when Joyce's hero taps his brow and says to himself : 'In here it is I must kill the priest and the king.'

The influence of both Jung and Freud on literature and novel writing in particular continued through the next thirty to forty years. At his seventieth birthday celebrations in 1926, Freud refused credit for the discovery of the unconscious. That, he said, properly belonged to the masters of literature who had always been aware of its presence. A new genre of literary criticism grew up, whereby earlier works of literature were read through the focus of psycho-analytic discovery. In Jungian terms, in *Pride and Prejudice* for instance, Elizabeth could be seen as Darcy's anima. He needs to bring himself in touch with this other side of himself, his feminine side, before reaching a fuller understanding of himself. Wickham can be read as his shadow side which again he must confront before he can begin to integrate himself fully. However, reading literature in this way interferes with the pleasure we get from it. To systematise Jane Austen according to Jungian or Freudian conceptions misses out on much of the subtlety and nuances of her writing. *Wuthering Heights,* on the other hand, can repay a Jungian explanation; for example, comparisons can be made between the individual personalities of Catherine and Heathcliffe and their archetypal representations.

The Jungian emphasis on dreams has helped writers in many ways. Writers tap into this mix of personal and collective unconscious and often use it as an impetus to their writing. For example, Borges (1974) calls writing a 'guided dream', and many writers have spoken of how their work has been shaped by dreams. Graham Greene kept a dream notebook by his bedside, and Robert Louis Stevenson explained that his Dr Jekyll and Mr Hyde came from a dream, which he jotted down the following morning. It might be of interest here to learn of Jung's own literary preferences. In his 1930 paper 'Psychology and literature', he mentions *Moby Dick* as his favourite English-language novel (with the pursuit of the white whale as a sort of negative dialogue with the Self). Goethe's *Faust* holds the same place in German literature for him with its mix of individuation and the attempted fulfilment of the collective dream of salvation so central to the Western psyche. In the same paper Jung writes of the creative process as having a feminine quality arising from

> unconscious depths – we might truly say from the realm of the Mothers. Whenever the creative force predominates, life is ruled and shaped by the unconscious rather than by the conscious will, and the ego is swept along on an underground current, becoming nothing more than a helpless observer of events. The progress of the work becomes the poet's fate and determines his psychology. It is not Goethe who creates *Faust*, but *Faust* who creates Goethe. (*CW* 15, para. 159)

The shadow side is a particular concept central to the Jungian view of artistic creation. The shadow is the darker side of ourselves, the part not exposed to light, the inferior side, the side of ourselves we do not like and often project on to others. *Hamlet* can be read as a play of shadows – 'oh what a rogue and peasant slave am I' – as Hamlet struggles with his private demons (Act II, scene ii, line 584). The Jungian view is that you have to acknowledge and recognise the shadow and accept it as part of yourself as a necessary step before achieving integration and self-growth. *Macbeth* is another Shakespearean play redolent with shadow. In this case the witches symbolise Macbeth's shadow, his darker side. In *The Tempest* it is Caliban that is Prospero's shadow that he has to accept before integration and resolution can occur: 'this thing of darkness I acknowledge mine' (Act V, scene i, line 271).

The work of literature that exemplifies the Jungian concept of shadow par excellence is Dante's *Divine Comedy,* especially the *Inferno* section, the descent into the depths, the inner journey into the shadow side of human nature. The poem starts with Dante facing the side of a mountain : 'In the middle of the journey of our life I came to myself within a dark wood where the straight way was lost' (Dante 1958). Note, too, the 'found myself again' – *mi ritrovai.* This is a mid-life crisis, a turning point, and hence a Jungian situation again, back to square one. On the hillside that he has to climb are three beasts: the lion, representing pride; the leopard, lust; and the she-wolf, greed. Each of these are shadow sides of himself which he has to encounter and deal with before he can proceed. He is frightened, trembling with fear. Help comes to hand with the presence of Virgil, his mentor (or therapist!), representing culture and tradition – perhaps the 'wise old man' in Jungian terms. With Virgil at his side he descends into the depths, encountering there various archetypal figures: the Minotaur, Ulysses, and so on. These are participants of the collective unconscious, as well as personal friends and enemies from Florence; in other words, his personal unconscious. T.S. Eliot echoes these lines of Dante in 'Little Gidding' in the *Four Quartets*: 'What, are you here too?', as Dante meets his old teacher Brunetto Latini (Eliot 1959). Dante's task is to reconcile the personal, the accumulated experience within his own history, and the collective, that which is omnipresent and universal. At the lowest point of hell, the point of inertia, to which the narrowing circles descend, sits Satan on his throne. Dante and Virgil see him from afar. Dante must confront him. Eventually he must pass under Satan's throne, through the dark and narrow, harrowing passage between Satan's hairy thighs and legs, the passage symbolising death and rebirth, before passing on to the other side. From this vantage point where he can look back safely at Satan on his throne. Satan is now much less menacing. Dante and Virgil now proceed with their ascent. The metaphor of climbing, of struggle, is important, and Jung himself often liked to quote Virgil's lines, 'the descent to Avernus [the underworld] is not hard ... but to retrace the steps and escape back to upper airs, that is the task and that is the toil' – *'hoc opus, hic labor est'* (*The Aeneid*, vi.126 [Virgil 1956]). Eventually Dante reaches Purgatory and heads towards Beatrice in Paradise, his source of love and redemption, a symbol of final integration.

The shadow, therefore, is the opposite side, the dark side. Reconciling the opposites is another Jungian focal point. F. Scott Fitzgerald said that the test of a good mind in a writer was the ability to hold two opposing ideas at once in consciousness. Nowadays, in our field, increasing interest is being taken in the notion of paradox, that is, the idea that two things can coexist simultaneously, or in a contradictory fashion, or even both be true, at once.

Creativity, or the creative process is, as we have seen with Jung's own experiences, something that emanates from the depths of our experience. It draws on many aspects of our nature. Here I find the Jungian writer Rosemary Gordon's definition of stages in the creative process very helpful. In her book *Dying and Creating* (1978), she marks out four stages of creativity. The first is preparation, where the author immerses him- or herself in his or her subject, reads all relevant books, literature, and so on. This is followed by a stage of incubation where the unconscious has its say, a sort of floating, letting go, time of confusion, pain, anxiety, waiting for things to happen. Next comes the stage of inspiration, when ideas and insights occur and there are flashes of illumination. Finally there is the stage of verification – testing out, organising, doing the actual hard grind, the writing out, selecting, sifting, editing, finalising. Of course, all these stages overlap and run into each other, but they are all dependent upon the centrality of unconscious processes.

This allowing for the interplay of conscious and unconscious forces is exemplified by Kipling's recommendation: 'When your daemon is in charge, drift, wait, obey' (Kipling 1937). This implies a certain surrendering of the ego, a giving up, a renunciation, a waiting. This may be unfamiliar to people used to doing things, to being proactive, focused and conscious. In order to access the unconscious, it is necessary to dig deep, or to allow things to happen. In his phrase, *'je ne cherche pas, je trouve'*, Picasso was indicating that being in touch with the creative process meant plumbing the depths of his unconscious until he found what he wanted. Clouzot's film of Picasso painting showed that he would suddenly rub out something that to others might seem complete or finished, saying 'that's not right', and so he would start off again. Paul Klee used to describe his drawing technique as taking a line for a walk (Klee 1953). Bertrand Russell stated that when he first started writing, each new piece of writing seemed to be beyond his powers. 'I would fret myself into a nervous state from fear that it was never going to come right. I would make one unsatisfying attempt after another, and in the end have to discard them all.' After a while Russell found that such 'fumbling attempts' were a waste of time. What he needed was a period of 'subconscious incubation which could not be hurried and was, if anything, impeded by deliberate thinking'. Sometimes he found he had to cancel the book he was thinking of writing, but often this incubation period produced results : 'having by the time of very intense concentration, planted the problem in my subconsciousness, it would germinate underground, until, suddenly, the solution emerged with blinding clarity, so that it only remained to write down what had appeared as if in revelation' (Russell 1965).

These techniques, or processes, link in with the Jungian idea of individuation, finding the path that is true to oneself. These are steps in the discovery of the Self, a form of self-actualisation and self-realisation (that is, making the self real), often by uncovering the God-images that we all carry around inside ourselves. The composer Aaron Copeland wrote: 'Each added work brings with it an element of self-discovery. I must create in order to know myself, and since self-knowledge is a never-ending search, each new work is only a part answer to the question "who am I?" and brings with it the need to go on to other and different part answers' (Copeland 1953, p. 41). Jung would have concurred with this view of Copeland's, embarking on the search for the self via the activity of creating.

As I wrote at the beginning of the chapter, Jung and the arts have often been associated with the second half of life, the post-mid-life years. Jung wrote in his paper 'The aims of psychotherapy' (*CW* 16, para. 83) that over a third of the patients who consulted him were not suffering from 'any clinically definable neurosis' but more from the 'senselessness and aimlessness of their lives'. This search for meaning underpins much of Jungian thought, and creativity can give the individual a meaning to his or her life.

The Jungian idea of creativity as a search for the self has helped me personally. In 1971 I helped start up Peper Harow in Surrey, a therapeutic community for emotionally disturbed adolescents. I was made head of education and took a leaf out of Jung's book by allowing the collective unconscious to get to work. Initially, I abolished all formal education and waited to see what would happen. A fifteen-year-old, with no educational background, started talking to me one day about the myths of Greece and Rome, which he had read about in a Ladybird book in a Remand Centre he had attended. I responded to him, told him some more and gave him a copy of Homer's *Odyssey* in the black Penguin translation to read. It started something rolling. After a while others became interested and so we formed a Greek literature group to read translations of Aeschylus, Sophocles and other Greek writers. The group understood immediately what these works were about since 'tragedy' had been so close to their previous experiences. The collective unconscious, the universality of human experience, had come into play. I then discovered an exam syllabus – Greek Literature in Translation – which they were entered for and all passed, the first exam any of them had ever taken in their lives.

They had thus found meaning in literature and had responded creatively to their discovery.

Jungian ideas and approach continued to inform my working life. In recent years I have become a writer, and a biographer, in addition to my work as a psychotherapist. Writing draws on the unconscious, and writing a biography can be compared to the process of therapy. Both are long-term and open-ended, with a sketched-in but uncertain outcome. In time, the journey becomes as important as the arrival. Biographies aim for cumulative truth, and there are hints, too, of the alchemical process at work, the transformational element. The biographer resembles the therapist in this way in his use of free-floating attention, of hovering, allowing things to be, suggestion and free association. Keats, speculating as to what led to achievement in literature, suggested 'Negative Capability'; in other words, 'the capacity to be in uncertainties, mysteries, doubts, without any irritable reaching after fact and reason' (Keats 1970). This is similar to Rosemary Gordon's (1978) second stage in the process of creativity.

In the biography I wrote of R.D. Laing (Clay 1996), the unconventional Scottish psychiatrist and psychoanalyst, I tried out certain Jungian perspectives to begin with; in particular, the concepts of individuation, *puer aeternus* and the trickster. In time, some of these Jungian ideas stayed and others were discarded, but they had all allowed me to evaluate material in an imaginative way. R.D. Laing was such an intensely mercurial figure that the research, the journey of the book, became quite precarious as Laing's personality threatened to take over. At one point the book seemed almost unmanageable and looked as if it would never reach its end, despite the known death of its subject. My publishers then reminded me of their deadline. During one long hot summer, I sat down and wrote out the last third of the book quite quickly, a private mantra on my lips – 'to hell with it', or words to that effect. It seemed to work. Once completed, the final section read as well as any other. Perhaps the unconscious, now allowed a free rein, was having its timely say.

Artistic creation is inevitably a struggle, and needs to be. Jung knew this and hence went in for his lengthy and fearsome confrontation with the unconscious. Others approach the struggle differently, using a process similar to Jung's idea of active imagination, a process of coming to know images from the unconscious by re-imagining them through various artistic media, such as painting, poetry, drama, sandplay, and so on. Creativity thus comes under many guises.

A special Jungian contribution for the arts is the notion of the trickster, which Jung borrowed from Native American mythology. The trickster is both a mythical figure and an inner psychic experience. He conforms to the archetype of mischievousness and unexpectedness, of disorder and amorality. He is an archetypal shadow figure. For someone bogged down in the sterility of an excessively entrenched, well ordered existence, the trickster can come as a relief, and can provide access to creative possibilities by helping to restore psychic balance. Jung found in the trickster a striking resemblance to the alchemical figure of Mercurius. He noted the trickster's fondness for sly jokes and malicious pranks, his ability to change shape, his dual nature (half animal/half divine) and he reminded him of the Swiss tradition of Carnival with its striking reversal of hierarchic order. Indeed, the trickster has found his way into contemporary literature, notably in the novels of Robertson Davies with their strong Jungian orientation and tricksterish heroes such as Magnus Eisengrim in the *Deptford Trilogy*, or in the writings of more postmodernist writers such as Martin Amis.

The relationship between artistic endeavour and therapy can be problematic. Not all artists or writers are prepared to lay themselves open to therapeutic intervention. The poet Rainer Maria Rilke, a contemporary of Jung's in the earlier part of the century, feared that going into analysis might cause him to lose his creative side, as he wrote in a letter to Lou Andreas Salome in December 1911: 'Psychoanalysis is too fundamental a help for me, it helps you once and for all, it clears you up, and to find myself finally cleared up one day might be even more hopeless than this chaos' (Rilke 1947).

Chaos can, in time, lead to order, and in this chapter I have sought to describe some of the background and historical origins of Jungian influence on the arts. I have focused predominantly on literature, but Jungian explanations can extend to all areas of artistic activity. We live in an increasingly fragmented world, where identity confusion is rife, and accepted standards are changing, and often lost. The *Zeitgeist* that Jung originally described as determining the course of artistic achievement is nowadays more difficult to ascertain. For instance, the collective, binding forces of religion, politics and mythology have been eroded, as have their symbol making capacity, their rites and rituals. Artistic activity can help to restore some of these.

The Jungian emphasis on individuation is a most valuable contribution in this area. It allows individuals to pursue their own artistic line in a way that will seem to them authentic and purposive. A Jungian perspective allows for a wide range of creative expression, geared towards the discovery of the self, that unique and inexhaustible treasure trove. In this way the Jungian viewpoint, as expressed in the arts, can be considered to have much relevance for us today.

References

Beckett, Samuel (1954) *Waiting For Godot*. London: Faber.
Borges, Jorge Luis (1974) Preface to *Doctor Brodie's Report*. London: Allen Lane.
Clay, John (1996) *R.D. Laing: A Divided Self*. London: Hodder and Stoughton.
Copeland, Aaron (1953) *Music and Imagination*. London: Oxford University Press.

Dante, Alighieri (1958) *The Divine Comedy*, trans. John Sinclair. London: Bodley Head.

Eliot, T.S. (1959) *Four Quartets*. London: Faber and Faber.

Fromm, Erich (1947) *Man for Himself: An Inquiry into the Psychology of Ethics*. New York: Holt, Rinehart and Winston.

Gordon, Rosemary (1978) *Dying and Creating*. Library of Analytical Psychology. London: Routledge and Kegan Paul.

Jung, C.G. (1963) *Memories, Dreams, Reflections*. London: Routledge and Kegan Paul.

Keats, John, (1970) 'Letter to George and Tom Keats', 21 December 1817, in *Letters*, ed. Robert Gittings. London: Oxford University Press.

Kipling, Rudyard (1937) *Something of Myself*. London: Macmillan.

Klee, Paul (1953) *Pedagogical Sketchbook 1*. London: Faber.

Rilke, Rainer Maria (1947) *Selected Letters 1902–26*, trans. R.F.C Hull. London: Macmillan.

Russell, Bertrand (1965) 'How I Write', in *Portraits from Memory and Other Essays*. London: Allen and Unwin.

Virgil (1956) *The Aeneid*, trans. W. Jackson Knight. London: Penguin.

15

Winter's Ragged Hand – Creativity in the Face of Death

Geraldine Godsil

Introduction

Jung's interest in the ever-present challenge of death is a central feature of his psychology. In 1930, he wrote:

> As a doctor I am convinced that it is hygienic – if I may use the word – to discover in death a goal towards which one can strive, and that shrinking away from it is something unhealthy and abnormal which robs the second half of life of its purpose. (*CW* 8, para. 792)

He describes the idea of life after death, so central in most religions, as an example of the 'primordial thoughts' that structure the unconscious (*CW* 8, para. 794).

Rosemary Gordon, in *Dying and Creating* (1978), builds on and extends Jung's work on 'the pervasiveness of man's concern with death' and her work has been a major influence in the Jungian tradition. It would be a mistake, however, to see Jung's emphasis on mid-life and beyond as a clear chronological division between Jungian analysis and psychoanalysis. An early paper by Jung, allegedly based on his daughter Anna's experience ('Psychic conflicts in a child', 1910), shows a little girl grappling with the events of death and birth through play and a sequence of nine dreams. The editors' note (p. 10) comments on the appearance in this early paper of the rebirth motif as a precursor to the concept of an 'archetype of rebirth' (*CW* 17, para. 7).

Jung's preoccupation with an archetypal component to all experience is the common thread that links this early paper with what was to follow. One of his most fertile ideas is that primitive structures in the mind influence the con-

244

struction of imagery, so that human experience is construed along particular, recurring lines. This concept is present throughout his work, constantly undergoing development and revision. Michael Fordham and the London School have further developed the ideas present in Jung's early paper on the nature of childhood development, 'Psychic conflicts in a child'. In the Jungian tradition, both classical and contemporary, the psychic experience of death is important throughout the whole life cycle.

However, outside this tradition infant development has often received more attention than the developmental tasks of mid-life and beyond. The reasons for our failure to observe the possibilities of psychic change in the elderly are probably connected to the psychotherapist's own defences. Nemiroff and Colarusso refer to this as 'professional ageism' and list six issues that contribute to the psychotherapist's resistance to take on and engage with elderly patients:

1. The aged's stimulation of therapists' fears regarding their own eventual old age (*and, we would add, anxiety regarding death*)
2. Therapists' conflicts about their own parental relations
3. Felt impotence stemming from a belief in the ubiquity of untreatable organic states in the elderly
4. Desire to avoid 'wasting' their skills on persons nearing death
5. Fears that an aged patient may die during treatment
6. Desire to avoid colleagues' negative evaluation of efforts directed toward the aged. (Nemiroff and Colarusso 1985, p. 25)

In this chapter I want to consider how personal recognition in mid-life and old age of the reality of death as an inescapable fate can propel the individual into new creative ventures. This flowering of mature creativity in full recognition of pain, loss, imperfections and deterioration of physical beauty and power is different from the forced creativity based on the wish to deny and replace rather than mourn.

Shakespeare's sonnets are full of protest and grief at the havoc wrought by the passage of time. My title is taken from one of them. His poetry provides him with some redress for the ravages of time. In Sonnet xv he uses a gardening metaphor to suggest how the loss might be acknowledged and made good by creative effort.

And all in war with Time for love of you,
As he takes from you, I engraft you new. (Shakespeare, (1609 [1986] *The Sonnets and 'A Lover's Complaint'*, Sonnet xv)

Seamus Heaney takes up this theme again in *The Redress of Poetry* (1995) with his discussion of the qualities that make poetry 'strong enough to help'. In a series of discussions of different poets he explores and illuminates poetry's power to rebalance the mind and restore the capacity to enjoy and endure. In a very interesting discussion and amplification of the meanings of redress he finds in the *Oxford English Dictionary*, he includes:

- Reparation – satisfaction or compensation for wrongs or losses
- Restoration – in the sense of setting a person or thing upright, raising them again to an erect position
- Repositioning – a concept that draws on a hunting term (now obsolete) meaning to bring back the hounds or deer to the proper course: a course where something unhindered, yet directed, can sweep ahead into its full potential. (Heaney 1995, p. 15)

Much of what Heaney says amplifies and elaborates the growing body of work in psychoanalysis and analytical psychology on how the acceptance of death can usher in a final life phase of great richness. Erikson (1981) defines the challenge of this stage of the life cycle as 'integrity versus despair'. Jung and Jungians have been pioneers in this area and it was interesting to hear from British psychoanalyst Pearl King at a conference in London in 1996, that her early papers on working with older patients were given at Jungian conferences and published in Jungian journals.

The disintegration of the body in death, a body that represents both a reference point and a container, can be experienced as obliteration and extinction unless the link with loved internal figures is secure. Shakespeare's Claudio in *Measure for Measure* expresses this fear eloquently.

> Ay, but to die, and go we know not where;
> To lie in cold obstruction, and to rot;
> This sensible warm motion to become
> A kneaded clod; and the delighted spirit
> To bathe in fiery floods, or to reside
> In thrilling region of thick-ribbed ice;
> To be imprisoned in the viewless winds
> And blown with restless violence round about
> The pendent world; or to be worse than worst
> Of those that lawless and uncertain thought
> Imagine howling – 'tis too horrible.
>
> (Shakespeare (1623 [1969]),
> *Measure for Measure*, Act III, Scene I, lines 118–28)

Sculpted Creativity in Jung and Blake

The rest of this chapter looks at the creative process at work in the successful working through of death anxiety in the cases of Jung and Blake. Both these creative thinkers shared a view that the symbol had its own momentum and that, however much individual psychic work is necessary, the sources of generativity in our minds are not wholly personal.

Blake called this phenomenon 'Jesus the imagination'. For Jung it was the archetype that had a numinous power that generated imagery and propelled individuation. The work and lives of both illustrate Jaques' hypothesis that there is a marked tendency towards crisis in the creative work of great men in their mid to late thirties. If the crisis is successfully negotiated, during what Jaques refers to as 'a period of purgatory', then a change from 'precipitate to sculpted creativity' can be noted in their subsequent work. This crisis is a universal feature, not just exemplified by the creatively gifted. Jaques believed that this developmental crisis is precipitated by awareness of the reality of one's own death. Death becomes a 'personal matter' (Jaques 1965).

However, I also want to suggest that after mid-life there may be other crises at moments when the recognition of death has to be faced anew with the possibility both of breakdown and of creative development. Jung experienced near-death twice: near-psychic death after his break with Freud, when he went on to chart the unknown territory of his unconscious, and a heart attack in 1944 after which he went on to produce some of his greatest work. Jung, like Blake, had a profound sense of the religious conception of life after death. This was not understood by either man in the weak sense of illusion and the turning away from reality, but in the strong sense as a powerful representation that struggle and effort release creativity. In *Memories, Dreams, Reflections*, Jung is reported as saying:

> A man should be able to say he has done his best to form a conception of life after death, or to create some image of it – even if he must confess his failure. Not to have done so is a vital loss. For the question that is posed to him is the age-old heritage of humanity: an archetype rich in secret life, which seeks to add itself to our own individual life in order to make it whole. (Jung 1963, p. 332)

The first creative crisis for Jung occurred at the age of thirty-eight after the break with Freud. The separation from Freud as idealised father left Jung unprotected and vulnerable. His crisis lasted for around five years and is described in *Memories, Dreams, Reflections* as an intense period of confrontation with the unconscious through dreams and creative activities. The material from this pursuit of his inner images became the '*prima materia* for a lifetime's work' (Jung 1963, p. 225). However, there was to be another critical period followed by a burst of creativity when Jung was sixty-nine. Again in *Memories, Dreams, Reflections,* Jung described his heart attack of 1944 and the visions that followed it. From this illness he emerged to write the extraordinary work of his last years ('The psychology of the transference' (1946), 'On the nature of the psyche' (1947), 'Aion' (1951), 'Answer to Job' (1952) and 'Mysterium coniunctionis' (1955/56)).

In one of these later works, 'The psychology of the transference', the rhythm of the human life cycle and the structure of the transference is imagined as a series of perilous *coniunctios.* New positions are established that constantly succumb to the pressure for further development as the individuation process gathers momentum. Although this is true all through life, there is a particular poignancy and urgency from mid-life on because the parental figures in the outside world are failing or dead and the possibility of new babies is waning or already achieved. The individual is left to face the reality of death with no buffering. In his commentary on the woodcuts of the sixteenth-century text *Rosarium Philosophorum,* which Jung used to illustrate his argument for the cyclical nature of the individuation process, he made it clear that the experiencing and integration of psychotic anxieties is an essential part of individuation. This process is, as a result, inevitably fraught with danger. At each *putrefactio* stage in the *coniunctio* cycle, the individual's 'specious unity' breaks down and the analyst has to contain an experience that is overwhelming in its intensity. 1913 and 1944 were moments of such breakdown for Jung, when his capacity to contain the feelings and impulses released was stretched to the limit. His weathering of the storm preceded a new *coniunctio* cycle which generated new theories and a profounder sense of the importance of internal and external links to significant figures and to the cultural world.

The uniqueness of Jung's contribution lies in his understanding that psychic life is a series of cycles of destruction and creation. His formulation of the transcendent function (*CW* 8, para. 131) as the capacity of mind that mediates opposites through an emergent but mysterious symbol is a profound intuition that has been increasingly validated in recent work in the cognitive sciences. For example, Mithen (1998) offers the view that it is precisely the development of cognitive fluidity between different domains that accounts for the unusual capacities of the modern mind with its powerful metaphoric functioning. It is Jung's understanding of the symbol as transformational of psychic energy that links him with Blake.

Jung knew Blake's work and references to it are scattered through the *Collected Works.* He recognised an affinity and spoke approvingly of how 'the poet must make use of difficult and contradictory images in order to express the strange paradoxes of his vision' (*CW* 15, para. 151). Both men were widely read in esoteric literature and mythology and knew the Bible well as a storehouse of imagery. Blake's notion of contraries parallel Jung's theory of opposites, and both men saw energy/libido as a form of loving curiosity with an instinctual component. Jung wrote of childhood as being a time when libido can 'constantly stream forth', but then has to be withdrawn in a 'process of re-collection' so that the individual can develop (*CW* 6, para. 428). Jung quoted from Blake's poem *The Marriage of Heaven and Hell* (1793) (Blake 1989) to illustrate his point: 'Energy is eternal delight'.

The Gates of Paradise

I want to develop these ideas further by taking Blake's illuminated text, *The Gates of Paradise*, as an example to illustrate the nature of the creative process at work as death anxieties are worked through. It was issued twice by Blake: first in 1793, when Blake was thirty-six, and then around twenty-five years later when he was sixty-one (Erdman 1974). The first edition of *The Gates* was directly connected with the death of Blake's favourite younger brother, Robert, who died in 1787. The seventeen emblems were selected from sixty-four drawn as a series in the notebook that had previously belonged to Robert and they follow on from his drawings.

The period when Blake was working on the emblems (from about 1787 through to early 1793) was a time of personal and political upheaval and a confrontation with death on the personal and political scene. The century was also coming to an end. His mother had died the year before *The Gates* was published; his father was already dead (1784). The French Revolution and the execution of Louis XVI dominated the political scene and England was at war with France. The theme of death is reflected in the content of the emblems. Erdman points out that in the sixty-four emblems drawn in Robert's notebook, over a third indicate ways of dying and that nearly as frequent is the motif of the grave represented as doorway, cave-mouth, prison, cage, coffin, tomb and earth (Erdman 1974).

The period when Blake was working on the emblems for *The Gates of Paradise* was one of intense creativity when several other major works were in gestation. The notebook emblems with all their narrative links seem to have functioned as a generative matrix or metaphoric resource. It was as if the task of responding to these powerful internal and external events involved intense psychic work to lay down the new matrix on which Blake drew for the rest of his artistic life. When he returned to his text in 1818 to make further additions, Blake was impoverished along with the rest of the country at a time of general economic depression which followed the end of the Napoleonic Wars in 1815. *The Everlasting Gospels*, *Jerusalem* and his great work, *Job*, were still in the future. Like Jung, Blake in his sixties seems to have drawn further creative strength from reworking in old age the themes of his mid-life crisis.

It is interesting that this text is tiny and would fit into the palm of one's hand like a talisman. 'To hold infinity in the palm of your hand', Blake wrote in *Auguries of Innocence* (1803) (Blake 1989). Perhaps this tiny book on which such labour was expended represents in external reality Blake's secure attachment to a creative world of internal objects. It has something in common with Jung's reference to 'the *prima materia* for a lifetime's work' mentioned above.

The 'sculpted creativity' of Blake's imagination in *The Gates* provides an illustration for Jung's thesis that at moments of psychic threat and change, the process of individuation is mediated by the emergence of a symbol. The symbol is both social and biological, having archetypal roots. It is personal and historical but not just determined by individual history. Symbols for Jung were challenges, riddles, intensely compelling and always meaning more than they say. They show deep unconscious sources propelling the mind's development (*CW* 15, para. 119). This sense of the infinite resource of symbols may be an important feature of a creativity that protects us from the despair engendered by death and must connect at a deep unconscious level to a phantasy of the parental couple engaged in infinite and joyful production. The sense of being benefited by this activity and not threatened by it must strengthen feelings of love and gratitude and sustain creative endeavour.

In Blake's illuminated text as he struggles with the psychic impact of death an outpouring of powerful imagery is accompanied by a sculpting that has energetic and ruthless elements in it. Creativity is clearly hard and painful work.

Erdman's edition of *The Notebook* (1973) gives an intimate view of the artist at work. The chaos and destructiveness of the creative process is clearly in evidence and when the working notes and sketches are compared with the final version what is striking is how much has had to be relinquished. Blake's title refers perhaps to Michelangelo's famous reference to Ghiberti's doors for the Baptistry in fifteenth-century Florence. Their panels make use of a narrative technique called continuous narration in which 'episodes of a story that are disparate in time are shown as though occurring simultaneously' (Avery 1970). Blake uses this narrative technique in his illuminated text but condenses the stories into one image. The image is both framed on the page but grows through the associations in the reader's mind beyond the boundary line as if, like Jung, Blake saw the symbol possessing the characteristics of a living organism. (Figure 15.1.) Meaning fans out to give both richness and ironic comment.

The Chrysalis/Baby Emblem

Drawing on Jung's ideas and some aspects of contemporary approaches to textual studies, I shall try to illustrate Blake's struggle against effacement, rigidity and meaninglessness as forms of psychic death in a discussion of Emblem 1

Figure 15.1

(Figure 15.2), which forms the frontispiece of *The Gates of Paradise* and later by examining three core myths that are constantly alluded to in the text.

Figure 15.2

In this emblem, captioned 'What is man?' in the 1793 version, a transforming chrysalis baby lies on an oak leaf with a caterpillar poised threateningly on another leaf that seems about to close down on the baby. This threatening overarching form is echoed again and again in the emblems that follow: branches of trees, rocky enclaves, caverns, scaley coverings, prisons – all produce a claustrophobic space.

Space and movement are two key features of metaphor. The word 'metaphor' comes from the Greek word *metaphora*, derived from *meta*, meaning 'over', and *pherein*, 'to carry'. The mind moves between two images reflecting on likeness and difference; it traverses boundaries, it explores identity, it creates something new. Jung writes that the 'symbol needs man for its development. But it grows beyond him, therefore it is called "God" since it expresses a psychic situation or factor stronger than the ego' ('On psychic energy', 1928). The idea of rebirth is intrinsic to metaphor which creates something new out of the already existing and familiar. The metaphoric use of space in *The Gates* suggests that life has the potential to be both journey and prison. There is a reversible pattern or *chiasmus* in the series of emblems: Blake's use of space shows figures caught in the encapsulated spaces described above and also hatching, travelling, rising, climbing. This reversible pattern is present in Emblem 1, in the closure of the leaf and in the emergence of the butterfly baby.

The butterfly's life cycle is one of the oldest images of transformation. The caterpillar/butterfly cycle suggests the 'regeneration of life from an outworn form and hence the survival of the soul after the death of the body' (Baring and Cashford 1993). This metaphor is given a further allegorical elaboration so that the emblem operates like an opening argument. By juxtaposing different narratives around this central organising metaphor of the butterfly cycle, Blake challenges us to think about likeness and difference in three myths central to Western culture: the biblical story of the Fall; Cupid and Psyche; and Oedipus. The reader is asked to participate in a discursive partnership. This is an allegorical usage very different from traditional allegorical forms where the meaning is fixed. Blake despised traditional allegorical forms with their cliched meanings and contrasted them unfavourably with the work of vision. Blake's overlaying of one story with another has much in common with postmodern conceptions of allegory and also with Jung's approach to the interpretation of dream images. In the context of discussing his approach to a dream series, Jung states:

> It is as if not one text but many lay before us, throwing light from all sides on the unknown terms, so that a reading of all the texts is sufficient to elucidate the difficult passages in each individual one. (*CW* 12, para. 50)

In Newman's discussion of postmodern approaches to allegory, he quotes the American critic Craig Owen: 'In allegorical structure ... one text is read through another ... the paradigm for the allegorical work is thus the palimpsest' (Newman 1989, p. 125).

In the palimpsest an original inscription has been erased and new words substituted. However, the original can often still be deciphered. Blake's stories, read through other stories, symbolise the constant recreation of meaning that both acknowledges and reworks loss and redresses the psychic terror of annihilation. Something of what is erased is retained, but it is transformed in its meaning by the presence of something new.

Newman makes a further point about this active, transformational process:

> Allegory, instead of presupposing a self-identical transcendental subject, allows for the constitution of subject positions which are dynamically entered into, or even repudiated by the viewer/reader/interpreter who participates with the author in the creation of the work. (Newman 1989, p. 130)

These ideas of participation in the creation of meaning, reading narratives through other narratives and taking different subject positions, are useful in trying to describe how metaphoric and allegorical processes *work*, not just what they are. They represent the common ground between Jung and Blake.

I shall argue that Blake links this living metaphorical movement with a quality of relationship and thought that is mutual, curious and forgiving and contrasts it with omnipotent, rigidly prescribed laws which dictate fixed meaning. He invokes his three core myths by metonymy, a figurative device in which the part stands for the whole. They operate as discourses of great power, but the palimpsest technique introduces a questioning dialectic which disturbs a simple compliance.

The metaphoric process at work in this layering of myth is a strategy for raising a series of problems. By using three myths where curiosity is punished, Blake is posing the dilemma: *the family and culture that nurtures us can also murder us.* This is an intimate process involving what happens to our minds and our capacity for thinking. These myths do not frame us; that is too external a metaphor: they permeate our conscious and unconscious phantasies.

The caterpillar membrane out of which the butterfly/psyche emerges symbolises this process. It has profound associations with the containing and separating functions of the vital membranes in the body. Membranes line or boundary the tubes, sacs, ducts, capillaries and passageways of the body. Just as the spatial imagery of the emblems indicates both entrapment and freedom of movement, so the body can be experienced as a womb-like enclosure or a sarcophagus.

The Myths of Oedipus, Psyche and the Fall in *The Gates of Paradise*

Distinctions between states of mind that lead to development and states of mind that hinder it are important in understanding the significance of the way in which Blake positions us in relation to the three myths and positions each myth within a complex interlinking narrative field. Curiosity, love and forgiveness, and acceptance of one's place in the life cycle, lead to creativity and development. Rigid morality, despair, retreat and fixed perspectives lead to psychic death. The palimpsest is a metaphor for the processes at work in the transcendent function. As links are re-established between different perspectives in multiple configurations, a sense of richness, depth and complexity makes the restrictions of our all-too-mortal bodies bearable.

But first, I want to take each of the three myths in turn, starting with Oedipus, and gradually illustrate my argument.

'Mutual forgiveness of each vice
Such are the gates of paradise' (title page of 1818 version)

Figure 15.3

Oedipus

The Oedipus references in Blake's text are

- to the riddle asked by the sphinx and answered by Oedipus
- to the sphinx herself appearing as a highly condensed figure, both sybil and sphinx with the sphinx's serpent tail
- to Oedipus at Colonus as the aged traveller enters the tomb of earth, and
- to the bound feet of Oedipus (one version of the myth) in the swaddling and constricting chrysalis.

The butterfly symbol is ambiguous. It is connected with the transformations and perpetual regeneration of the soul, but the chrysalis/baby lies on and is overshadowed by oak leaves. In Blake's work the oak leaf also symbolises an authoritarian and oppressive Druid priesthood. The transformation of the soul may be restricted by the chrysalis of oppressive ideas.

The sybil/sphinx is another ambiguous figure. The origins and history of these two figures have been studied extensively (Pollock and Munder Ross 1988, Warner 1994). The sphinx has been seen as a monstrous maternal figure, linked with Jocasta and Hera, and a relic from the older matriarchal religions. As a representative of these matriarchal religions she reminds the arrogant young hero of the importance of human relations rather than power, violence and domination. In condensing the sphinx with the sybil, Blake introduces another dimension. Although the sphinx can be seen as linked with sadistic trickery and death, the sibyl has a more positive provenance. The sibyls were noted for prophecy, and Pausanias (quoted in Warner 1994) reports that the Lamia, the snake woman celebrated by Keats, bore a daughter after coupling with Zeus: 'they say she was the first woman to sing oracles and was named Sybil by the Libyans' (Warner 1994, p. 67). Marina Warner's fascinating book goes on to trace the legend of the sibyl, its development in folk lore and legend and its incorporation into Christian mythology as prophesying the birth of Christ. Feisty, tough, tricky and clairvoyant, sibyls represent powerful female figures of a benign kind. Warner links the sybils with the legend of the Queen of Sheba – another famous asker of riddles – who, in the Bible, comes to prove Solomon with 'hard questions'.

This ambiguity, which is rich and complex, rather than undecided, is an aspect of the symbol that Jung also sees as characteristic of life: 'One face looks forward, the other back. It is ambivalent and therefore symbolic, like all living reality' (*CW* 12, para. 74). (Figure 15.4.)

Figure 15.4

The sybil/sphinx figure who presides over the earthen tomb of the pilgrim/Oedipus at the end of Blake's text has another association – with the

Eumenides. As Kanzer writes, the grove of the Eumenides as the setting for *Oedipus at Colonus* has profound significance. The Eumenides are the Furies who, in Greek mythology, are 'older and stronger than the gods'. These female representatives of a prehistoric matriarchy maintained their hold on the popular imagination long after the rise of a father state, with its high valuation of reason and discipline, had been established in the later Greek culture (Kanzer 1948, p. 77). Oedipus is both punished and finally accepted back into the womb of these primitive mother goddesses. From the grove of the Eumenides he disappears into the earth at the end of the play.

Blake would have known these stories and their various versions. What has been left out of Sophocles' Oedipus story but would have been known to his audience are the earlier Oedipus stories that link him to the cult of Demeter and the spring vegetation rights. This different relationship to the mother, away from the cycle of revenge and retaliation, is suggested in *Oedipus at Colonus* by the grove of the Eumenides. The religion of the old mother goddess is also evoked in Blake's poem by the psyche and sybil motifs.

In his use of the Oedipus myth Blake seems to be drawing our attention to two systems, presented not as alternatives but as states of mind to be negotiated and recognised as essential to human experience. There is the butterfly cycle of perpetual regeneration and there is the cycle of retribution in which the exposed child is sacrificed as a consequence of the punishment ordained for his father Laius' homosexual rape. Young Oedipus is the victim of priestly vengeance. Blake's strategy is to build up, by a process of juxtaposition, ambiguity and irony, an awareness and experience of several perspectives simultaneously. The tension of these opposites generates new meanings for the reader who participates in a form of active imagination to discover the 'unknown terms'.

Psyche

It is in the myth of Psyche that we find most clearly the ancient archetype of rebirth in a new form. The story of Psyche is linked with Egyptian stories of destruction and rebirth. The Egyptian cult of Isis, with her beauty and beneficence and her act of gathering together her partner Osiris' fragmented body, contrasts with the vengeful envious destructiveness of Venus in the story.

The story of Venus' birth links her with the old Titans. She is said to have been created from the severed phallus of Uranus when it fell into the sea. Uranus, son and husband of Gaea and father of the Titans, hated his children and confined them in the body of the Earth who begged them to avenge her. His son Kronos castrated him with a sickle as Uranus' phallus blocked the birth canal, replacing him as ruler.

Psyche's birth is different. She is born from the Earth and impregnated by a drop of heaven's dew (Neumann 1956). Blake suggests that she is not linked as Venus is to the old Titans with their themes of castration, immolation and transgenerational destruction, but to new imaginative possibilities which draw on the regenerational aspects of the Isis, Demeter and Innana mysteries (see Baring and Cashford (1993) for an account of how these Greek, Sumerian, Cretan and Egyptian myths influenced each other). The offspring of Psyche and Eros is Pleasure. Again and again Psyche nearly succumbs to suicidal despair as she struggles with the tasks set by Venus. But she finds help: from the ants, from the reed, from the eagle, from the tower and finally from her husband and lover Eros. Eros, in turn, is helped by Zeus, albeit in a comic, lecherous way.

Blake deploys alternative positions revealed in his three myths so that different systems can be explored and experienced. The Psyche myth draws into the frame myths of birth and rebirth: Aphrodite and Adonis, Isis and Osiris, Demeter and Persephone. In this context Psyche's curiosity – looking at her sleeping husband against his command and then looking in the box she was bringing back from Persephone to give to Venus – challenges the existing order but brings about new developments and relationships. The dominant narrative of the Oedipus myth – disobedience, punishment and expulsion/ death – is recast as curiosity, suffering and rebirth. Blake is drawing our attention to different systems of meaning and their interplay in which different identifications are constantly at work. As Blake's pilgrim enters death's door he enters in a surge of energy, echoed in the whorls of the oaken door, its frame and the pilgrim's cloak (Figure 15.5).

Death's Door

Figure 15.5

The myth of Psyche parallels the myth of Oedipus in many of its features, but with quite a different outcome. By juxtaposing the two myths Blake develops the suppressed narratives of the oedipal story in a way that serves as a commentary and critical evaluation of it.

Blake would have been fully aware that there were *different versions* of the myths that he studied and often illustrated. He uses this in *The Gates* to undermine fixed positions and suggest their limiting effect on the mind. This aspect of the symbol as 'a perpetual challenge to our thoughts and feelings' is another link with Jung (*CW* 15, para. 119).

The Snake and the Fall

When Blake juxtaposes the story of the Fall with the stories of Psyche and Oedipus, he deploys the foundational myth of the Judaeo-Christian religion and he does it from within an antinomian tradition where *different versions* of Genesis were currently debated. Blake would also have been aware of different versions of the Fall in the Gnostic tradition (see Thompson 1993, p. 35, for an account of his sources). Thompson writes: 'the Naasenes and some of the Gnostic sect of Ophites venerated the serpent, and interpreted its role in the Fall as a benefaction, since it first raised human beings to higher knowledge' (Thompson 1993, p. 34).

Pagels also comments on another Gnostic source: *The Testimony of Truth.* She summarises the Adam and Eve story in this text as follows.

[T]he serpent, long known to appear in gnostic literature as the principle of divine wisdom, convinces Adam and Eve to partake of knowledge while 'the Lord' threatens them with death, trying jealously to prevent them from attaining knowledge and expelling them from Paradise when they achieve it. (Pagels 1979, p. xvii)

When Blake juxtaposes Forgiveness with the Law he is developing an antinomian theme:

The Ten Commandments and the Gospel of Jesus stand directly opposed to each other: the first is a code of repression and prohibition, the second a gospel of forgiveness and love. The two might have flowed from the minds of opposite gods. (Thompson 1993, p. 14)

In *The Gates of Paradise* Blake was envisioning a return to an unfallen state. The old myths of regeneration and rebirth find a new expression in which expulsion is followed by return and renewal. However, this was no endorsement for institutional religion. *Mutual forgiveness* of each vice opens the gates of paradise but these are not Ghiberti's magnificent gates through which one entered into the cathedral in Florence. Blake's return to paradise is essentially a state of mind, characterised by mutuality, questioning, the acceptance of uncertainty, individual responsibility and participation.

This aspect is explored in great detail by Larrissy's reading of Blake. Larrissy sees Blake's irony and ambiguity as a strength, for it makes it hard for readers

> to establish some authoritative intention which they may feel secure about: these works provoke, question, suggest varying interpretations. Reading Blake demands a labour of interpretation. (Larrissy 1985, p. 155)

Alternating meanings of the serpent, the enclosing membrane within which we hatch out or suffocate, are fully exploited by Blake. The snake is linked both with a state of mind characterised by oppression, corruption, hypocrisy and exploitation and also with change, activity, curiosity, the 'holiness of the heart's affections' and renewal. It is characteristic of Blake's psychological subtlety and political realism that both are held in an unresolvable and

Figure 15.6

necessary tension. The individuation process that was central in Jung is here demonstrated in the way symbolic meaning is formed by the mind's capacity to hold together conflicting opposites.

In the final emblem added to *The Gates* circa 1818 Blake seems to suggest that all forms of external religion and ritual are potentially illusory distractions and that only the inner processes of imaginative life are essential. In this final emblem he shows a magnificent bat-winged Satan covered in stars separating itself out from the sleeping pilgrim, reminiscent of the vision of Isis in her star-covered robe in the original Psyche story (Figure 15.6). Satan is a dunce, an ass, and only the traveller remains. All external sources of authority are repudiated; false Gods are seen for what they are and illusion is relinquished.

Blake uses the palimpsest of his three myths to circumambulate the themes of psychic death and rebirth and the conditions for symbolic life. Death and ageing are not evaded but seem to generate new symbolic energies and a greater capacity to engage strenuously with psychic complexity. What might have been effaced and suppressed becomes restored. Jung called this process being 'ready to die with life' ('The soul and death', 1934).

Conclusion

> What goes on four feet, on two feet, and three,
> But the more feet it goes on the weaker it be?
> Sophocles, *Oedipus Rex, The Theban Plays*

I have tried to show, by reference to Jung's life experience and through a detailed examination of Blake's *The Gates of Paradise* using Jungian theory as a frame, that the recognition of death as an immediate and personal fact can stimulate creativity. The fecundity and intellectual potency of the symbol and symbolic forms which Jung placed at the centre of his psychology represent the possibilities of meaning and growth even at the moment when death is inescapable. It is impossible to rejuvenate the body – the pain and the loss of that has to be faced. But if acceptance of ageing and death can be accomplished, then a rich harvest can be reaped in later life.

We are living in a world where people are living longer than ever before, where at the age of fifty one can expect to live for a further thirty years. The social and psychological implications of this are still being absorbed. Jung stood out among the early psychoanalysts, wanting a broader perspective than Freud – at least than the Freud of 1913 – could allow. He was aware, from the beginning, of other themes to be addressed at different stages of the life cycle, death being one of them.

The image of the Grim Reaper/Death encapsulates our fear of mutilation and castration. In Blake's illuminated text he reworks that image by elaborating the suppressed narratives in the bleak and tragic myths of Oedipus and the Fall. He restores through the poetic allegory the effaced tradition of the older religions represented by the Demeter/Psyche myth.

Death removes permanently. We cannot bring back the dead or prevent our own death, but creativity is abundantly possible in later life if we can suffer the pain of relinquishing our omnipotent illusions. The same may be true of our theories. As the second century of psychoanalysis begins, the Oedipus complex has already been elaborated in many different ways. Perhaps as the body fails and the genetic and psychic linkage between the generations is put under strain by the body's imminent disappearance, creative activity both in art and analysis, that symbolises the infinitely creative couple, makes it possible to look death in the face. The blind eyes of Oedipus are linked with political and transgenerational traumas in which parental love and concern has been undermined and distorted. Jung and Blake both recognised that there were restorative sequels to the human story that these traumatic narratives had suppressed.

Figure 15.7

References

Avery, C. (1970) *Florentine Renaissance Sculpture*. London: Murray.
Baring, A. and Cashford, J. (1993) *The Myth of the Goddess*. London: Arkana Penguin.
Blake, W. (1989) *The Complete Poems*. London: Longman.
Erdman, D. (1973) *The Notebook of William Blake*. Oxford: Oxford University Press.
Erdman, D. (1974) *The Illuminated Blake*. New York: Dover Publications.

Erikson, E.H. (1981) 'Elements of a psychoanalytic theory of psychosocial development', in *The Course of Life* (Vol. 1): *Infancy and Early Childhood*. Washington, DC: US Department of Health and Human Services.

Gordon, R. (1978) *Dying and Creating*. London: SAP.

Heaney, S. (1995) *The Redress of Poetry*. London: Faber and Faber.

Jaques, E. (1965) 'Death and the mid-life crisis', in E. Bott Spillius (ed.), *Melanie Klein Today* London: Routledge.

Jung, C.G. (1963) *Memories, Dreams, Reflections*. London: Collins/Routledge and Kegan Paul.

Kanzer, M. (1948) 'The "Passing of the Oedipus complex" in Greek drama', in G.H. Pollock and J. Munder Ross (eds), *The Oedipus Papers*. Connecticut: International Universities Press, 1988.

Larrissy, E. (1985) *William Blake*. Oxford: Blackwell.

Mithen, S. 1998) *The Prehistory of the Mind*. London: Phoenix.

Nemiroff, R.A. and Colarusso, C.A. (1985) *The Race Against Time*. New York: Plenum Press.

Neumann, E. (1956) *Amor and Psyche*. New York: Princeton University Press.

Newman, M. (1989) 'Revising modernism, representing postmodernism: critical discourses of the visual arts', in L. Appignanesi (ed.), *Postmodernism: ICA Documents* London: Free Association Books.

Pagels, E. (1979) *The Gnostic Gospels*. London: Weidenfeld and Nicholson.

Pollock, G.H. and Munder Ross, J. (eds) (1988) *The Oedipus Papers*. Connecticut: International Universities Press.

Shakespeare, W. (1609) *The Sonnets and 'A Lover's Complaint'*. London: Penguin, 1986.

Shakespeare, W. (1623) *Measure for Measure*. London: Penguin, 1969.

Sophocles (1947) *Oedipus Rex*, in *The Theban Plays*, London: Penguin Classics.

Thompson, E.P. (1993) *Witness Against the Beast*. Cambridge: Cambridge University Press.

Warner, M. (1994) *From the Beast to the Blonde*. London: Chatto and Windus.

Suggested Reading

Baring, A. and Cashford, J. (1993) *The Myth of the Goddess*. London: Arkana Penguin.

Gordon, R. (1978) *Dying and Creating*. London: SAP.

Cited Works of Jung

Jung, C.G. (1957–79) *Collected Works* (*CW*). London: Routledge, and New Jersey, Princeton University Press.

Volume 1, 'Psychiatric studies'.

Volume 2, 'Experimental researchs'.

Volume 3, 'The psychogenesis of mental disease'.

Volume 4, 'Freud and psychoanalysis'.

Volume 5, 'Symbols of transformation'.

Volume 6, 'Psychological types'.

Volume 7, 'Two essays on analytical psychology'.

Volume 8, 'The structure and dynamics of the psyche'.

Volume 9i, 'The archetypes and the collective unconscious'.

Volume 9ii, 'Aion'.

Volume 10, 'Civilization in transition'.

Volume 11, 'Psychology and religion: East and West'.

Volume 12, 'Psychology and alchemy'.

Volume 13, 'Alchemical studies'.

Volume 14, 'Mysterium coniunctionis'.

Volume 15, 'The spirit in man, art and literature'.

Volume 16, 'The practice of psychotherapy'.

Volume 17, 'The development of personality'.

Volume 18, 'The symbolic life'.

Volume 19, 'General bibliography'.

Volume 20, 'General index'.

The Freud–Jung Letters (1974) *The Correspondence Between Sigmund Freud and C.G. Jung*, ed. William McGuire. London: Hogarth.

(1916) *VII Sermones ad Mortuos*. Trans. 1925, H.G. Baynes. London: Watkins, 1967.

(1958) *The Undiscovered Self*. London: Routledge and Kegan Paul.

(1963) *Memories, Dreams, Reflections*. New York: Pantheon.

(1964) *Man and His Symbols*. London: Routledge and Kegan Paul.

(1973) *Letters of C.G. Jung*, Volume I, 1906–1950. London and New Jersey: Routledge and Kegan Paul.

(1976) *Letters of C.G. Jung*, Volume II, 1951–1961. London and New Jersey: Routledge and Kegan Paul.

(1978) *Modern Man in Search of a Soul*. London: Routledge and Kegan Paul.

Jung, C.G. and Pauli, W. (1955) *The Interpretation of Nature and the Psyche*. London: Routledge and Kegan Paul.

Index

Compiled by Sue Carlton